ɔɧ

WHAT I LEARNT

WHAT I LEARNT

What My Listeners Say –
and Why We Should Take Notice

JEREMY VINE

WEIDENFELD & NICOLSON

First published in Great Britain in 2017
by Weidenfeld & Nicolson

1 3 5 7 9 10 8 6 4 2

A CIP catalogue record for this book
is available from the British Library.

HB ISBN 978 1474 60492 5

Typeset by Input Data Services Ltd, Somerset

Printed and bound by CPI Group (UK) Ltd, Croydon, CR0 4YY

Weidenfeld & Nicolson

The Orion Publishing Group Ltd
Carmelite House
50 Victoria Embankment
London, EC4Y 0DZ
An Hachette UK Company
www.orionbooks.co.uk

In memory of my mother-in-law Margaret Schofield
(1948–2015), who would have disagreed with half of this,
and still encouraged me

Contents

Contents

Before We Start

One of my dearest friends had a terrible fear. Reaching fifty-seven, and loving red wine, he realised that he had got to the birthday his father never saw. The friend – let's call him Austin – had taken his dad's place running the family business. His responsibilities had been handed to him prematurely, and in tragic circumstances. Austin's father died suddenly from a massive heart attack. He was fifty-six.

These days everyone knows that family history is a vital indicator of good health. Strengths and weaknesses are bequeathed in our genes. News items carry stories about 'genetic splicing', the first attempts by scientists to edit those genes. But they are in their infancy.

My friend is perceptive and thoughtful. He celebrated his fifty-seventh without joy. In the work he does, and which his father did, he cannot avoid stress. He must see many clients and all must feel they have his undivided attention. I see him juggling fifteen different projects and wonder how he does it. Thinking of his father, Austin began to wonder too. He started to avoid starch, eat raw nuts and cut desserts. There was an increase in exercise. But you cannot outrun your own DNA.

However, Austin is successful – his father's business has bloomed under his watch – and thus he has two great advantages: money and information. He went to see his GP.

'I want treatment for a heart attack.'

'You have had one?' The doctor looked astonished.

'No. I want treatment before I have it.'

The doctor was puzzled. 'What are your symptoms?'

'I have no symptoms.'

'Breathlessness, shooting pain in your arm?'

'No.'

'In that case you are not ill. Why have you come to me?'

'Because,' replied Austin, 'I have just passed the age at which my father died of heart failure. He and I lived the same life. We run the same business and we drink the same wine. So I know I will have a heart attack, and I want you to treat me for it.'

The GP laughed. 'That is rather putting the cart before the horse! A doctor can only treat you for an illness you have.'

Austin was not thrown. *'I want you to treat me for my father's heart attack.'*

Eventually the physician was persuaded to refer Austin to one of the finest cardiologists in Harley Street. But the referral must have been lukewarm, because once again my friend found himself having to argue for attention.

'I really don't know why you're here,' said the eminent cardiologist.

'I would like the gold standard heart tests. Cameras, dye, everything.'

'We don't do that without some cause.'

'Never?'

Possibly deciding an examination would be less exhausting than the argument, the cardiologist finally agreed. A camera was inserted into Austin's right wrist and fed upwards through a major artery to his chest. Dye illuminated the chambers of the heart.

Waking from the anaesthesia, Austin saw a change in the cardiologist's expression.

'I'm glad you came. Your vessels are unusually narrow. Your heart may tick reliably for five years but I doubt it would last longer. Cardiac arrest could be in years or months. Or it could be in weeks.'

'So treat me now,' insisted Austin. 'I want the operation you would normally give a patient the day after their heart attack, except I want it before.'

I visited him in hospital. The triple bypass took five hours. When he arrived for the operation, Austin heard the surgeon joke that he was the first heart patient to arrive in the hospital carrying his own suitcases. His private insurers had needed a little – shall we say – persuasion to fund the procedure. But Austin was now sitting up in bed, happily talking to me. The vivid wound down the centre of his chest seemed like a detail. Successful surgery had saved the life his father lost.

The most surprising part of the story is not that Austin asked for an operation the doctor thought he didn't need. To me, the most surprising part is the astonishment of the doctors – do they not know their patients are arriving in consulting rooms armed to the teeth, tooled up with information like Jason Bourne carries guns?

A year after his heart was repaired, Austin's radical approach was vindicated in the worst way possible. A heart attack claimed the life of his elder brother, who died in his sleep.

Austin had shocked the physicians because he inverted the normal relationship. Their patient was now the expert. The medics protested because they were no longer in charge. But they should get used to the creak of the tables turning. Others will follow.

All around us, power balances are shifting. 2016 and 2017 were years of similar inversions. The winners were Brexit, Corbyn, Leicester's football team. Plus Trump and very nearly Ed Balls.

But this story is more personal to me. It starts the year before.

Part One

1. The 25,000th Call

During the summer of 2015 I was sitting outside a café in hesitant London sunshine when something happened that made me think. I saw a tweet saying we were nearly at 21 June – the 172nd day of the year, and also the longest.

Now, if you are not a fan of Twitter, the news that people use it to announce the date to strangers probably confirms your worst fears. But it made me curious.

Working back from 172 showed me that this particular day was 166, and I scrawled the following formula on a napkin:

$$n = d \times c \times w \times (12 + 166/365)$$

where 'd' is the number of Radio 2 programmes I present in a week, 'c' is the number of callers we take per day, 'w' is the number of broadcast weeks in the year – and 'n' is the total number of listeners who have been put through on air to my show. I then took a second napkin and wrote numbers where the letters had been, which gave me this:

where the last number is the most significant.

I had taken 24,909 calls.

Yep. Really.

I looked at the napkin again and again and eventually realised it should say 24,908.

But still. This was dramatic.

Since starting on Radio 2 in January 2003, taking over from the indefatigable Sir Jimmy Young, an 82-year-old household name who famously had his higher-quality 'toupée for special occasions' packed into an airtight box and couriered by motorbike to a last-minute interview with Prince Charles, I had spoken live on air to that truly humungous number of listeners. 12.45 years and 24,908 on-air conversations.

People often say: 'How does the delay work?'

I reply: 'Delay? There isn't one. We just have to trust the caller not to shout SHAT MYSELF IN MY WAGON or BIG BOSOMS.'

(Someone did once pull the 'shat myself in my wagon' line on us actually, a lorry driver who rang during a discussion about indigestion, but at least it was well meant.)

Now, only ninety-two calls short of the magic 25k, I became more than a little excited. Occasionally in the days that followed I would say to myself, 'Ah, that was call number 24,930', or 'Now we only have fifty to go', or maybe, 'I really am glad *that* wasn't call 25,000.' Chris Evans, you were wondering why a mug in your studio was marked with

like the wall above a prison bunk? I was counting to 25,000.

And so it came to pass that on 26 June 2015 I worked out that Jane in Leigh, near Wigan, was caller 24,994. She rang us to complain about migrants.

'We had a nightmare last year. We brought two of them back in with us on the axle of our motorhome. They were risking their lives because I was driving at seventy miles an hour down the M20 with two Somalian lads hanging from my back axle.'

The item focused on the drama in Calais caused by thousands of African migrants trying to enter Britain. Call 24,995 was Trevor Hope in Crook: 'The French, if they had their way, would move the border to Carlisle.'

Caller 24,996 was Linda Shawcross in Glasgow, a well-spoken lady who launched an attack on the UK benefits system while throwing in a stray fact about her own situation that was completely distracting: 'We have to be hard line. When I claimed benefits in Belgium I had to prove exactly who I was.'

(In radio this is known as a Witch's Post – later I will explain what exactly this is, and soon you'll be hearing them everywhere.)

We changed the subject. News had emerged that London Pride, not the beer but the parade, had banned UKIP's gay chapter from marching. Again, the power of the stray fact – *UKIP has a gay chapter?* UKIP seem about as likely to have a gay chapter as Robbie Fowler's autobiography. But they do. Campaigner Peter Tatchell agreed UKIP should be banned until they 'apologise for past homophobic statements'. London Pride had made the excuse – I'm calling it one; it certainly sounded like one – that someone on Twitter had threatened to spray urine at the UKippers from a water pistol, which had unsettled the volunteer stewards, which made the ban inevitable. Thus Richard Moyes in Glastonbury became caller 24,997.

'I couldn't be more – probably what Peter Tatchell doesn't like. Having said that, I'm extremely liberal. I don't have a racist, sexist, ageist bone in my body. But this is gross hypocrisy.'

Richard's first line, 'I couldn't be more what Peter Tatchell doesn't like' . . . er, right, what does that mean? *I spend eight hours a day in the gym, and the other four having sex with busty women, reading Russian motorbike magazines and bringing up phlegm in theatres?* I guess we may never get to the bottom of it. And it doesn't matter. Callers are hand-picked by the twenty-somethings on our switchboard simply for passion. They may create more questions than they answer, and crucially *they may be wrong* . . . but once in a while they give you a precious fact that can be recalled and reused for ever.

So it was with caller 24,998. Louise Morales in Woking rang after we began discussing the death of a young gardener in Hertfordshire who had brushed his hand against the poisonous flower Devil's Helmet. Five days later the poor man succumbed to multiple organ failure. Louise, herself a professional gardener, had a customer who wanted the same flower planted.

'He called it Monkshood. I said you do realise this is very poisonous? We mustn't let children near it. So we put it at the back of the border where it won't get brushed by anybody. There are no children, and the clients never go to the back of the border.'

I love the simple wisdom of that: if you grow a poisonous plant, put it at the back of the flowerbed. The same with poisonous colleagues, I guess. Louise brought us one inch closer to the magic 25,000, albeit via a story of personal tragedy. Migrants . . . Marchers . . . Monkshood . . . I was going to say 'all human life is here', but it turns out we seem to restrict ourselves to stories that start with the letter M. The item was only slightly spoilt for me when I saw the Radio 2 homepage, which underneath a large picture of me had placed the words

JEREMY VINE:
Devil's Helmet.

It hardly mattered. Because now my own butterflies were starting to flutter. A forester in Richmond, North Yorkshire, was put through.

'I've come out in a rash gathering ragwort. The sap gets into your skin, and affects your liver and kidneys. And when you crush or burn cherry laurel it gives off cyanide gas. That's why you don't find laurel plants being eaten by rabbits.'

Dave the Forester was 24,999. A little dour, but never mind. I liked the line about the rabbits.

The next call would be the watershed moment for my show.

I had visions of champagne suddenly being produced by managers jumping out of cupboards, bunting hung above the checkout like they used to do in American supermarkets: YOU ARE OUR MILLIONTH CUSTOMER. Except you don't have cash registers on a radio show, just a mixing desk crammed with faders. I slid one upwards and there was Nick Brown, business guru, talking about what to do if the bank won't lend you money. We gave out the number and waited for calls. '0500 288 291,' I kept saying urgently.

It seemed to take a very long time. The editor shook his head on the other side of the glass: 'Nothing yet.' We played a record. Sister Sledge. Then the producer brought through a piece of paper saying *STUART BRUCE IN NEWBURY. Wants to ask about where he can borrow money as bank said no.*

Perfect. So here we go.

'We have Stuart in Newbury on the line,' I announced, just seeing the figure *twenty-five thousand* swim into my field of vision, imagining a queue of zeros bouncing like beans, fluorescent pennants sagging from the ceiling, managers offering me a huge rise in salar– no. That last part was pure fantasy.

'Go ahead Stuart.'

On he came, the historic caller, our 25k-man.

Maybe this would be the moment I became a legend in the same league as Sir Jimmy Young. The caller began to speak, slowly at first.

'I am a small franchise. I went to a bank for a loan. I got turned down, so I managed to go to the sperm bank. TO GET LOTS OF SPERM.' (*Loud laughter, caller hangs up.*)

I looked at Nick Brown. He looked at me. His eyebrows went up. Mine went up higher. You went to a *sperm bank*? Of course, the silly man was messing around. My 25,000th call was a joke.

Had it been a good hoax – and we have only had two of them over the last decade – then it might have been worth celebrating. Had Stuart said, 'My business idea is to paint ferrets bright red and use them to search for Viking treasure', then he probably would have got ten minutes of airtime while presenter and expert unpacked the idea with boggle-eyed fascination. But just to shout SPERM BANK! and hang up . . .

So now I got a little cross. What a buffoon, I thought, with a restrained internal *grrrrrrrrr*. What a – Devil's Helmet. My watershed moment was ruined.

But actually the Sperm Banker did me a favour. He forced me to take stock. No modest way to say this: if my show were a news programme, it would be the number one in the country. It regularly beats Radio 4's *Today* programme, the nearest competition. The problem is that we aren't really news. They announce stuff; we discuss it. Even 'current affairs' puts it a bit too strongly. And it is more than a phone-in. Perhaps we could just call it 'water cooler radio', and settle for that. A place where people gather to laugh or chat, to hear things, and mainly to get entertained.

In the nineties I interviewed the prisons campaigner Lord Longford. 'And what is your autobiography about?' I asked him.

'Me,' he said. One word.

And then he laughed.

That was basically the start and the end of the conversation. *Private Eye* printed it as a Colemanball and I thought my career was over.

Well, this book is not about me. It is about them – my listeners, and all the surprises they spring, and what they tell us. Often they communicate pure joy. Just as often they are furious about something. A small number adopt the line taken in a letter published by the *Evening Standard* on 15 August 1979:

Dear Sir,
    I wish to complain most strongly about everything.
      Yours sincerely,
      Henry Root

Root was a made-up person. My listeners are real and I love them. They are capable of great compassion but when they react with anger it blows every thermometer. Among subjects which have infuriated them in recent years are:

- Lollipop ladies
- Old people using buses
- Old people not using buses
- A vicar who complained about the amount of hardcore porn on battleships
- Tony Blair saying anything at all, even breathing
- Goldfish being given away as prizes at fairs
- Russell Brand
- Cellophane

But there are other, supremely tender, moments. I am writing this at five to three on a Wednesday afternoon. A little earlier – at ten past twelve – I welcomed to our Cardiff studio a Welsh listener, Rowena Kincaid, and wished her a happy fortieth live on air. Those birthday wishes took precedence even over an item on the previous day's House of Commons debate on the bombing of Syria. Why? Because two years earlier Rowena had been told her breast cancer meant she had no more than six months to live. We had spoken on the radio back then, and she had said her ambition was simply to get to forty. Now she had. Not cured, still terminal, but shining with a special kind of optimism. So we marked the day.

'Unfortunately my chemotherapy session falls on Christmas Eve – the next day I never feel like doing anything, so Christmas is a bit of a write-off this year,' she told me without a shred of resentment.

'But I think I was born happy. I stay positive. I am dealing with it head-on. It is really difficult because you always have to be prepared for the punch in the face and then the fall, then getting back up and dusting yourself down again. But it is just one of those things. You just have to keep on going. I enjoy my life and I just want to keep it. Stay positive and keep on going. On days when I feel good, I can go out and have a drive and see my friends and have lunch, and just feel okay.'

I listened to her voice, and was transported. Maybe you thought there was nothing much dramatic in what Rowena said. Or maybe, like me, you saw those ten sentences and thought they told us almost everything we need to know about who we are and how precious our life should feel.

2. Horse Day Combat

I was wheel-clamped in Acton. I had parked perfectly properly overnight in a west London car park, then in the morning neglected to buy a ticket. At noon I suddenly remember the car and start looking for it.

Sure enough, the front wheel is visible from two hundred yards away because it is now luminous yellow. The man who applied the clamp is retreating hurriedly.

He is a strapping fellow with a West African accent and is still holding the key to the padlock when I catch up with him.

'You should have bought a ticket,' he insists.

As courteously as possible, I give him my answer. 'Forty-five minutes ago, behind the third-floor hospital window you can see up there, I became a father. My wife has been in labour for twenty-four hours. When dawn broke and I was supposed to be getting your pay-and-display sticker, I was instead having to accompany her up to the third floor in a wheelchair as she got ready to be – ' I paused, searching for the right phrase. 'Surgically encouraged.'

The car park attendant says: 'Oh my God. Please forgive me.'

I smile magnanimously, thinking: *Remain calm*. 'Listen, it doesn't matter at all. I am not even slightly upset. The wheel clamp cannot compete with these developments.'

The attendant smiles. 'Was it a boy or a girl?'

'A girl. And they're both doing fine.'

'Here is your ticket,' he says in broken English. 'I am sorry for my part in this.'

I wave the piece of paper. 'I shall pay it – with elation.'

He replies: 'You must pay it with cash.'

You have to laugh. The conversation came back to me when

I forgot to send a cheque to the VAT people and within days got a letter from the taxman entirely in red, written in the style vigilantes use when they spray-paint the front door of the neighbourhood paedophile. The letter did not contain the phrase DIE BASTARD DIE but it came close. I showed it to my wife. 'All red ink, all capital letters. They even wrote their own address in red. You have to laugh,' I said.

She pointed out that people only say *You have to laugh* when they are almost speechless with fury. There is a British laugh that is exactly the same as the noise chimpanzees make before they attack. The laugh is just diverted anger. It might explain why so much of the tragedy on my radio show seems to release itself as comedy. During an item about vehicles catching fire while being driven, Ian from Oxford left this message.

'I was in an ambulance. Being rushed to hospital after a suspected heart attack. Drivers were sounding their horns and pointing at the bottom of the ambulance. It was on fire. The driver pulled in at the next opportunity – BUT IT WAS A PETROL STATION. They all got out and forgot about me, lying in the back.'

Fortunately someone saw Ian, raised the alarm and pulled him clear before the vehicle was consumed. 'The ambulance was burnt out,' he concluded with an impressive lack of emotion.

Patricia rang from Ryde to complain about loft extensions. 'I have a bungalow and my neighbours have very tall houses and have extended their lofts towards the sky,' said Christine. 'Now I can't see anything. They have left me in darkness. And this is the second time I have called you, Jeremy.'

'Oh, when was the first time you called?'

'A year ago.'

'And the subject that time was loft extensions?'

'No, it was when your children are murdered by their father.'

At some point the penny quietly drops for us all, and we learn that life is precious. You might be listening to the radio and make the sudden switch between loft extension and murder. Or you are with the abandoned man in the burning ambulance. Or you hear

Rowena. Or you wheel-clamp a guy who just became a father. Or maybe it was in the moment that you became a parent yourself that the truth suddenly dawned:

So many important-seeming things are not very important at all.

I always think there are two ways of getting a sense of how brief life is. One is to study history and philosophy, not just modern history but ancient and medieval too. Cicero and the Tudors. The philosophy should encompass different cultures; for example, the Chinese teaching of the Shang and Zhou dynasties. That is the first way.

The other is to cycle in London. I started when I hit forty-five, shocked by the speed at which my natural gawkiness deserted me. But I got a greater shock from the way teams of trained assassins, disguised as ordinary motorists but actually working in well-organised hit squads, would converge at particular junctions to kill me. Most mornings on my bike I feel like Yasser Arafat cornered by Mossad. I tell friends that cycling in our capital city either lengthens your life by ten years or shortens it by twenty.

A doctor responded: 'But Jeremy, you do need your exercise. You are in sniper's alley right now.'

'Sniper's – what?' I asked.

He put the pen down on his desk as if this was serious. Sniper's alley, he explained, starts when a person turns forty-seven.

'At that point the bullets start flying. People get taken out by all kinds of illnesses between forty-seven and fifty-two. It's a dark and scary five-year corridor where, if a person is still behaving like they're twenty-five, all the wear and tear, all the stress and strain suddenly catch up with them. But get through the alley without being hit,' he went on confidently, 'and you're good for two or three more decades.'

At Radio 2, we are often reminded of our mortality. The station has a commendable approach to ageing presenters – it seems to feel the added years somehow make them more valuable.

Gloriously, that means we have some of the oldest working broadcasters (Alan Keith set a UK record: born in 1908, still on Radio 2 when I arrived, finally died aged 94 without ever actually having retired). The sadness is that some DJs pass away with their headphones on.

In 2017 we lost both Desmond Carrington and then Brian Matthew, whose relationship with the Beatles meant he could genuinely claim to be a part of their story. Just before noon on 5 April 2017, various senior people rushed into my studio to give me the news that Brian had lost his fight against a short illness.

'Am I announcing this myself?' I asked.

'The newsroom are being told now,' came the reply. 'They will do it.' For us it was on the level of a royal death.

At noon Ken Bruce handed over to me. I read the list of stories we would be covering and then said there was some sad additional news which the newsreader would now give us. She read the bulletin: 'Much-loved Radio 2 presenter Brian Matthew has died at the age of eighty-eight.' There would, she added, be a special programme tonight with tributes from people who had worked with Matthew during his illustrious career.

As listeners began to email and text emotional responses to the loss of their radio companion, the newsreader handed back to me. Asked by the producer to deliver a tribute myself, I said this was very upsetting news for the Radio 2 family, and talked a little more about Brian's career – the way he had championed the Fab Four at such a crucial early stage of their career, and his remarkable sixty-three years behind the microphone which brought us shows ranging from *Saturday Club* to *Round Midnight*, as well as the famously long-running *Sounds of the Sixties*.

'He will be much missed by all of us here,' I concluded, and played his theme tune.

A few minutes later there was a blur of activity on the other side of the studio glass. The editor Phil Jones came in during a record.

'Don't mention Brian Matthew again.'

'Why not?' I asked.

'I can't tell you.'

'He definitely is dead?'

'That's the point.'

'What do you mean?'

'He may not be.'

'HE MAY NOT BE?'

'We are hearing Brian is alive.'

So despite hundreds of tributes flooding into our various inboxes, there was, confusingly for the listeners, no further reference to my admirable colleague that lunchtime. Some hours later the BBC formally admitted that the announcement of Brian's death was the result of someone, somewhere, getting their wires crossed when speaking to the presenter's close relatives.

Unfortunately a similar misstep had occurred at the start of the year, when the BBC announced Brian Matthew had stepped down from *Sounds of the Sixties*. A newspaper contacted him in hospital and reported his answer: 'That's absolute balderdash. I was ready and willing and able to go back, and they've just said they are going to put the programme in the hands of other people.'

Social media was typically brutal when it emerged that we had botched the announcement of the presenter's death. One person tweeted –

'BBC: "Brian Matthew has retired." Brian Matthew: "No I haven't." BBC: "Brian Matthew is dead." Brian Matthew: "No I'm not."'

The following weekend, the presenter sadly passed away.

Of course the doctor who warned me about what he called 'sniper's alley' was referring to a younger generation – people in their late forties and early fifties. A glance at friends around me in the BBC suggests he may be right. Almost simultaneously, Andrew Marr had a stroke; Nick Robinson got a tumour on his lung; the newscaster George Alagiah had bowel cancer.

I heard gunshots myself, but got off lightly. In 2009 I suffered a dose of abject misery. An expert said it sounded like burnout. I didn't know whether it was burnout or Burnout, with a capital

B, so I decided to escalate experts and walked round the corner to Harley Street. A psychologist with kindly eyes that twinkled behind her spectacles said I might need time off work. I responded: 'No. Your job is to keep me working.' As a result of that kind of idiocy, I wandered around for a long time as if wearing a gigantic blob of freshly spun candyfloss on my head. Nothing, not even hearing The Smiths sing 'Heaven Knows I'm Miserable Now', gave me pleasure. There is something powerfully comic about a radio presenter delivering a two-hour talk show to seven million, then leaving the office and paying one person £120 to listen to him for a further forty minutes.

In all I spoke to seven different professionals. 'I feel like Debenhams after a fire,' I told one. 'The entire store has burnt to the ground except the shop front. There's no stock, escalators, cash registers, staff. They're all just ashes. There are only the dummies in the shop window. That's the last bit of me that exists – the bit at the front.'

'The presenter,' he said.

It might have been a midlife crisis. It certainly doesn't compare to the brutal illnesses my friends suffered. But, to trouble you for an extra second on the subject, the whole business taught me a lesson. Which is that misery can be positive.

The French phrase *hors de combat* [pron.: 'or decomba'] was a favourite of my late mother-in-law, who made a joke of constantly mispronouncing it 'Horse Day Combat'. Her version meant the same thing: off the battlefield. I reckon burnout is the body's way of taking you Horse Day Combat before you suffer physical injury. In the instant that the evil gods of stroke and heart attack have decided you will be their next victim, you are suddenly forced into hibernation – crashed in bed and out of their clutches. Misery is a circuit-breaker. It may not be tidy, but I would rather lie under my duvet staring into my own heart than be opened up on a trolley with surgeons doing the staring instead.

When I awoke one morning and knew I was better, I was overjoyed. I was through Sniper's Alley. But the trough made me reflect. I began to realise what was important. Gradually, rediscovering elation, I decided I should do the oldest and simplest thing: count my blessings.

Some of them are obvious. Fronting a radio show in the UK is a great gig. If I did one in Wyoming, my audience would only be moose and bison. Wyoming is bigger than the UK if you count in square miles:

WYOMING	97,818 mi²
UNITED KINGDOM	94,058 mi²

but the population is just an eyelash over half a million, so there are fewer people in Wyoming than Bristol. I went to the state once, which is why I mention it. I only saw what wasn't there — the sheer space. An empty sky that moons at you like an inescapable blue buttock. All British men over forty secretly want to become cowboys and gallop into that Wild West horizon. But I ended up with a talk show in Britain and discovered it is the Wildest West of all – sixty-four million people jammed onto one tiny island, all waving their Colt 45s and yelling over their fences, me stuck in the middle. I feel lucky.

You are lucky if you can laugh at stuff. And I realised I am also lucky because I can still learn. Laughing and learning: the two most important things in a life. Oh, and love. Make that three. The third one is the biggest. Laughter and learning and love.

When my crisis was over I turned fifty. Years ago, the night before my youngest daughter's birthday, I sat on her bed and told her: 'Anna, isn't it amazing? You're four tomorrow.'

She replied, so sweetly: 'Yes daddy, I was surprised as well.'

I laughed as the doting father. But now, hitting my own half-century, I realised that although I could have written 'turn fifty' in my diary at any point since I learnt to hold a crayon . . . *I was surprised as well.*

We had a family get-together for the occasion. My brother gave me an Apple Watch. My mum wrote a fiftieth birthday poem. She tried to read it in front of the whole family and burst into tears halfway through the first line. Mum had a quick walk round the block to compose herself, and I thought: life has come full circle. On 17 May 1965, it was me who got upset and popped out suddenly.

But fifty made me look back. I was born only two decades after Hitler's suicide. My brother – the comedian Tim Vine – arrived twenty-two months after me. When we played soldiers as kids, we called them German and British. We put the soldiers away and I grew up. Tim brilliantly refused to. He never wanted to get any closer to university than supportively watching me being awarded an honorary degree. He held out against adulthood all those years: I never realised you could do that.

It hit home when I went to see his most recent tour. My little brother's name in the huge lightbox above theatre entrances! As the 49-year-old me drew final breaths, I brought Anna to watch a show. She and I presented our complimentary tickets and slid past other knees to reach our seats. I held her hand – she is eight now – and wondered why the word *childishness* is always negative. Why does every parent say *Don't be silly*? The other day I heard one school mum sigh to another: 'Well, I'm afraid we had a slight outbreak of high spirits.' My brother's act is childish and silly and it makes your spirit soar.

Back when Anna was three or four, she only understood two professions — firefighter and comedian. So Uncle Tim was her hero from the start, because I have never driven a fire engine. That night at the theatre he unleashed a torrent of nonsense so overwhelming it almost washed us away. I whispered to Anna: 'Look, darling. The old guy in front of us is about to die laughing.' He was a sergeant-major type with broken veins in his cheeks who groaned and gasped and doubled up so violently in his cricket sweater that I honestly thought he would peg it right there in Row Q of the Fairfield Halls.

Afterwards I asked: 'What was your favourite joke tonight?'

Anna replied: 'I had a map of Italy tattooed on my chest, but I've got really sore Naples.'

A line purer than poetry. Yet I felt a sadness – I had robbed myself of the childhood Tim managed to continue. After my birthday party I glanced at his gift on my wrist and reflected that if the Apple Watch was bought by comedy, perhaps every second of my life was now a joke.

Which was when I decided to go on *Strictly Come Dancing*.

3. Could You Do That Again Without Clutching My ******

I was told to come to a secret room in Roehampton. But the date was in August during a family holiday in Edinburgh. So I said no, sorry, I would have to come to the secret room another time. And the response was: If you don't come, you can't dance.

That was the moment I realised I wanted to dance. I mean . . . desperately. Aged fifty, dressed like the main suspect in a raid on Peter Crouch's laundry basket, I needed to embark on the whole *Strictly Come Dancing* adventure for a whole host of reasons:

- My daughters had discovered that I had said 'no' three times and were not going to rest until they got an assurance that, if *Strictly* asked again, I would take up the offer
- At fifty your brain starts to narrow. If we don't force ourselves outside our comfort zones, by sixty the surface of our minds is glazed as hard as a builder's mug
- Over the years I had faced serious allegations of dad-dancing
- I wanted to do that face people do in the tango, the one where it looks like your whole family just died
- They had given me the codename 'Nemo'. Basically I really just wanted a codename

The secret room in Roehampton was actually the size of a tennis court, a sort of ballroom with a bouncy wooden floor. On arrival in a cab — which had turned up outside my home with the words MR NEMO stuck in the windscreen — I had my first paparazzi experience. A man with a long lens rushed towards me. I got ready to throw that *I-Wish-I-Wasn't-This-Famous* pose which I had seen in magazines, but the photographer asked in a foreign accent: 'Where . . . is Peter Andre?'

I said I had not even met Peter yet.

He followed up with 'Where . . . are the celebrities?' (to be honest that was a little crushing) and I said I was trying to find them myself.

Inside the secret room were all the people I had heard of. Anton du Beke and Brendan Cole, plus female professionals like the Amazonian Natalie Lowe, Janette Manrara and Kristina Rihanoff, a Russian bombshell known as the 'Siren from Siberia' after a series of competitors had their hearts broken. The description was unfair, as Kristina is not from Siberia. I wondered what my wife would say if I was paired with her. Cross that bridge when we come to it.

Also in the ballroom were the so-called celebrities. I say 'so-called' because the weather forecaster Carol Kirkwood and I bonded over the fact that we didn't feel like we had any right to be there, either on the basis of fame or dancing. I reassured her – bookies had made me the favourite-by-a-mile to go out first, and that was *before any other celebrity name had been announced*. I was also a very long 160-to-1 to win the contest. So on paper I was toast before I had even danced one cha, let alone three of them.

The Roehampton process began in a stop-start fashion. We were asked to 'do a few waltz steps', at which point I realised I didn't know a single one. Then a sweet fellow with silver hair and a sweatshirt tried to teach us the Charleston, and Peter Andre slid across the room as smooth as natural yoghurt. I moved more like muesli. The Charleston takes six months to master. After six minutes I was definitely the worst in the building. I felt the panic rise in my throat.

Out of the corner of my eye I could see actresses from *Call the Midwife* and *Coronation Street* gliding around majestically. Carol and I shot each other a glance. Had we been stitched up, dropped into a contest with all these brilliant movers? Iwan Thomas, the beefcake sprinter, looked as focused as he did when he won

Olympic gold. There was a boxer and at least three pop stars.

Oh God, why was I here? During an item on Radio 2 about what the guest had unwisely called 'public sector non-jobs', an irate listener rang to ask, 'Jeremy, what sort of a job is it where you just read out other people's emails?' and now, recalling the way I felt stripped bare by that comment, I was naked again. The panic in my throat rose till it became almost edible. Suddenly 160-to-1 seemed generous.

If you don't watch the show – *Strictly* is now, I reckon, the biggest and most successful format the BBC has ever devised – it is pretty simple. Fifteen celebrities (shorthand: 'slebs') are paired with a pro dancer. Every week they dance. Four judges roast, toast and score them; the public vote for their favourite couple. The judge/public votes combine and the two couples with the lowest scores dance against each other, with the judges eliminating the weakest. For the slebs it is like being in a hostage situation where their captors execute them one at a time.

The show hurtles on to a final edition where the four surviving pairs face each other for the prized BBC Glitterball, which is made of plastic.

None of the above would matter were it not for two things I have failed to mention – half the country watches, and the whole blooming thing is *broadcast live*.

Why is it so successful? The veteran host Sir Bruce Forsyth put his finger on it. 'When it started, we didn't think the celebrities would try. How wrong we were.'

As everyone knows, the word 'celebrity' is interchangeable with 'personality disorder'. Put fifteen broken souls into a dance contest and they will do anything to avoid the humiliation of being thrown out, even the Argentine tango.

One thing I should add – a complicating factor. Contrary to appearances, *Strictly* is not purely a technical contest. The judges score on ability, but the audience vote with their hearts. And it is very hard to work out where the two intersect.

For example, in 2014 Dave 'Hairy Biker' Myers stormed along as the loveable amateur for weeks until the viewers decided he was unfairly taking the place of more competent dancers and pulled the plug. Similarly, the über-cool Pixie Lott was the finest dancer of her year but somehow failed to connect with the audience and was wordlessly defenestrated. Gabby Logan was voted out early when she drifted into view at the back of a camera shot doing stretching exercises, which, combined with a thousand-yard stare when she was about to dance, gave the off-putting subliminal message: 'I am taking this very seriously.'

So in combining the votes of judges and audience to see who wins, the programme creates a complex space between being technically effective and being liked – which is where politicians operate every single hour of the day.

You'll think I'm crazy to draw the comparison between acts on a dance floor and Acts of Parliament, but my next chapter is about a general election programme that took place in the very same network of studios in Elstree . . . so in Britain there are already mysterious connections between dancing and politics.

The main lesson from *Strictly* is probably summed up like this: the programme is not judging you on what you do. It is judging you on who you are.

Now the good news. I was told my partner would be Karen Clifton, a Venezuelan born Vanessa Guedes Cardenas in 1982. She came at me with every single part of her body dancing, even her hair. It is no exaggeration to say that Karen is one of the most gifted, hypnotic, expert dancers on the face of this planet. Her whole physique is expressive. Her grace is amazing. Her hamstrings are as tight as a Greek budget. She is Latin to the end of her immaculately painted nails.

You can probably sense that I was bowled over.

In the introductory episode, when our names were paired, she jumped out of the crowd of dancers with a loud yelp and hugged me. Bless, Karen actually managed to look delighted at being paired with the favourite-to-be-first-out. I had the sudden thought that the show might be more fun than expected.

I called this book *What I Learnt* because if I look back on *Strictly* – where Karen kept us in for a staggering eight weeks, being eliminated only a fortnight before the god Andre – the dance lessons and the life lessons blend so you can barely tell them apart. Presenters like me are trained to think that dance is not serious because it rhymes with 'prance' – as Iwan Thomas said in his introductory video: 'I have always thought dancing is for wallies' – and also because moving your body around to music has no obvious point. It will not unblock a drain or dialyse a kidney. Dancing will not plough a field. It will not catch a murderer, unless you do it as part of a police operation.

But the same could be said of all sport and all entertainment. We could even argue that different colours or differently shaped buildings serve no purpose, so why have them? Frequently on Radio 2 we will be doing a feature on an expensive item – the statue of *The Three Graces* in Edinburgh, say, or Wayne Rooney – and a listener will comment, 'For that price you could buy forty kidney dialysis machines!' as if that means the large immobile object . . . or *The Three Graces* . . . has been massively overvalued.

It is very powerful, the argument that nothing has a value unless it has a use. Yet following that logic lands you at all sorts of surprising destinations. The royal family rehoused above a petrol station. Hairdressers abolished. The World Cup cancelled and Wimbledon called off. Ed Sheeran working as a forklift driver. All comedians forced to retrain as soldiers.

A friend once asked me, 'Have you ever been late to work because you were having sex?' and when I said no, I had always been on time, she just murmured: 'Tragic.' She felt I had missed the point – that life is more about fun than function.

So dance is definitely something. The remaining question, and one that came back to me daily on *Strictly*, is whether dance might be *everything*. Whether, as in the phrase Bill Shankly used about football: 'It is not a matter of life and death – it's much more important than that.'

For Karen, it was as big as life itself. Her mum moved her from Venezuela to New York when she was six, then almost by accident into a state-sponsored dance programme set up to help kids with poor English two years later. 'So you started dancing at eight,' I told her, 'and I started dancing on August the eighth.'

In a whisper I confessed I was terrified we would be eliminated immediately. Not because I would have minded getting my autumn back, but because it would have been hard for my girls, aged nine and eleven, to see dad come straight home with the crease still visible in his brand-new tracksuit bottoms. Might we be out first?

'Do what I tell you, and we won't be,' was Karen's exhilarating response. I loved her for that.

Our first encounter in a private gym was, frankly, an embarrassment. I came in dragging a heavy object in a four-foot cardboard box. We did not really know each other at all. After we had been practising for an hour Karen asked me, just to make conversation: 'What's in the long box?'

I replied: 'An axe.'

A look crossed her face, as if she was wishing she had chosen a room with a fire escape.

'An axe?'

I was about to explain that we had done a radio feature that day on the joy of using an axe to cut wood and the axe-enthusiast arrived at the studios bearing one as a gift in a package I had not yet even opened. But instead of saying that, for some reason I just blurted: 'Don't worry, I am not a murderer.'

We managed to put the axe incident behind us.

The first televised dance was to be the cha-cha-cha. When I arrived at the studio to see the set being built I was told it would be 'based on your work for the BBC election programmes'. That in itself was hilarious – I had never imagined any possible link between elections and ballroom, between Dimbleby and Tonioli. But when I walked into the studio on the day of the programme I could hardly stop giggling. My appearance would be introduced with an 'election Swingometer' projected onto the floor. With Dave Arch's band ready to play, the producers said I should announce something political 'which does not mention any party'. Now I giggled a bit more; how on earth was that even possible? As I stood in front of the musicians, multicoloured graphics swirling around my feet, behind me were two tall curtained-off wooden kiosks with the words POLLING STATION above them. So I would say something about politics . . . the music would start . . . and a curtain would fly back to reveal Karen, who would roll her hips seductively and shimmy out of the voting booth.

I was giggling again. For a hard-news guy this could not, by any stretch of the imagination, be more unreal.

Or more fun.

What we decided was this. I would wear a formal newsreader jacket. I would point at the *Strictly* Swingometer and cry in a very serious voice: 'Oh dear, only sixteen per cent! But I wonder if that would be different in — *September*?' I did not really understand what any of that meant, but nobody minded. As I said 'September' the song of that name by Earth, Wind & Fire would start with a deafening crash. I would throw off the jacket. The curtain would shoot back and Karen would begin her polling-station-gyration.

Suddenly it was thirty seconds away. We were about to be on live TV.

Lights, cheering, and the breathless announcement: 'And now — dancing the cha-cha-cha — Jeremy Vine and Karen Clifton.'

I am afraid I had a rush of blood, not just to the head, but to every other part of my anatomy. The result was not nervousness. The opposite. The combination of adrenaline and joy made my whole body surge. The audience erupted. Instead of focusing on what I had been told — by a German dancer friend of Karen — was the magical 'vun millimetre' of extra space I needed between my head and shoulders, I moved across the dance floor with all the finesse of a man running down a mountain to escape a volcanic eruption. A group of women from Tewkesbury, who sat near the right corner of the floor and whom I had met earlier, started screaming as we passed.

At one point I had to stretch out my arms as Karen, with her back pressed against me, sank to her haunches. For some reason, as this happened, I just shouted: 'YOWZERS.' There was even a photo of me shouting 'YOWZERS', which is not a word I have shouted since school.

The dance was given two points out of ten by judge Craig Revel Horwood, who said – at least this is what I think he said through all the audience shouting – 'You would not even get booked at the national dad-dancing championships in Devon with that.'

But we were through.

Others were having their own revelations. The pop star Jay McGuiness danced a jaw-dropping jive to the music from *Pulp Fiction* in week two. Afterwards he wandered into the costume room and was surrounded by me, the Irish singer Daniel O'Donnell and Ainsley Harriott. We understood what Jay had done because we now knew that the impact of the live dance floor flushes thirty per cent of your technique on the spot. So Daniel, Ainsley and I congratulated the star of The Wanted with pats on the back and heartfelt sincerity.

Something powerful passed between us. Jay said nothing in reply. He simply turned and walked out of the room. As he left I realised he was crying.

The contest gathered pace. I felt like I had woken up in someone else's dream. I was shedding weight so quickly my wedding ring fell off my finger as I walked down the street.

My partnership with Karen was to be the central part of the experience. You expect a dancer to be a little vague and mystical, rolling up late in lacy outfits, wafting around scented with lavender, constantly humming the tune to 'Wuthering Heights' and unsure what month it is. But Karen was the opposite. Bang on time every day and sharp as a razor. More gorse bush than Kate Bush. Being partnered with her was like going on manoeuvres with the SAS.

After I raised her awkwardly above my head for our second dance, the American Smooth, she asked: 'Jeremy, could you do that lift again, but this time without clutching my vagina?'

That's when I started to write down her best one-liners.

During a waltz I had to approach her, stroke her face and take her hand. But I kept moving too early. 'Don't come with me because you want to come with me,' Karen said. 'Come with me because it's the right time.'

31

On another occasion: 'Do that again. But don't approach me with the frightening hands.'

Or: 'You came to me and you took me. But you ended up disappointing me.'

There was advice that could work for the whole of life: 'Don't look at your feet. Never look at your feet.'

Or, simply: 'Dance your height.'

It was not all sweetness and light. The quickstep demanded that I keep my shoulders in place and not let my arms sag. When they did, she told me: 'LOCK IN THAT FUCKING SHIT NOW.'

During the waltz, when a couple's heads have to face in starkly different directions, I sneaked a glance at her. The immediate retort came in a heavy Bronx accent during the most romantic section of the song: 'DON'T YOU DARE FUCKING LOOK AT ME.'

None of which should make Karen sound harsh. In fact she was exactly what I needed: a demanding teacher, a kind of genius. She managed to remain patient even in the opening fortnight, when the journalist in me insisted on bringing a reporter's notepad and slowed her teaching to a crawl by thinking up a name for every step and writing it down with arrows and sketches alongside. The notepad lasted a fortnight. Whatever part of my reporter's brain demanded a written record of the dance, it was not the part that would be controlling my dancing.

Mind you, Karen recognised my need for labels. When I asked her if a particular tight turn had a name: 'Yes. "Squash your balls" is what we're calling it.'

It was in about the fourth or fifth week of the competition that an elderly listener rang my Radio 2 show from her home in Yorkshire. Her voice was frail but full of excitement.

'Jeremy, I think you can actually win *Strictly*.'

'Really?' I said, genuinely touched.

'Yes. You can win the whole contest.' Then she continued: 'I was born blind . . . '

The television shows were overwhelmingly scary because of the live element. Contestants like Kirsty Gallacher and Daniel O'Donnell, who were both absolute sweethearts to me, freely admitted that those Saturday nights left their nerves in tatters. Katie Derham said that when she first took to the dance floor: 'I couldn't feel my legs.' One by one we were eliminated, as in an Agatha Christie novel where lots of posh dinner guests pretend not to notice the corpse on the floor.

First Iwan went, after a spectacular attempt to pass off his breakdancing as a salsa. 'I don't know what that was,' said chief judge Len Goodman, angrily pointing at the spot on the floor where Iwan had landed after bravely jumping off the stage with an injured hip. With appalling timing, Iwan then had to drive from Elstree to Southampton to attend a party thrown to celebrate his first appearance.

The following week the boxer Anthony Ogogo left, then Daniel and Ainsley Harriott. With every programme the stakes rose.

The press seemed to fixate on *Strictly*, and in the absence of stories simply made them up. Carol Kirkwood opened one newspaper to discover she was 'battling to save her sight' – bravely dancing despite rapidly encroaching blindness, which she told me she never knew she had. A magazine reported 'a fist-fight between Peter Andre and Jay McGuiness over Aliona', Jay's pro dancer. Georgia May Foote and Jamelia were not speaking 'because Georgia told Jamelia she couldn't dance'. Helen George was 'aloof' and the *Daily Mail* reported that I was 'known to be hugely demanding with the costume department', which made my wife laugh. If only!

During one interview Karen said, as a joke, that I had a six-pack that was 'better than Peter Andre's' (he was famous for his abdominals in the 1995 'Mysterious Girl' video). Karen went further: 'I know Jeremy has a better six-pack because I have touched it.' This gained more traction than anything ever written about me during my entire career. When I saw 'Karen Clifton has touched Jeremy Vine's SIX-PACK' headlining in the *Mirror*, I was startled. Interviewed by a magazine, I rashly said that if I reached the *Strictly* final I would 'recreate Peter Andre's "Mysterious Girl" video with my abs exposed'. At the time there seemed to be no chance whatsoever of getting to the final. When, in weeks six and seven, we hit a sweet spot, I started to panic.

Karen kept us on track. She was so brainy she seemed to have a sixth sense. During one of the last rehearsals for our foxtrot, performed in the studio with all the cameras tracking us, I messed up a step.

She had not noticed, I reckoned. But afterwards she asked: 'What happened there?'

'Nothing,' I said, feeling like a naughty boy.

'You missed a step, Jeremy. Did something distract you?'

'No.'

'Was it Jamelia? You were chatting to her earlier. Did someone say something to you?'

'No, honestly.'

'Anita Rani?'

'No.'

'Did someone wave or something?'

'No. Nothing happened, Karen, honestly. It was just one of those things.'

At that moment the programme editor, Louise, walked over. 'That was brilliant, Jeremy. The wink.'

'The *wink*?' Karen repeated, looking at me. 'You winked?'

'Yes,' said Louise happily, 'when Jeremy came down the right edge of the floor there, he did a big wink at the camera. We loved it in the gallery.'

When she had gone, Karen said: 'You don't do a wink unless we rehearse a wink, okay? That wink was not authorised. DO NOT WINK UNLESS WE PRACTISE A WINK. Otherwise it'll throw you off.'

Nothing in life is more exhilarating than being rocketed by a dancer.

The jive was a fine showcase for Karen's talents as a choreographer. She remembered a moment in *Grease* which lasted only two seconds, where Travolta pounced on the floor and spun himself in a circle while lying sideways. By the time I had practised it sixty times, I had worn a hole in the outer edge of my shoe – not the sole, the side – which baffled Megs in the costume department.

'We have literally never seen this before,' she laughed, holding the shoe up in the light. I kept it as a memento.

But again, I was my own worst enemy. Dancing to 'Splish Splash', the Bobby Darin song, I had to start behind a shower curtain. Minutes before we were due on stage, I was offered a pink shower cap by Billie from the costume department.

'Don't take it,' said Karen.

'But – all I have to do is appear, throw the cap off and start dancing.'

'It'll throw you off. Even a tiny thing can do that. Remember the wink.'

'Honestly, it won't.'

I took the cap.

Sadly, when the shower curtain opened to reveal me standing in a bathtub, I was so taken up with removing the hat and throwing it into the audience I made a mess of the first ten seconds of the dance, where I was supposed to turn at ninety degrees twice and move my arms in an organised way.

The result was that Jonathan Ross showed the shower cap incident to Darcey Bussell when she appeared on his TV chat show. Darcey, bless her, just laughed when Ross said: 'This is basically a man having a nervous breakdown live on television, isn't it?'

So we did the cha-cha-cha. The American Smooth. The jive. The waltz (which was awful – I felt like I had Locked-In Syndrome, where a person can only communicate by blinking). Somehow we survived that episode. Then we had a salsa and a tango.

The tango was the big one.

Karen said: 'I want you to appear on a horse.'

'A real live one?'

'No, but an enormous one.'

Indeed, our fibreglass monster was huge (with testicles the size of tennis balls, if that is a guide) and I needed a ladder to mount it. When the music started I would climb down and pull the angry-face. Apparently cowboys needed a fearsome expression when the tango was first invented; in the absence of women they had to practise with each other out on the plains, and the face was their way of showing they weren't romantically interested in other cowboys.

I probably overdid the tragic expression. I did not just look like my whole family had died, I looked like their bodies had been minced and eaten by buzzards.

Afterwards the audience went crazy. Bruno jumped up at his desk, ready to drop a Tonioli of manure on me. 'That was how the West was LOST,' he cried, but the rest was drowned out by booing from the far-too-generous spectators. Craig Revel Horwood, wonderfully, offered an extra point 'because of the way your little bottom tweaked just as it passed my desk'.

I have to give Craig credit for his one-liners. I am convinced that the more brutal they were, the more people voted for me and Karen. When he made the remark about my cha-cha-cha and the dad-dancing championships, we were saved. When he said I danced 'like a stork hit by lightning', the viewers spared us again (one even sent me a T-shirt with a picture of an electrocuted stork on it). After I did a rather uncoordinated salsa to Michael Jackson's 'Thriller', Horwood said: 'The problems really began when you started to dance.'

Constant bad scores made me grateful for small mercies. When our 'Thriller'-salsa finally got a four from Craig – *a four!* – Karen and I were so uncontrollably jubilant on the balcony that it looked as if we had won the whole contest. Karen screamed, grabbed Claudia Winkleman and put her in a headlock. It was the only time I ever gave her advice. 'We may need to give a little thought to our balcony etiquette,' I said gently. Cheam meets Caracas.

People kept asking me, 'Why were you always laughing when you were getting those insults hurled at you?' and I replied that I could never believe where I was: standing in that famous end-of-desk spot being given both barrels from Horwood & Tonioli after dancing on the BBC's biggest show. I never minded the gunpowder burns.

And there was even the occasional pleasurable moment too. After that incident at Roehampton where I realised just how hard the Charleston was, I had spent every waking moment perfecting its central toe/heel slicing motion. When we actually pulled it off, the head judge Len Goodman pointed at me and said: 'One word from the old man. Genius.' I almost wept with surprise.

Afterwards Karen quietly asked me: 'It was good, but do you remember your final position?'

'Yes,' I said, and showed her what she had taught me. The right arm neatly stretched out, fingers carefully arranged. One leg straight, the foot resting on the base of the big toe.

'That's what I taught you, yes,' Karen confirmed. 'Your actual final position when we did the dance was a kind of star jump.'

Once again, I apologised.

Still, the quickstep was probably our most solid dance; it got the least criticism and we were thrown out in an elimination show watched by ten million people. But even our exit was made joyful by this personal message from a young mum:

Tweet on Monday Nov 16th, day after elimination

22:11   40%

Mentions

Catherine
@theJeremyVine On Sun my heartbroken 4yr old said she was going straight to sleep because no one could stop you dancing in her dreams.

All in all, I loved my time on *Strictly*. There was one particularly telling moment that happened outside the studio, which we will come to in a later chapter because it needs a bit of thoughtful unpacking.

But most of it was plain madness. In fact, by the end of the contest the madness had become sanity. Bizarre was the norm, and the world beyond *Strictly* looked very grey.

Our tango night with the horse, for example, was a facer from start to finish. An hour before broadcast I was in the costume department wearing only a pair of purple Y-fronts. I looked up to see a long line of people walking into the room. Three civil servants led the way for John Whittingdale, Secretary of State for Culture. Behind him were the BBC1 controller Charlotte Moore, head of BBC entertainment Katie Taylor, and Peter Salmon, the controller of BBC Production. They all saw me in my pants.

The senior executives, civil servants and Cabinet Minister all stopped in their tracks, alarmed at my semi-nude state, and made to turn around. Automatically I said, 'No, don't worry, come in. This happens all the time', which it didn't, not with a Cabinet Minister anyway. There was a piece of chewing gum in my mouth and I pulled it out – big mistake. The gum turned out to be in its stickiest stage and I could not get it off my hand no matter how violently I flicked it at the dustbin. As the others talked, studiously ignoring the agitated journalist in the purple Y-fronts flicking gum at the bin, I grabbed my outfit for the night and pulled it on as fast as possible.

Finally I was dressed.

I straightened up and approached Whittingdale. 'There we are,' I said. 'Dignity restored.'

The minister replied: 'Yes, although you are wearing a cowboy outfit.'

At that point Peter Salmon intervened in a way that I thought was rather telling.

'John,' he started, 'last time Jeremy was broadcasting from Elstree was for the general election in May. He was doing the graphics. Now he's back dressed as a cowboy to dance for *Strictly*. And that, if I may say so, demonstrates the range of what we do at the BBC.'

4. Eaten by Sharks

Four or five hungry sharks entered the room that evening, along with the man in charge of the BBC.

Election Day, 2015. No dance floor now. Instead we are in a small room off the main studio in Elstree. Beside me on the sofa the Director General, Baron Tony Hall. All BBC chiefs should come with a title, otherwise the staff have to make one up. Sat around us that supercharged night: James Harding, head of news. Nick Robinson, political editor. David Dimbleby, my producer.

Whoops – let me adjust the misleading comma. It's not 'David Dimbleby, my producer'. Maybe on another planet there is a David Dimbleby who is the producer of a Jeremy Vine, but not this one. That would be like asking Attenborough to hold my microphone while I whispered something about arachnids. Mr Dimbleby is of course the presenter. My producer is Ben Watt.

Also there: Sam Woodhouse, election editor. I shall return to the sharks in a moment.

Sam was in charge of making sure we all entered the room at exactly 9.30 p.m. on Thursday 7 May, half an hour before the voting ended. It sounds like an easy job – it's traditional in the BBC for the most senior people to be given the simplest jobs – but during a rehearsal of entering the room the previous day, Sam had been locked in.

After being released by security in scenes reminiscent of the in-house comedy *W1A*, Sam declared it was very important the same thing did not happen to the team on election night itself, because the only people free to take our places in the Elstree studio as the show went live at 10 p.m. would be students on work experience. So tonight two security staff waited on the other side of the meeting room door, in case it had to be forced. I noticed that one of them was laughing.

It was not the only unhinged element of that election night. British law on voting days is properly batty. Broadcasters cannot discuss an election on the day itself (even though everyone else is doing so). We can only say 'it's raining'. Punishable by imprisonment is the offence of airing any prediction before the polls close. So the idea of a bunch of people going into a room to *discuss the election and share an exit poll* – a rocket-fired class of prediction – is understandably terrifying for those in charge of the BBC in this era of the social media leak. To be on the safe side, I entered the room with just one sheet of paper and a biro. There is no retweet button on a sheet of paper.

The door snapped shut. Were we going to be trapped, only emerging during the first Miliband term? Sam produced his smartphone and placed it on the table in front of us . . .

And it buzzes almost immediately.

Sam switches it to speaker.

We all lean in.

First we hear the voice of Sue Inglish, head of Westminster. She says she is passing the phone to the polling boffin Professor John Curtice, who has been barricaded into a separate building all day. We can fairly assume not all of that time was spent teasing his election hairstyle into place.

At exactly that moment, on the other side of London, another polling expert, Lord Ashcroft, is declaring at a dinner that 'we are about to see a hung parliament with Labour the largest party'. He has spent many thousands of pounds polling marginal seats – it would have been quicker to spend the money on eggs and spread them all over his face – but at this point, with eighteen minutes till ballot boxes across the UK are thrown into vans and ferried to the counts, it is very hard to find anyone who does not agree with Ashcroft.

To confess: as Sam's phone buzzes, I am equally convinced Ed Miliband will emerge from the 2015 election as Prime Minister. That is because I did not listen carefully enough to my mum.

41

A week before the election the mum-phone rang at home – like most households, we have a landline that is only ever used by our mums. My parents live in the Conservative/LibDem marginal of Sutton & Cheam and rarely express any political views. But during the call on the mum-phone she suddenly exclaimed, 'They cannot be allowed to run us down here', which turned out to be a reference to Nicola Sturgeon's Scottish National Party.

It seems the hypnotic Conservative chant – 'vote Miliband, get the SNP', repeated a thousand times during the campaign – had even penetrated Cheam. I should have realised, as my mother uttered the words 'they cannot be allowed to run us', that Ed Miliband had not just had his bacon sandwich, he had had his chips as well.

And there was another incident, actually one of those 25,000 calls to my show. Dale Aston in Pontypridd rang to complain about Miliband's panicky demeanour during the referendum on Scottish independence. 'That man,' he told my listeners, 'is as weak as whisky down water.'

He added: 'He is about as much use as a boil on the scrotum.'

I did not pay close enough attention to my listener or my mother – two, as they say, *#EpicFails*. Like Lord Ashcroft, I assumed Labour had edged the election.

So the numbers that came out of Sam's mobile sounded like an earthquake. What was even more bizarre is that Professor Curtice read them from the other end of the line in the bored-but-precise voice you use when you are telling someone where a restaurant is and they really ought to know.

'Conservative three hundred and twenty, SNP fifty-eight, Liberal Democrat eleven, Labour two hundred and thirty-eight.'

We all look at each other. The Conservatives have *won*? Labour crushed? The SNP . . .

I remembered a surreal moment on the first day of rehearsals. I was talking to David Dimbleby in a corridor when a woman with horrible injuries appeared through a side door and started walking towards us. I felt my heart beat faster. The left leg of her jeans was sliced all the way from the ankle to the hip. A deep wound in her thigh gaped wide open. Blood covered the woman's trousers and shirt. She also had her head bandaged so thoroughly that only her mouth and one eye were visible.

Dimbleby stared at her and roared with laughter. 'Did you survive?' he shouted.

The woman, drawing closer, replied: 'I'm afraid not.' They were both laughing, and now I understood. The election team shared the building with the actors and directors of the hospital drama *Holby City*, and this lady was an extra.

But if that was Magritte-level surreal, the Professor Curtice forecast was the full Salvador Dalí.

His voice on the mobile cuts in on our thoughts.

'Labour support will be stronger in the north, so don't be alarmed when the first results from Sunderland show Labour performing well. Trust the data.'

The significance of that was not lost on me.

In the 2010 general election Curtice came out with a stunningly accurate prediction showing Labour decimated. But strangely the first results (from Sunderland) suggested an improvement for what was then Gordon Brown's party. At the main table Dimbleby's guests all went in to bat on the assumption that the 'exit poll must be wrong', which had the professor tearing at his shirt backstage and making animal noises. As he explained to us afterwards, Labour had done better in their core areas but correspondingly worse in tighter seats – piling up extra votes in safe Sunderland, where they won easily, but not in places like marginal Nuneaton where they most needed them. Labour's 'core boost' only made Brown's problems worse, and Curtice finished the night vindicated.

For that reason, when the Prof ends his mobile call in 2015, we are not about to question the numbers. The room breaks into animated chatter. I turn to the Director General, sitting to my left, and say: 'So Scotland goes independent and the BBC gets shut down.' Just instinct speaking. Lord Hall responds with the merest nod of his head, not even enough to buy a painting at an auction.

Now I stare at the television. There they are, the sharks, swimming in silent circles ever since Sam shut the door. Any pinprick, any drop of blood from one of us, I think, and we will all be high-definition dinner. The images are part of a perfectly timed BBC documentary called *Shark*. The TV sound is down, but there is something about those jagged sets of teeth that reminds me of Liberal Democrat conferences.

Then we do what journalists do in a crisis – all jump up and start charging about. The programme goes live in thirteen minutes.

A little background. My role at election time is to front the virtual reality graphics. During rehearsals in 2015 I realised we were having a major breakthrough. For the first time the computerised imagery that showed me walking along Downing Street, or inside the House of Commons, actually *made it look like I was there*.

For years, both Peter Snow and I had rather self-consciously arm-wheeled our way around graphics that looked like graphics. They were not virtual reality at all – in a famous sequence where cartoon versions of the party leaders ran up Downing Street, Charles Kennedy looked more like Charlton Heston after being mangled by a chariot in *Ben-Hur*. Snow's famous phrase to explain the charade was: 'Just a bit of fun.' But the new-generation graphics made it all more serious. On election night I would be outside a Number Ten door, or inside a Commons chamber, that looked so real no one could see the joins.

In fact our 2015 Downing Street was so convincing that as the election programme extended into the following morning, a viewer would complain that: 'Vine's sequences have obviously been pre-recorded, because he is in Downing Street at night but the sun has come up. This is an appalling deceit by the BBC.'

For the graphics team, the complaint was a breakthrough moment of historical proportions.

As we leave the Curtice briefing at 9.47 p.m. it strikes me our new turbo-realism has a downside. The professor's numbers do not sound right – they are out of line with eighty-nine out of ninety pre-election polls – but Ben and I have to feed them, coughing and spluttering, into my ultra-real House of Commons, so I can offer Dimbleby 'the chance to see how the new chamber will look with all the MPs inside' – *and it really will look like the chamber*.

If we have messed up the election result, the BBC's enemies will argue that there is no point having us at all. My virtual Commons (which even shows the Prime Minister on the benches, blinking and fidgeting) will be screengrabbed to death as the boot goes in. 'If they can't even get a general election right . . . '

The clock strikes ten.

Our exit poll causes a murmur of shock in the studio from the camera crews – you can go a lifetime in broadcasting without hearing that sound.

A minute earlier, Ed Miliband had been so certain he was going to walk into Number Ten that a well-connected friend of mine said Labour had asked Cameron and Osborne to be out of Downing Street by 11 a.m. on 8 May.

In an instant, as Dimbleby theatrically pulls a postcard from an envelope and reads the numbers – 320, 238, 11, 58 – all expectations are dashed. The forecast does not just drive a coach and horses through the polls. It threatens to end political polling as a business (the only poll which correctly forecast the result had not been published because the pollster felt it was too far out of line with the others). Over my left shoulder, on a balcony with Andrew Neil, there is a loud laugh from Paddy Ashdown: 'If your numbers are right I'll eat my hat.'

Alastair Campbell shakes his head in the seat beside Lord Ashdown and goes one better. 'If your exit poll is right I'll eat my kilt.'

From his giant illuminated desk in the middle of the studio, Dimbleby calls across to me.

'Jeremy, show us what the new House of Commons will look like.'

The remote control in my not-very-dry palm fires up the graphic and I am surrounded by a gasp of green leather.

'And there it is, David, the new House of Commons – as we are forecasting it – although remember, not a single result is in yet.'

At that point a nine-foot hologram of David Cameron is beamed into the studio, next to the forecast: 320 SEATS.

I look at Cameron's face as his suited body looms over us like one of the spooks in *Ghostbusters*. It is an odd expression he wears, as if a bad smell has just wafted past him.

And I remember the reason.

In order to make the graphics look super-real, some weeks before the election we asked the party leaders if they would pose for us inside a temporary green tent so we could get a 3D image of them.

Someone told me: 'The PM needs to know we are not wasting his time, Jeremy – can you turn up for the imaging session to ensure he feels good about it?'

So early one Sunday morning I arrived in a basement room on the third floor below ground in New Broadcasting House. The Prime Minister was due to see us before an interview on *The Andrew Marr Show*. At 8.45 a.m., bang on time to the minute, he comes through the door with his communications chief Craig Oliver and two security people.

Knowing Mr Cameron's time is short, I greet him with a brisk: 'Thank you for coming! We just need you to stand here and not move for ninety seconds.'

At this point the producer intervenes.

'While the PM stands there, Jeremy, can you stand in front of him – just here, yes – and talk to him – if that's okay, Prime Minister – just to make sure you have something to look at and listen to while we map you in three dimensions. You don't need to say anything yourself. Okay, over to you Jeremy.'

Being suddenly confronted by an extremely famous person, and needing to say something, can have awkward outcomes. I read somewhere that when the Olympic rower Steve Redgrave met Nelson Mandela, he just panicked and asked the world's most famous symbol of moral and political courage: 'Can you drive?'

When Radio 2 got me tickets to see a Taylor Swift concert and meet her backstage, I was bowled over. But as the moment came,

I suffered a similar seizure. My kids were with me, but I was more nervous by far.

Swift came up to us backstage and said: 'Well, who have we here?'

I wanted to say, 'My daughters Martha and Anna', but no words came out so I just coughed and pointed.

There was a lull. I knew I should make conversation. Noticing Taylor Swift was very tall – in her heels almost as tall as me – I meant to say: 'You're very tall.' Unfortunately, as that thought came into my head I remembered a clip on YouTube where she had sung 'Dancing in the Dark' backstage with Bruce Springsteen at a concert in America, and Springsteen was much less tall.

All of these thoughts came together as Taylor Swift looked enquiringly at me, and I blurted: 'Is Bruce Springsteen very short?' Those five words were all I have ever said to Taylor Swift. I saw her look of confusion before aides swept her away.

In the BBC basement a whirr and a buzz signal the start of the graphics filming. The 3D camera starts to revolve around the Prime Minister. I am staring at Mr Cameron and he is staring at me, and I realise I have just been given a quite remarkable opportunity. The Prime Minister of the world's fifth-biggest economy has to look directly at me for two full minutes, and not speak, while I can say whatever I like.

Today, of course, writing this, I can summon up a whole series of important things I should have said:

- Call for an end to world famine
- Call for all children to receive food and education
- Massive homebuilding programme to solve UK housing crisis
- An end to all war

Instead, I panicked.

'We had a gardener ring my show, Mr Cameron, and he was in the middle of gardening – potatoes I think – or – no, it might have been leeks – definitely a vegetable – and he looked up and someone was using a drone to spy on him while he was hoeing – yes, the sort of drone you can buy in Maplin – hovering above him – that close. Sorry, Prime Minister, please just keep looking straight at me. Anyway, the gardener tried to swat the drone with his hoe, he was jabbing at it, and he missed, but what if someone – see, what I thought – what if someone flew one over Buckingham Palace and dropped something – and the Queen probably isn't too handy with a hoe. Basically I was wondering if they should be banned – from Maplin, anyway, from high street shops – because, in the situation this gardener had –'

I chuntered on. Credit to the PM, he stared directly at me throughout. Now I began to worry that banning drones from Maplin was the wrong choice of campaign and wondered about changing the subject, yet all I could think of was something I had joked about with my daughters – that Beatles music should be played on buses.

From Maplin to Lady Madonna? I could chance it. Maybe rescue the situation. But then I saw a subtle expression cross the Prime Minister's face. The expression said something like – *Please get this berk out of the room.* His features displayed a weariness that looked almost like physical pain.

Which was the face that ballooned over our studio in 2015. Greeting the news that Mr Cameron's party had won a shock majority at the general election, the nine-foot prime-ministerial hologram showed us a man looking a little queasy, a little fed up with life, a little like he wanted to go back to bed and not get up again all day.

*   *   *

In *Fawlty Towers* there is a fabulous moment that is the definition of surprise. Under the slogan 'No Riff-Raff', Basil invites the great and good of Torquay to sample his best cuisine. But there is a disaster in the hotel kitchen. In a panic, he has to collect the promised main course, duck, from a local French restaurant.

Everyone loves the bit where Basil's car breaks down and he

climbs out and thrashes it with a branch. When he finally gets back to the dining room and his impatient guests, he proudly announces: 'The duck.'

Fawlty lifts the big domed lid on the silver tray with a flourish. Then he looks in horror. It is not duck but a large trifle.

Shocked, Basil pauses for a second with the lid – known as a cloche – in his hand. Then he does a brilliant thing. He replaces the cloche and lifts it a second time. As if looking again will change the dessert from trifle to duck.

Once, travelling with a cameraman, I saw this very move. We were due to film in Birmingham for *Newsnight*, having driven from London. My colleague opened the boot of his car when we arrived. The boot was empty. He had forgotten to pack his camera. His reaction was to shut and reopen the boot, as if the camera would now appear.

Let's call that move – *open, look, not what you expected, close, reopen* – The Cloche.

The general elections of 2010, 2015 and 2017 made us all do The Cloche. The same when Jeremy Corbyn was elected Labour leader. But they were nothing compared to the shock of Brexit, where I really did slam the lid back down and lift it again, expecting (though not necessarily hoping for) a different result.

The unexpected victory of Leicester City in the English Premier League in 2016 was everyone's best national Cloche moment.

The election of Donald Trump was of a different order. That had the whole world doing The Cloche. *Open, close, open again.*

Still trifle.

During the presidential campaign only one opinion poll in the States consistently put The Donald ahead, and I love the story. Its title was a mouthful – the 'USC Dornsife/Los Angeles Times Daybreak tracking poll' was consistently ridiculed by people who noticed the all-important sample of voters contained a 19-year-old black lad in Chicago, who had surprisingly declared for Trump. For technical reasons this teenager was heavily weighted in the sample and could not be removed. Throughout the campaign the *LA Times* poll was scoffed at for having been 'disrupted' and 'corrupted' by the real responses of this real person. Even the newspaper's own readers, residents of liberal California, complained that the *LA Times* was giving such nonsense printed space. As we now know, the poll turned out to be one of very few that accurately predicted the result.

In the run-up to the presidential vote, I was on my guard. I fully expected Hillary Clinton to triumph, probably by a Reagan-sized landslide, but Brexit had made me wary of the dangerous rhythms of the unexpected. So two days before the election I tweeted: 'Every single number looks good for #Hillary. And that is exactly how it looked for #Remain.'

And we know what happened. Trump's victory was the Cloche moment to end them all. We will never expect duck underneath that lid again.

After the American election programme, the BBC graphics team toasted the new quality of politics – surprise. Not just Wimbledon-commentator 'Oh I say' surprise, but proper bare-naked-lady-jumps-out-of-birthday-cake-holding-machinegun surprise. Donald Trump has continued a run of electrifying nights in our green space that confirm this really is the best time in the entire history of the BBC to work on elections.

But there is a bigger lesson for me.

Having done The Cloche so many times, your elections commentator finally and belatedly realises – those 25,000 callers to my show have not just arrived on the line to entertain us. They have taken control.

5. The Witch's Post

A geography lecturer brings his students on a field trip. He takes them to a fast-flowing stream to show the distribution of rocks and stones on the riverbed. They stand on the bank and look out at the water as the professor explains.

'The highest set of stones are pale or light grey in colour, and smoother. They are in shallow waters, so the sun has bleached them over the centuries. They are known as Dolostone.

'The set of stones in the middle of the stream, right below us, are a dark red or even black, with small bubble-holes. They are known as Scoria and have been here since the 1700s – oh, and by the way, that wooden post you can see sticking out of the water is what they would tie witches to. As the river rose, the witch would drown.

'Further along you see the last set of stones, and these are the most interesting. These rocks are brown in colour and have a glassy appearance. They are known as Brown Quartzite. They were left here in . . .'

It is no use. The students around him are not listening. They heard Dolostone, and they heard Scoria, but when their hapless lecturer mentioned the witch's post – and added those electrifying eight words, 'as the river rose, the witch would drown' – the minds of his students were gone. Later that day, none of them will recall the third, most interesting set of stones. In years to come, they will have forgotten the professor, the river, their classmates. Everything except the post.

Frequently on Radio 2, a caller will give us a magnificent example of this phenomenon. The editor will catch my eye, mouthing: 'Witch's Post.' A stray remark that is not part of the central story has completely overwhelmed the rest of the sentence, the item, or, once in a blue moon, the whole of that day's programme. In

51

Chapter One I mentioned caller 24,996, the well-spoken Linda Shawcross in Glasgow, who as part of an attack on so-called spongers in the UK benefits system threw in the phrase: 'When I claimed benefits in Belgium . . .'

As the presenter you want to say: 'Wait, Linda – what? How come you, a rather (if I may say so) posh lady now criticising benefit claimants, were ever *on the dole in Belgium*?' But you fear that when she replies, 'Because I am a trapeze artist and my top was torn off during a jump that went wrong, which meant the audience saw my naked breasts, and in Belgium that is a serious crime which triggered a public prosecution for in-decency during which no Belgian circus would employ me . . .' you have the equivalent of several dead witches on your hands and will be lucky if any of that day's programme survives the drownings.

We had one just two days ago. During an item about hygiene in doctors' surgeries, an expert in the studio said that 'hand gel has been removed from many GPs' surgeries because alcoholics were drinking it'. Suddenly we all forgot what the original item was supposed to be about.

Every Witch's Post creates a rule you didn't know existed. I have changed the names of some programme guests in the examples below, but the rules are immutable:

If you're talking about something else, never mention an air crash.

During an item about the danger of cats and dogs catching the hospital superbug MRSA from humans, and then reinfecting other humans who pet them, I did not think there could be any risk of a Witch's Post since the starting point of the discussion was endlessly fascinating. But the Post came in the form of a glancing reference to the husband of a woman whose dog had died.

JV: 'Were you and the dog close?'

Felicity: 'Lola and I were incredibly close. She got me through an awful time in 2000 when my husband, who was a pilot, died in a plane crash. But then I noticed Lola began to have symptoms . . . '

Felicity made no further reference to the air disaster. But for some reason the concept of *the pilot who dies in a plane crash*, which combines personal tragedy with a reminder that nothing in our lives, not even a pilot at the controls of a plane, is as dependable as it appears, knocks pet infection into a cocked hat.

In an item about severe hallucinations, the caller who told me 'I am now so well recovered from profound psychosis that I have begun training as a pilot' also deserves recognition: that's great news, but which airport, just out of interest, do you fly out of?

There seems to be a particular issue with fireworks. In 2006 the Radio 2 newsreader John Marsh, known to Sir Terry Wogan's fans as Boggy, began reading an item about a man who had suffered life-changing injuries on Guy Fawkes Night. He did not, for reasons that might become clear when you see his script, reach the end of this extremely serious item before collapsing into gales of laughter.

Have a look at the text in front of the newsreader and see if you can work out which particular phrase caused him to lose control:

Safety campaigners have repeated their warnings about the dangers of fireworks after a prankster tried to launch a powerful rocket from his backside.

The 22-year-old man suffered serious internal injuries when the Black Cat Thunderbolt rocket ignited during the Bonfire Night at Monkwearmouth in Sunderland.

Did you get it? John was completely composed and professional until he had to read out the name of the firework. 'Black Cat Thunderbolt' caused the meltdown.

Another distraction was created during the live interview with a villager about catastrophic flooding on the Somerset Levels.

JV: 'Describe where you are.'

Harry: 'I can see nothing but water. I am standing, tragically, next to the location of the Taunton fireworks disaster, and it looks like it will be weeks before anyone gets back into these flooded homes.'

Rock. Paper. Scissors. Any disaster involving fireworks – even though at the time I couldn't place the reference – beats a flood, *no matter how much water the flood involves*. Suddenly we are not thinking about the Somerset Levels. We are thinking about what a fireworks disaster must look like. It is like the moment in the movie *Naked Gun* where a truck carrying a missile ploughs into a fireworks factory, causing the biggest release of pyrotechnics you have ever seen in your life, and the policeman played by Leslie Nielsen shouts at the crowd: 'Please disperse! Nothing to see here!'

The rest of the interview is lost.

It looks like we were establishing a rule that you must

Never refer to a story bigger than your story

but actually that is not quite how the Witch's Post works. In March 2015 the journalist James Delingpole came on to talk about the experience of suddenly arriving in the NHS with a pulmonary embolism. His concern was the number of elderly people on the ward, some with dementia, who could not leave the hospital because there was nowhere safe for them to go. As we know, this is a huge and important story – sometimes rather rudely referred to as 'bed-blocking'. James talked about his medical emergency and the four days he spent in hospital. He then described other patients in some detail before, fatally, ending with a stray reference to the incident which had caused his health problems.

'And it was all because I fell off a horse,' he concluded.

For some reason I felt I should explore the role of the horse.

JV: 'It occurs to me that I should have asked you how exactly you became ill.'

James (*defensively*): 'The horse.'

JV: 'I didn't know you rode horses.'

54

James (*nervously*): 'Oh, it was one of those things.'

JV: 'Were you just galloping around?'

James: 'No. I was fox-hunting.'

Wipeout. The phrase 'I was fox-hunting' is the Witch's Post to end them all. Even the statement 'I broke into Buckingham Palace to look inside the Queen's fridge after a morning spent fox-hunting' diverts your attention from the fridge to the foxes. It might be something to do with our DNA as an animal-loving nation; it is also the way it brings in class. Any reference to class can trigger a fight in an empty room. Fairly or not, 'I was fox-hunting' emerges from the radio as: 'I'm posh. And cruel. I dress in exotically silly outfits and I think the oiks who listen to your show shouldn't even be allowed to polish my toecaps.'

I felt bad for James. He was evidently trying to avoid the Witch's Post. Pushing him towards it was entirely my mistake. The first listener reaction to his compassionate insider's account of an NHS ward was: 'Get this toff off the air.'

So perhaps we need a new rule, one that says

Do not refer to any animal unless it is the main subject of the discussion.

When it came to the item about a restaurant threatened by wildlife activists for serving squirrel, a Witch's Post seemed impossible. The central story, which focused on the lunch menu at the Hadley Bowling Green Inn in Droitwich, was simply too compelling. The staff had listed 'squirrel terrine' for £7.95 and were promptly told by activists that the premises would be firebombed and their cars vandalised. The animal rights campaigners said the menu was cruel to squirrels.

The restaurant's response was perfectly logical.

'But we already serve pork, lamb, beef and chicken. Aren't pigs, sheep, cows and chickens animals too?'

Sadly that only inflamed the situation. The activists were angry because of the unspoken rule that *Squirrels are special because squirrels are furry*. At this point we are safe from a Witch's Post, aren't we? What could possibly distract us from this eye-popping confrontation between the unappetising and the irrational?

A caller, Joyce from Cumbria, managed it. 'There is absolutely nothing wrong with the restaurant menu,' she began. '*Elvis Presley used to eat fried squirrels.*'

Somehow, after those seven words there was nothing more to say. I gulped air. A similar swerve befell us in a discussion about the *Daily Mail*'s description of Ed Miliband's father Ralph as 'the Man who Hated Britain'. After a perfectly sensible conversation, a listener called in to say: 'This may or may not be relevant, but Ralph Miliband's first name was actually Adolf.'

Rule:

Hitler and Elvis leave you nowhere else to go.

Now that I am looking at all the Witch's Posts on my show involving animals, I sense a theme. When we asked whether farmers ought not to treat rabbits as pests, the interviews went perfectly to plan until David in Leigh-on-Sea rang. 'Rabbits are a much more prominent pest for farmers in Australia than they are here. I remember watching a programme on television that showed farmers backing rabbits into a corner of the field and then using a flamethrower to kill them.' As soon as I was handed this piece of paper . . .

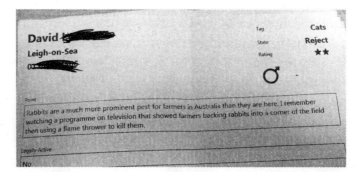

. . . I remember thinking, *The only fact anyone will remember about today's show is that Australians kill rabbits with flamethrowers.*

Even better, an item about the over-regulation of abattoirs had this show-stopping comment from Angie Watt on Twitter.

'Our primary school is right next to an abattoir. Seagulls regularly drop cows' ears into the playground.'

Sorry, what were we talking about again? It's a great rule for public speakers, this –

Never forget the power of the visual image.

Flamethrowers-on-rabbits and cow-ears-falling-from-the-sky are all you need to make everyone forget what it was we were actually talking about. We have had them all – when the distinguished Professor Colin Green came on to talk about the water quality in Aviemore he said, without warning, 'I like to swim in hot springs myself, but I eat a lot of rhubarb', thus drowning the rest of the item. And one of the best was Steve Feltham, a listener who rang after we posed the question: 'Do you speak with an accent which confuses people?' His was a peculiar mix of Midlands, Scottish and American.

'So where are you actually based, Steve?' I asked.

He replied: 'I am living in a mobile library on the edge of Loch Ness while I try to spot the Loch Ness monster.'

Boom.

Yet the Witch's Post need not be a physical distraction like a fireworks disaster or Loch Ness monster. It can be emotional.

We covered a piece of research suggesting more and more parents were letting their children win at board games, and this was not good for the children. A dad rang, indignant. 'I would absolutely never do this! I used to play Connect Four with my daughter all the time and was determined to keep beating her. Then one day she was in hospital, aged fourteen. I played her and she won for the first time. And her face just lit up.'

'In hospital?' I repeated. 'Hopefully she's okay now.'

'Sadly she didn't make it. She died the following week. And I will never forget the expression on her face when she won that game.'

That conversation must have been seven years ago. I have written the exchange down word for word from memory because, like the dad, I won't ever forget it.

If that was a Witch's Post, it shows they are not necessarily a bad thing. Perhaps the geology professor, pointing out the original post in the river, is pleased that his students remember it decades later; they would have forgotten the three different types of stone anyway.

I will spare you the other 146 examples – the day pop star Billy Ocean came on to talk about the legacy of slavery, but instead launched into a denunciation of the Congestion Charge in London because he had just been fined; an item about nursing homes derailed when someone said their favourite resident was 'an old man who likes to be called Parsnip'; the interview with the BBC's distinguished foreign correspondent Lyse Doucet, where we discussed how much news she could report from warzones when there are children watching the bulletins, and she came out with the ultimate Witch's Post: 'It is like telling them Father Christmas doesn't exist. You have to. One day they're going to find out.'

That's definitely a rule, by the way –

Never, ever say Father Christmas doesn't exist.

At least we are not alone. When BBC1's *Watchdog* ran a feature about viewers let down by special offers, a man spoke on camera about an advert promising a free MP3 music player. Indignantly, he explained how he should have been sent the free gift after collecting labels from three-litre Coke bottles.

'I drink two of these three-litre bottles a day, sometimes three if I am under stress. But I sent off the labels and nothing came back.'

Sorry – *You sometimes drink nine litres of Coke in 24 hours if you are under stress, and you think your life would be improved by a small music player?*

A contender for Greatest Witch's Post Ever came during a Channel 4 special on a by-election in Eastleigh in 2013, where the

Eurosceptics of UKIP were mounting a strong challenge against the Conservatives. As I watched it on TV at home the presenter, Krishnan Guru-Murthy, called on a UKIP supporter from the audience.

KGM: 'Elizabeth Hill, you were a Conservative supporter.'

Elizabeth: 'Yes. Zis goes back down to a lot of zings.'

It becomes clear that Ms Hill is German – she has a very strong accent.

Elizabeth: 'Under Ted Heaz's government I vus a young Conservative. I remember being seventeen years old ant wearing ze T-shirt: "Say yes to Europe". It vosn't in my idealistic days zat I envisaged zat ve could lose so much sovereign-etty.'

This now becomes confusing. Elizabeth Hill is a German resident in Eastleigh who will vote UKIP because of Britain's loss of sovereignty? Just when I think she is making no sense, she explains: 'Incidentally, I have just to say zat I am Eastleigh-born ant bred, and I haff lived here all my life. I haff a medical condition, Foreign Accent Syndrome, so you might zink I am an immigrant here. I am not. To go back to vot I vas sayink – '

I watched at home, mesmerised. My mind went the way yours might have gone. She woke up one morning, as a Conservative Eurosceptic, and found she now spoke in a German accent? The poor lady. What must that be like, continually having to explain to people: 'I am actually not German, this happened to me overnight and no vun knows vy'? And of course in straining to hear more of her accent I missed everything else she was telling Krishnan about why she had shifted her vote from the Conservatives. We could search another ten years of archive material and not find a better example.

But maybe there is one. When the geology professor pointed out the stones in the middle of the river and the post protruding from the water he was only doing a version of what my agent accidentally did in Japan. Alex Armitage, who is also one of my closest friends, runs a theatrical and broadcast agency named Noel Gay. It was the pen name of his grandfather, the supremely gifted writer of the musical *Me and My Girl*. One of Alex's missions in life is to ensure Noel Gay's inspirational song list – including 'The Sun Has Got Its Hat On' and 'The Lambeth Walk' – is not forgotten. On this occasion he was in Japan to promote a rock band.

One day he spoke to an audience of wealthy businessmen and theatre people. He began conventionally, introducing himself, talking a little about the legacy of Noel Gay and the work of his agency.

However, at an early point during the speech, Alex noted: 'I seemed to have lost the audience.' Afterwards he asked the translator why the people in the room had been really fascinated at the start, and then the mood suddenly changed. 'They laughed in all the right places to begin with, but then an awful silence descended.' No matter what Alex said, he could not get their attention back. 'They had this look of horror on their faces.'

The translator replied, with beautiful understatement, 'I think perhaps your comment, "I am here to ensure everyone remembers the joy brought to the world by Enola Gay" was quite surprising to them.'

Enola Gay has come up a number of times on *Eggheads*, the quiz show I host, and it is a very long way from Noel Gay. All pub quizzers can give you the answer to the question: 'What was the name of the plane which dropped a nuclear bomb on Hiroshima in 1945?'

Alex gets the award for the Witch's Post to end them all.

6. 'When Does He Learn to Box?'

Speaking of quizzers, Rachel and I sat down to watch the movie *Rambo* the other night.

I had seen it a couple of times, but my wife never had. I never get tired of the story of the lone Vietnam vet who falls out with the police in a small town – understatement of the year – and takes to the hills. Sylvester Stallone ends up in a battle in which he appears to defeat the entire US army using only a hunting knife, a short length of rope and a dramatic mullet.

So my wife and I sat beside each other on the sofa as Stallone went through his early traumas with the cops. Half an hour into the movie he had been locked in a cell by the local sheriff and was starting to have the stare of a man who is about to lunge for the nearest bandana and disappear through a window. But something was puzzling Rachel. Eventually she asked the question. 'I'm really enjoying the movie, but – erm – when exactly does he learn to box?'

I laughed. Quite loudly. And then apologised for laughing quite loudly and explained that *Rambo* is the movie where Sylvester Stallone uses guns and knives and stuff – it is *Rocky* where he boxes. There is no point in *Rambo* where the hero rushes out of the forest wearing a pair of boxing gloves, inserts a gum protector or weighs himself.

It took us on to a discussion about quizzing. 'I'll never be a quizzer,' Rachel bemoaned. 'If I mix up my Rambos and my Rockys I'll never know my Gladstones from my Disraelis.'

'But I'm the same,' I reassured her. 'I host *Eggheads*, I listen to all those questions and answers, and I still don't know the stuff that quizzers know. They are built differently. That's all there is to it.'

In case you have missed *Eggheads* during its thirteen-year journey from the quiz-nobody-knows-about to the quiz-hardly-anyone-knows-about-but-some-people-quite-like, I can bring you quickly up to speed. Each day at 6 p.m. on BBC2 our home team of 'Eggheads' – sometimes that seems far too polite a word – takes on keen amateur quizzers from around the country. Five against five. Mostly the Eggheads win. Um. That's it, really.

Anything else?

I am struggling to think of one or two dramatic facts to spice up my description. Okay – deep breath – here we go. We film it in Glasgow, often five editions a day (record: sixty-six in a fortnight). When the Eggheads win, they look a bit bored and the spotlights do a sort of swirly pattern across the studio wall. Sometimes the lamps break and we have to get them repaired and a man appears who looks like a member of Slade. Often I have soup for lunch. The Eggheads once got through forty bags of crisps in two days. The floor manager is called Jady and he supports Newcastle United. Judith Keppel I like a lot, but NOT because she once took a million pounds off Chris Tarrant.

That really is all I can think of.

Oh – there is one other thing.

Eggheads is one of the most successful daily quizzes in the history of British TV. It may yet become the all-time number one.

And that is the peculiar feature of the show. It positively screams its modesty. It yells its invisibility. It acts as if no one has heard of it and no one should ever be expected to. We have had several instances of Chris Hughes and Barry Simmons falling asleep during recordings. Yes, actually nodding off as they sit facing the competitors and cameras, and *some have even been broadcast*. Yet *Eggheads* has become a powerful, powerful television product.

Here is how it was born. One day, at around the turn of the century, a bright spark in a London TV company read a magazine article where the reporter described rounding up a posse of keen general knowledge buffs (*Mastermind* champions, British Quiz winners, etc.) to see what would happen if the gang wandered into random pub quizzes. The resulting story was hilarious. The travelling brainboxes found the pub questions so tedious they were yawning and rolling their eyes. At times they could barely stir themselves to answer. It helped that they were all, shall we say, slightly unusual personalities. The TV producer who read the piece wondered: 'Could that be a television format?' And here we are, more than 1,700 shows later.

The game is different every day, and strangely unchanging. The Eggs, as I affectionately call them, seem not to care very much whether they get their questions right – but strangely they do. They are men and women who are quite normal. Yet strangely extraterrestrial.

I can report, having surreptitiously examined Kevin Ashman and Lisa Thiel up close while posing for photos with them, that they do not have small green trumpets protruding from their temples or suckers where their elbows should be. Yet they still do not seem human like the rest of us. Kevin knows from memory the date Shostakovich was born. Dave 'Tremendous Knowledge' Rainford was once banned from pubs with quiz machines in Manchester because he won the cash jackpot so many times the landladies feared for their livelihoods. Barry specialises in constant awareness of every element in the periodic table, as well as Rugby League. To me that looks suspiciously like non-humanoid behaviour. Chris 'The Locomotive' Hughes talks a lot about liking Carol Vorderman, but he could just be pretending to be human. When I asked him, 'Do you have any photos of Carol?' he replied, in a very serious voice, 'Don't go there.'

CJ de Mooi, who came to fame as the eccentric youngster on the panel with the explosive ego and a face that contorts if anyone else guesses wrong, takes an interest in movies, tennis and American Vice-Presidents. One day I asked him about *Tootsie*. A favourite film of mine, I said. Maybe one of the best. Could I test him on it?

'Sure,' he replied.

'Year?'

'Nineteen eighty-two.'

'Starring alongside Dustin Hoffman?'

'Bill Murray, Jessica Lange, Teri Garr, Dabney Coleman, Charles Durning, Geena Davis,' he answered.

'Oscars?'

'Nominated for ten, but only Jessica Lange won – for Best Supporting Actress.'

Now I asked: 'Director?'

'Sydney Pollack. Who also appears in the film as Tootsie's agent.'

'Name of Dustin's character?'

'Two names. Michael Dorsey, Dorothy Michaels.'

'Best line?'

He paused. 'That's not a quiz question.'

'I was expecting you to quote Sydney Pollack, as the agent, when he tells Dustin Hoffman: "Michael, *no one* will hire you. *No one.*" That's my favourite line,' I said.

'Oh.' CJ looked baffled.

'What's yours?'

'I don't have one,' he replied airily. 'I've never actually seen the film.'

As I say, *extraterrestrial*. To know about *Tootsie* by learning a list instead of spending ninety minutes watching it?

'It's a little longer than that, around a hundred and twenty minutes,' CJ corrects me. He knows running times as well.

I had a similar moment with Pat Gibson, who in 2016 was the #1 ranked quizzer in the world. A former *Mastermind* Champion of Champions, he is another Egghead who won *Millionaire*. He excitedly told me he had a seventeen-page document listing questions on Ibsen, the Norwegian playwright, 'which basically covers every fact that could ever come up in a quiz'.

'And what's your favourite Ibsen play?' I asked.

'Oh, I've never seen one.'

CJ de Mooi returned to the studio from Macclesfield after playing Abanazar in forty-eight performances of the pantomime *Aladdin*.

'Wonderful!' I said. 'And who was playing the Princess?'

'I've no idea,' he replied.

We sorely missed CJ after a series of catastrophes engulfed him. All were preventable. The whole thing began when, for reasons I never really understood, he announced that *Strictly Come Dancing* had refused to have him on as a celebrity because he insisted on dancing with a man. Accusing his employer's most popular show of homophobia is not likely to end well. The problem was compounded when a junior BBC press officer decided to fight what was still a relatively small fire with an extinguisher full of petrol. The official BBC statement, '*Strictly* is a family show and we have chosen the traditional format of mixed-sex couples', led to outrage on social media, with tweets like this:

> **J**
> @Kingofjedlions
>
> *Follow*
>
> So it was because Strictly is a 'family show'...
> LGBT people exist in families, you
> know!Disappointed in the BBC.

Sometimes you can hear the BBC thinking, and the sound is like the quiet ticking of a bomb. After a tense two weeks, the ticking stopped with no explosion. *Strictly* put out a terse comment: CJ had never been approached.

But the quizzer's talent for rapid self-immolation was not easy to tame. I take some responsibility for the next disaster. CJ had given me a draft copy of his autobiography to read, and I returned it with praise and half a dozen suggestions, all of which he naturally ignored. I am still baffled as to how I missed the danger of a story he told, buried on page one-hundred-and-something, about a tramp in Amsterdam. The paragraphs did not stand out when I scanned them. Maybe I went too quickly. The story was about a homeless Dutchman coming at CJ with a knife and trying to stab him in the eighties. (This reminds me of the BBC newsroom editor, standing beside me, who turned away to announce into the breaking news tannoy: 'Attention all outlets. Liverpool Police say a man has been shot in the Croxteth area.')

Being stabbed in the eighties or shot in the Croxteths are two fates worth avoiding. CJ told how he pushed the tramp into a canal to avoid being knifed. The autobiography was given to the *Mirror* to serialise. They pounced on the tramp-in-canal story. Asked to elaborate, CJ described how 'he caught me on the wrong day and I just snapped. I punched him so hard in the face, knocked the knife out of his hand and threw him in the canal. I fully suspect I killed him. I've no idea what happened to him.'

He added: 'This is the one incident of my life I do regret.'

When your job is to be a fun presence on a daytime show, the headline

EGGHEAD CJ FEARS HE KILLED A MUGGER AFTER ATTACKING HIM

threatens to overshadow general knowledge questions on stag beetles and land speed records.

During one of our filming blocks in Glasgow, I tweeted a picture of a smooth-as-glass River Clyde. A bright spark replied: 'Who did CJ throw in today?' The quizzer was the subject of regular jibes on the social network – *Must be difficult for the media to find a picture of CJ de Mooi looking like a murderer, apart from every picture of him ever* – and just when we thought it had all blown over, we heard that police in Amsterdam had started asking questions, and they were not of the 'Where were the 1976 Olympics held?' variety.[1]

The explosive ticking started again, and again it stopped. The BBC would stick with CJ. But it would really rather there weren't any more attacks on *Strictly* or homeless men.

Unfortunately the final straw followed soon afterwards. I remember the morning well, because I had come in to work at BBC Scotland – for one of our exhausting 'five-show days' – and was worried about a slight swelling around my right eye.

'I don't know what's happened,' I told the *Eggheads* producer,

---

[1] Montreal.

Rob Dean. He has managed the show almost since the very start and over the years has taken on the role of editor, social worker and friend to us all. 'It might,' I continued gravely, 'be an allergic reaction to popcorn.'

Rob apologised if my relationship with popcorn was not concerning him unduly. 'In the last twenty-four hours one member of the team has had a medical emergency and spent the night in A&E, then Chris Hughes tripped over the ramp we have on hand for wheelchair users in the studio and had to be lifted back to his feet by no fewer than four researchers – at which point Chris said, "It takes more than a disabled ramp to take down Chris Hughes" – and,' Rob continued as my jaw dropped, 'CJ is being questioned by the police.'

'Eh?' One of my eyes widened.

'Something about sexual assault.'

The story emerged over the following days. The quiz star, happily married to Andrew, had spent the evening with friends who had platonically shared his hotel bed 'to save money'. Unfortunately, the second of the friends was someone CJ did not know very well. There was some suggestion the two had met on Twitter. Initially all seemed fine between the three. But early in the morning the third man left early and went straight to Strathclyde Police to complain that during the night he had unexpectedly been fondled by the quiz champion.

For various reasons I have no doubt that CJ was innocent. When the police got round to investigating it properly – which took months – the whole thing melted away. But at the Beeb the explosion finally happened. The combination of murder, *Strictly* and now the Mysterious Moment in the Hotel Bed created so much static that even CJ's formidable knowledge of mixed doubles winners at Wimbledon could not drown it out.

The upshot was that, despite being officially cleared six months later (with CJ convinced he was the target of a malevolent individual who wanted to destroy his career in quizzing), the larger-than-life Egghead announced he was leaving for South Africa to pursue a career in acting:

There the story stayed. But then CJ returned to the UK in 2016 and was pulled out of the arrivals queue at Heathrow. The non-urgent department of the Amsterdam Police had become interested in the British homelessness campaigner (yes, that is his main focus outside quizzing), who had apparently confessed to the killing of a Dutch homeless person. Worse still, they had reportedly taken a look in a stretch of canal which fitted the story CJ had told and found *twelve bodies*.

On entering the UK, de Mooi was apprehended under an international arrest warrant, which triggered headlines of the sort you would be hard pressed to imagine even in your worst nightmare. Eventually the Dutch warrant was shown to have been issued in error, but the quizzer seemed badly damaged by it all.

The whole story felt like a terrible shame to me. De Mooi – a Dutch surname he adopted, meaning 'the beautiful one' – is a unique and unfettered broadcast character. It is as if someone opened his personality inside Photoshop and pressed the maximum-saturate button. He makes no concession whatsoever to anyone, not even the television audiences who employ him. He does not mind being loathed and is the opposite of bland. He is full of what the poet Yeats called 'passionate intensity'. Many of the worst people are the opposite of that, so I genuinely liked him.

I had direct experience of CJ's extraordinary qualities when we made a failed attempt to spin out the *Eggheads* brand in 2014, launching a show called *Revenge of the Egghead*. The premise was gloriously simple. The Egghead in question was de Mooi. He would adopt his most extreme James-Bond-villain persona and lay into individual contestants, who went into a huddle and tried to beat him using their combined knowledge. The show was similar to *Eggheads*, but without the buffering that softer souls like Judith Keppel and Daphne Fowler gave CJ by sitting around him.

But he went beyond James-Bond-villain. He took his clever clogs and bashed competitors over the head with them. Instead of a mildly unsettling Blofeld or Dr No, he gave us Anthony Hopkins in *The Silence of the Lambs*. Those clogs were made of hard material. We actually had to ask CJ to dial back on the withering remarks – 'Please do not refer to anyone's appearance, especially not their weight, or hair, especially not the clothes the women are wearing.' The superbrain played so rough with ordinary mortals that the BBC switchboard took literally hundreds of complaints, possibly thousands. Several people described *Revenge* as 'the most unpleasant programme the BBC has ever ever produced'. One went further – CJ was 'the most obnoxious man in the universe'. The only programme which came close to the level of complaints was the BBC's coverage of the Royal Regatta organised for the Queen's Jubilee. As it progressed down the River Thames, an underprepared commentary team told viewers again and again: 'We can see a lot of boats.'

I remember precise words and phrases from the reaction to

Revenge because I present the veteran complaints show *Points of View*.

Oh. I should say a word about the adorable old friend that is *Points of View*, the in-house complaints programme first broadcast during the reign of Henry VI. Not just my friend – yours too, I hope. After more than half a century the programme virtually wears a badge announcing it as 'The One The BBC Would Love To Close But Doesn't Quite Dare'. Doubtless on a wet Tuesday at some point in the future an executive with a free afternoon will ignorantly pull the plug on our weekly car crash of viewer complaints and nervous-looking managers. But the show is so much a part of the national fabric that the late Victoria Wood included it in her act. 'If the Russians feel strongly about an issue they launch a bloody revolution,' she said. 'The British write a strongly-worded letter to *Points of View*.'

When I look back at the history of *POV*, as the team call it, I am as proud to have been asked to present it as I was the other old lady, *Panorama* (launch year: 1953, so the oldest current affairs show in the world). The *POV* presenters include Terry Wogan and more Robinsons than the Swiss Family – Robert, Anne, Kenneth and Tony.

Audiences are extremely healthy, as TV types like to say, which I think is because this strangely masochistic BBC offering ('Tell us what you hate about our programmes') has the same get-on-board DNA that has made Radio 2 so joyous. If my radio show has taken 25,000 calls, *Points of View* has probably had a quarter of a million letters.

The flak goes both ways. Because it goes back to 1961, *POV* has been the butt of jokes since before I was born. *Monty Python* made us a target more than once. The eighties satire *Not the Nine O'Clock News* featured a furious viewer's letter saying: 'I think the licence fee is far too low. I would willingly sell my house and all its contents to help the BBC.' In another episode a woman claims she has had two letters read out on *Points of View*, and says that if you get a third on air you are automatically placed in an asylum.

But the CJ de Mooi quiz took us into tricky territory. I was fielding complaints about one of my own programmes and having to interview the channel controller with the question: 'Why on earth was this [programme starring me] even made in the first place?'

Furious viewers called it a waste of airtime, dire, obnoxious, disgusting, a horror, patronising, sanctimonious, cynical, cheap, awful, terrible, unwatchable, shocking and ghastly. Poor CJ was described as arrogant, unpleasant, rude, egotistical, appalling, posturing, sanctimonious and cynical. Social media was like that Manet painting of Emperor Maximilian in front of a firing squad. 'He is sat in the chair as if he was a king,' said one viewer, not quite realising that was the point of it. Someone else rang in about the 'offensive attitude of the Egghead de Boor'. A pensioner messaged *Points of View* to say the show 'made me want to puke'. CJ's behaviour unleashed so many adjectives I thought there might be a national shortage. He was said to be dismissive, superior, smirking, cruel, smug, big-headed, dreadful, insufferable, objectionable, off-hand, rude, ignorant, inconsiderate, sarcastic and belittling.

'Contestants were insulted by this complete prat,' said one viewer. 'CJ took on five contestants. He belittled the contestants and is too full of his own importance and smirks when mistakes are made. CJ made the viewers and contestants very uncomfortable. I felt CJ was most rude to Jeremy Vine.'

The famous BBC duty log – whose contents are so secret they must never be directly quoted – racked up fourteen pages of telephoned complaints in a single day. There were thirty-four different uses of the word 'obnoxious'.

The following day, CJ called me.

'I think this is all going rather well, isn't it?'

In Chapter 1 I said this book was called *What I Learnt* because I calculated that I had taken 25,000 calls from Radio 2 listeners and so I must surely have learnt something. At the time of writing this I am twenty-five shows into series eighteen of *Eggheads* – typing in a café in Glasgow on the single day off we get in our fifteen-day run. That means I have now presented 755 editions. Each has roughly thirty questions. Get out my napkin and felt tip, and I discover I have posed a total of 22,650 questions.

To me, that is an incredible figure. If each question takes twenty seconds, that would be – wait, *125 hours of my life* spent just asking stuff! So, assuming that I listen when I go on to give the correct answer, I must have superb general knowledge, right? My brain must be full of Mexican athletes and Russian assassins?

How I would love to say: 'Yes – I have amassed knowledge to rival the Eggheads. Having paid close attention, I now know the name of Alanis Morissette's daughter, as well as the element on the periodic table with the abbreviation In, and whether William III came before Edward II.'

I wish, wish, wish it were true – *Answers: Onyx Solace, Indium, no he didn't* – but unfortunately I think I have an emotional brain which remembers conversations as colours, and dumps facts as brutally as old fridges. I can't recall the number of the bus that stops fifty yards from my front door but I know exactly how I felt when I was travelling on it, bumped into a man I recognised, assumed it was a friend, shook his hand and introduced him warmly to my mother-in-law – only to realise as they chatted happily to each other that the fellow was Patrick Magee, the Brighton bomber, a mass murderer who had been released under the Good Friday Agreement.

The world divides into accountants and poets: fact people and emotion people. I am not sure what the current unemployment figure is to the nearest million but I know the exact phrase used when I got fired from a summer job in the States in 1986 ('I punched your card out, Jeremy – please leave'). I am well aware that Sylvia Plath put her head into a gas oven and I think I understand why, but I will never remember the year or even the decade. I once travelled to St Petersburg for the *Today* programme but because I never consulted a map I was under the mistaken impression for the entire trip that I was east of Moscow (*Answer: you are 444 miles north-west*). The emotional brain is great for some things – you are hypersensitive to other people's moods and you cry when someone dances – but it is a hopeless quality in a quizzer.

In 2014 we covered a story on Radio 2 which we bizarrely labelled 'chicken crash'. A truck carrying 6,500 chickens down the M62 hit the central reservation and turned over. No humans were hurt but 1,500 chickens died. Concerned residents and emergency workers rounded up as many of the dazed survivors as they could. Animal rights activists were said to have raced to the scene to help 'save' the wandering chickens (one slight problem with that – the rescued animals were then taken as planned to an abattoir). Many hundreds of chickens managed to break free from their pursuers and leg it across nearby fields.

We covered the story because the animal campaigns charity People for the Ethical Treatment of Animals, disgusted by what the incident said about the horrible conditions chickens routinely endure, were demanding a statue be erected in Warrington in memory of the chickens who died. A PETA spokesman told me they had already designed the statue, which would depict 'an angry chicken' in stone.

Now, without looking at the last two paragraphs, tell me the total number of chickens, the year and the name of the road in the story? If you can, you are a quizzer. I know I'm not a quizzer because my emotional brain just gets overloaded with the drama of it all – the workers who chased the chickens, the statue designed by PETA and what an angry chicken might look like, the fact that the rescued chickens were all slaughtered the next day. The beautiful and complicated thought that maybe the chickens sensed they would die if they allowed themselves to be saved by the animal rights activists. Every fact is submerged in a flurry of feathers. But a quizzer will walk away from that story with four key pieces of knowledge:

M62
6,500
PETA
Warrington

Meanwhile I'm wondering how the truck driver is, what he saw the instant before the crash, whether he has kids. By now I have even forgotten that the statue is supposed to be in Warrington.

But quizzing is not only about knowledge – and here I can help you if you are permanently despondent about your performance in the annual village quiz or the weekly Q&A at the pub. The Eggheads, remember, include *Mastermind* and British Quiz Champions, as well two quiz millionaires. So, as Yogi Berra said: 'You can learn a lot by just watching.' Here, then, are my five rules of quizzing. How to be an Egghead yourself.

*   *   *

Rule #1 – *It's always the Pacific*

This rule was established by Judith Keppel, who became the first person to win £1,000,000 on *Who Wants To Be a Millionaire?* by identifying, from four options, the husband of Eleanor of Aquitaine. The answer 'Henry II' made her wealthy. Tempted as Judith was to give the same reply to every question put to her since then, she noticed, as she took a greater interest in quizzing and joined us as an Egghead, that the Pacific came up all the time. So she created the Rule of Judith.

A large number of quiz questions ask, 'In which ocean is . . .' and then give the name of an obscure island or a tiny country or an even smaller sea. 'Which ocean does the Ceram Sea run into?' was an example we had recently on *Eggheads*. 'In which ocean are the Gilbert Islands?' 'What did the Spanish explorer Vasco Núñez de Balboa discover when he crossed the Isthmus of Panama in 1513?'

Answers: Pacific. Pacific. Pacific. The Rule of Judith is: *Always Pacific*. If you are asked for an ocean, the sea that covers one-third of the surface of the world is probably the answer you are looking for.

But the rule extends. Just today I filmed an edition of *Eggheads* with the question: 'Where is the ethmoid bone? Is it in the foot, the elbow or the skull?' The Rule of Judith tells us – *Always go skull*. The skull has eight cranial bones and fourteen facial skeleton bones. It is the Pacific of the human skeleton.

It helps with food as well. Frequently a competitor is asked, 'What type of food is . . .' and the blank will contain something unbelievably obscure like pule, or casu marzu, or akkawi. The names are baffling and you don't know where to start. Here the Rule of Judith tells us – *Always go cheese*. So a multiple-choice question along the lines of 'What kind of food is Airag? (*Cheese, Soup, Canadian vegetable*)' is actually quite straightforward. Judith sums up her tactic thus: 'If I have the chance, I always choose Pacific, cheese or antelope.' There are ninety-one species of antelope.

She has probably spoken about her rule too loudly. We wear microphones and the producers overhear everything. One day the quiz-setters on *Eggheads* will give her the following question – 'What is Lechwes? (*Pacific island, Cheese, Breed of antelope*)', and Ms Keppel will be completely lost for words. Over to you for the answer.

Rule #2 – Mnemonics are your friends

Mnemonics, the scary-looking word that looks like a spelling mistake, are actually there to make the hardest quiz question easy. A mnemonic is a friend: an easy-to-remember sentence that gives you a sequence of letters that leads to something more complicated. The one we all learnt in school, 'Richard of York Gave Battle in Vain', so famously gives us the order of the colours in the rainbow that I won't even waste your time by spelling them out. But watching Barry Simmons – who I always introduce with 'Barry, known as "The Brain" because he wears glasses' – I have come to understand that a vast amount of knowledge can be quickly underpinned with a mnemonic.

Barry's strangest and best is *Pregnant Camels Often Sit Down Carefully – Perhaps Their Joints Creak? Early Oiling Might Prevent Permanent Rheumatism.*

75

This sequence of letters, PCOSDC–PTJC–EOMPPR, spells out the following geological eras: Pre-Cambrian, Cambrian, Ordovician, Silurian, Devonian, Carboniferous, Permian, Triassic, Jurassic, Cretaceous, Eocene, Oligocene, Miocene, Pliocene, Pleistocene, Recent. Believe it or not, those eras have come up several times among my 22,650 questions. The answer to one was 'Eocene', and Barry got it.

Some are pretty tasteless. The sentence 'Michael Jackson Really Makes Small Boys Nervous' is used by wine experts to remember the names of larger bottles in the correct order: Magnum (2× the size of a normal bottle of wine), Jeroboam (4×), Rehoboam (6×), Methuselah (8×), Salmanazar (12×), Balthazar (16×), Nebuchadnezzar (20×).

Now it is true that you still have to remember which words are signified by the mnemonic – but, with the help of Michael Jackson and the pregnant camels, the hardest part, the sequence, becomes a cinch.

Rule #3 – Half the kings are Henry VIII

There are no shortcuts to being a brilliant quizzer. Well . . . maybe there are one or two. The sequence of kings and queens comes up all the time. And here you need, not a mnemonic, but a simple rhyme to carry you through:

> Willie, Willie, Harry, Stee,
> Harry, Dick, John, Harry three;
> One-two-three Neds, Richard two,
> Harrys four-five-six, then who?
> Edwards four-five, Dick the bad,
> Harrys twain and Ned the Lad;
> Mary, Bessie, James the Vain,
> Charlie, Charlie, James again,
> William and Mary, Anna Gloria,
> Four Georges; William and Victoria;
> Edward seven next, and then

George the fifth in 1910;
Ned the eight soon abdicated
George the six was coronated;
And if you've not lost all your breath
Give a cheer for Elizabeth.

Learning that might seem like a lot of work. In which case, focus on line six only – 'Harrys twain' refers to Henry VII and Henry VIII. Now take the second of those, Henry VIII.

Henry VIII seems to account for fifty per cent of all king-&-queen quiz questions. If you know his wives and what happened to them (divorced, beheaded, died; divorced, beheaded, survived) and his birth and death dates (1491–1547), you are some way down the track. You might also ensure you know:

It was his marriage to CATHERINE OF ARAGON that led to his break with the Catholic Church.
He was painted by HANS HOLBEIN.
He was SEVENTEEN when he became king.
His divorce was refused by POPE CLEMENT VII . . .

and so on, making certain you include Thomas More and Cardinal Wolsey and how Henry got injured in 1536 (jousting: his horse fell on him when they were both in full armour). The rule sounds crazy – *Henry VIII is half the kings* – but it really is quite incredible how often the big man (weight 28 stone, waist 52 inches) comes up. Even the Spanish Armada in 1588 (130 ships, 2,500 guns, 30,000 soldiers and sailors) is Henry VIII territory in some ways, because although it happened during the rule of his daughter Elizabeth I, it was Catholic Spain trying to rein in Protestant England.

The only other King-Fact you might need is that Henry I died in 1135 because he ate a surfeit of lampreys.

Rule #4 – It's NOT before your time

This will sound like an ageist comment, but I feel I have to make it. A team of retired financial advisers arrive in the *Eggheads* studio and are asked: 'When was the Antikythera Mechanism, thought to be the world's first computer, found?' They think hard about it, chunter a bit, scratch their beards, run fingers along their frown lines, groan, gurgle – they never smile – and if they are very clever, by which I mean Egghead-Lisa-level clever, they come up with 1901.

Or they say: 'A long time ago. We aren't sure when.'

Or: 'Was that the seventeenth century, Jeremy?'

Or maybe: 'Nope. Drawn a blank. We have no idea what the Antikythera Mechanism is.'

What they *never* say is: 'We are sorry, that's before our time.'

For some reason, younger quizzers – students, or recent graduates at the start of their careers – will constantly use the phrase 'that's before my time' when confronted by a question that lies beyond their direct experience.

As I say, I hope I don't sound ageist. But given that the scope of human knowledge takes in about the last forty thousand years, there is no logical reason why a 25-year-old is more justified in saying 'That's before my time' than a 75-year-old. The missing fifty years is a blink.

Yet they *are* more likely to say it. They say it all the time. Harry, nineteen, from Sheffield, was fresh from a degree in marketing management when he entered the *Eggheads* studio a couple of years ago. I read him the question below from my card:

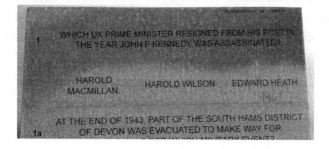

Harry replied: 'Well, I've never heard of Harold Wilson or Edward Heath, so I'm going to go Macmillan.'

'I can see you're struggling with this,' I said.

'It's a bit before my time,' he grinned. I couldn't help but like him and he beamed even more broadly when I told him Macmillan was right.

After Harry came his teammate Kate. Also a student, also nineteen. She was asked:

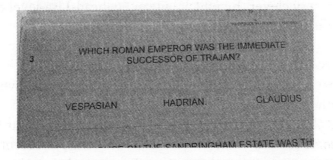

Choosing between Vespasian, Hadrian and Claudius is not easy. Roman emperors started in 27BC with Augustus ('I found Rome a city of bricks and left it marble'). His successors ruled for more than 400 years until the whole thing fell apart as each new emperor commanded less loyalty than the last. It is true that the three on the question card were in the stronger part of the sequence. Claudius ruled from AD41 and Vespasian from 69. Hadrian was from 117, so a little later. But really the only way of getting to the answer is in having some knowledge of Hadrian and the fact that he came to power because he was the adopted son of . . . Trajan. So it's a hard question.

But Kate's response – 'I'm sorry Jeremy, Trajan is a bit before my time' – made me flinch. A retired civil servant or vicar's widow will not hear the question about lampreys or the Antikythera Mechanism and say: 'Before my time.' Older contestants quiz with the innate understanding that the world existed before they were born, that the rest of the world is more important than even the greatest of us, and knowing what was going on in the decades and centuries before you lived must surely be a higher state of existence than not knowing.

That said, I do relate to the younger players. I remember, as a teenager, thinking it was impossible that anything before my own birth year of 1965 could have any relevance to me, for which reason I treated British history like a series of fairy stories and dropped the subject as soon as I had the chance to, which I regret.

Now I wonder whether my arrogant sense of immortality is re-exhibiting itself even more forcefully with the i-generation. It is not so much that a tree falling in the forest makes no sound unless they are there – it is more that no one cares whether the tree fell or not.

More times than I can remember, younger competitors have responded to a question about the Beatles by saying, 'That's a bit before my time', and I think to myself: if the *Beatles* are before your time, then there is no reason at all to know about Hitler or Emmeline Pankhurst, and even less to give a flying fig about the days when people tipped pots of urine out of their upstairs windows and Portugal conquered Brazil and Julius Caesar fell to the floor in a bloodied toga and there were dinosaurs and a big bang that we now understand was more like a 1970s engaged tone.

I say this with puzzlement and not malice. I tell my children, 'The only thing you need to know about rock music is that the most important chord ever played on a guitar is the open G at the start of "Honky Tonk Women"', fully expecting them to junk my wisdom when a better chord comes along. More than any other category of challenger, the Eggheads and I love to have younger teams in. They pour life into our airless recording studio.

But I have to make it a rule – *It doesn't matter when it was, it's NOT before your time.*

Rule #5 – Use the Gokiburi method

Let's say you are given a multiple-choice question of the sort we use on *Eggheads*. You look at the question – 'What is the Japanese word for cockroach?' – and you think, I have not a clue. You shrug and laugh and are about to give up. But then the three options pop up – *kackerlacka, gokiburi, cafard* – and you realise *kackerlacka* and *cafard* are not even slightly Japanese-looking; they happen to be Swedish and French cockroaches. This method of answering questions – which I call the Gokiburi method – means asking 'what is it NOT?' and ruling out the wrong answers to get to the right one. Using elimination is far and away the most effective weapon in a multiple-choice game like *Eggheads*.

With that in mind, try this question to see how powerful it is: 'In which year was the Anglo-Saxon poem *Beowulf* written – 722, 723, 724?'

Impossible. Super-difficult even for the Eggheads. But now use the Gokiburi method to find the answer below: 'In which year was the Anglo-Saxon poem *Beowulf* written – 722, 1570, 2011?'

Straight away we eliminate 2011 because it's unlikely Anglo-Saxon poets were breaking through under the reign of the mighty double-headed king, Cameron 'n' Clegg. We head back to 1570 – and here we might pause, because 1570 is *a very long time ago*. But then we remember that it was the reign of Henry VIII, and we picture him in that Holbein portrait wearing all his embroidered robes and think he probably wouldn't be impressed by people who write 'wulf' as wolf, and anyway, wasn't Anglo-Saxon *even longer ago*? Wasn't King Alfred who burnt the cakes an Anglo-Saxon? Wasn't he around (easy date to remember) in 888, and while he was running from the Vikings didn't he take shelter in the swamps of Somerset, which is where a busy woman told the old guy to watch her cakes, and he got distracted by his thoughts, and they burnt, and she tore him off a strip while completely unaware he was king?

This is what I discovered while doing *Eggheads* and posing all those questions. Knowledge is such utter joy. History, in particular, is just a collection of stories, each a little more distracting than the one before.

Anyway – Alfred *was* an Anglo-Saxon, and I am not even sure how we got to him. Henry VIII, much as we love him, was a Tudor. The poem was Anglo-Saxon so we need to locate it as near as possible to Alfred. Thus, *Beowulf* was 722. Bingo.

I was recording five episodes of *Eggheads* today and one question showed perfectly how useful the Gokiburi method is. 'In which Shakespeare play,' I asked, 'are Lucius, Quintus, Martius and Mutius the sons of the title character?'

May the gods of the stage save us! We are about to be humiliated, think you and I. Chances are we have not read that play. It is not one of Shakespeare's best-known. But the options were *Titus Andronicus, Othello, Julius Caesar*, and here we start to get a foothold. I have seen *Othello* and cannot remember him ever referring to four children. Caesar was stabbed by his colleagues, not his kids. So *Titus Andronicus* it is. And it is the right answer. The Gokiburi method.

Rule #6 – Norway means Munch or Ibsen

This is a rule I actually feel bad about telling you, because it is such a staple of the quizzer and feels almost like cheating. It came out of a conversation with 'Tremendous Knowledge' Dave. He told me, quite frankly: 'If a question starts, "Which Norwegian painter . . . " the answer will *always* be Munch. If it starts "Which Norwegian playwright" the answer will always be Ibsen.'

It is not cheating. It just shows how experienced quizzers have answered so many questions on Norwegian painters that eventually the rut from the question to the answer – Edvard Munch – is so well worn they don't even need to think about going down it. Thus they can sound tremendously, superhumanly smart. Take this question: 'Which Norwegian playwright wrote a letter to Georg Brandes with the line, "Who can guarantee to me that on Jupiter, two and two do not make five?"'

It makes no difference that you have not heard of Georg Brandes; you haven't heard the quote; even that you haven't heard of Jupiter. You only need three words, 'Which Norwegian playwright . . . ', to trigger the answer IBSEN. And you are right.

'Which Norwegian painter created a cycle of paintings called the *Frieze of Life*?'

Answer, Munch.

I asked the Eggheads for other examples of this. They gave me so many I was amazed.

If any question mentions Greek sculptures, the answer is always the Elgin Marbles.

If any question uses the phrase 'Which skateboarder . . .' the answer is always Tony Hawk.

If any question describes a kind of painting called 'impasto', the answer is always Frank Auerbach.

If any question uses the word 'cosmonaut', the answer is Yuri Gagarin. (Cosmonaut is the word for astronaut used by the Russian Space Agency, but beware – if the phrase is *female cosmonaut*, the answer is always 'Valentina Tereshkova'. She was the first woman in space. An Egghead would know her craft was called Vostok 6 and took off in June 1963.)

Let's speed this up:

Economist – Keynes
Pastry – Choux
Female discus thrower – Gabriele Reinsch
Metaphysical poet – John Donne
NASCAR racing – Dick Trickle
Archbishop – Thomas Cranmer (not, as Judith once said, 'Archie Cranmer')
Airship – Hindenburg
Umbrella – Sarah Gamp*
High Jump – Javier Sotomayor.

Oh, can I say something quickly about Mr Sotomayor? Just really quickly? This guy is beyond incredible. My sports hero. His

---

*The character in *Martin Chuzzlewit* whose name became the nickname for 'umbrella' because she always carried one. The word was still being used as late as George Formby: 'And though the weather's damp I can do without my gamp.'

record is easy to remember – he is the only person in recorded history to jump higher than eight feet.

In 1988, at an athletics meeting in Salamanca, Spain, the Cuban jumped 2m 43cm, which is 7 feet 11.7 inches. The Seoul Olympics got under way only four days later but very sadly for him, and for us all, Cuba's political boycott removed him from the Games.

Nevertheless, he increased the record twice. He jumped 2.44m in 1989 in Puerto Rico: 8 feet 0.0625 inches.

Then came an even more extraordinary day in 1993, back in Salamanca. This is what he did:

2.32m – jumped and cleared the bar
2.35m – decided to pass
2.38m – cleared on first jump
2.45m – knocked off bar on first jump; cleared on
       second.

Because his records were not set in the glare of the Olympic Games, the video of Sotomayor's jump is grainy. He takes a bouncing run with three unconventional extra-long strides in the middle of the approach. He seems to catch the bar full on with his shoulder blades, but amazingly it does not fall. As he lands he realises instantly what he has done, spins around on the landing mat and runs underneath the still-vibrating bar towards his supporters – an action which, I always think as I watch it back, carries the horrifying risk of jolting the bar off its mounting and undoing his record jump. But the bar is not jolted and everyone realises what he has done. I drew a mark on my kitchen wall to show where the eight-feet point was . . . and it is near the ceiling. I look at it and cannot believe how any human will ever jump that high again. How did Sotomayor do that? *More than eight feet?*

And there I show why I am not a quizzer. I have gone too deep into a single subject, because it interested me. I have done the equivalent of watching *Tootsie* or seeing an Ibsen play. I do the same with British politics (fascinating) and John Peel's Festive Fifty countdowns between 1977 and 1982 (still wonderful). What

I do not have is an all-over awareness of queens and oceans and cheeses and legends. I forget who killed the Minotaur and what part of a Roman soldier's body was protected by his greaves. I do not know if the *quebradita* is a Brazilian sausage or a Mexican dance. No matter how much gameplay I have picked up after watching the brilliant Eggheads over 20,000 questions, I am aware there is no substitute for their rock-solid certainty when they face a question.

If there is one thing I know for sure, it is that I am not a quizzer. I simply do not know enough.

7. My Malignant Melanoma

Here's another question: what do you do when you look at your reflection and you see a mole you have never noticed before?

Just after the whole *Strictly* madness came to a juddering halt, I stood naked in front of the bathroom mirror and noticed a deep brown freckle under my left collarbone.

The freckle was the size of the nail on your little toe.

Not big, but had it been there before?

I have fair skin, just like the Radio 2 doctor Sarah Jarvis. She is also a 1965 baby. Regularly we bemoan the fact that we burnt ourselves to a crisp as teenagers in the days before factor 50 was invented or anyone knew the danger of sunrays.

'You and I are at the very top of skin cancer risk in later life,' advises Dr Jarvis, a redhead. 'We have to watch for moles, freckles, anything unusual.'

'When is later life?' I asked.

'Now.'

This blemish was definitely unusual. Was it a new arrival? It had appeared in that lull between Christmas and New Year when there is no one around to ask for help. After a couple of days of inaction I went hunting for holiday photos. Clicking on a folder marked 'Devon–2009', I found some snaps of me coming out of the sea in Sidmouth (think Ursula Andress, without the hunting knife). I zoomed in on my collarbone, shining white in the sun, but the pixels became big blurred squares. I thought I saw a freckle in the same place, *but it was much smaller*.

I knew not to panic immediately. I am very wary of diagnosing myself. Google has turned us all into amateur doctors. I had already had a particularly embarrassing experience of what is called 'cyberchondria'. A year earlier, I had felt a constant ache in a private area. Let's be upfront about this: *in my balls*. The ache did not go away, although it tended to ease a little overnight. Like most blokes, I did not want to trouble my GP. So I typed a description of my pain and its location into Google and discovered there were 'nine possible conditions' and 'your symptoms should NEVER be ignored'. One website helpfully said:

> As much as you might want to avoid a visit to a doctor's office, testicular pain isn't something you can disregard. There are a number of reasons why the egg-shaped sex glands in your scrotum may be hurting, and none of them are good. In many cases, trying to pretend the pain away could mean worsening your problem -- even to the point of needing surgery or getting your testicles removed. So sit up and take notice -- and click to the next page for a very

What the f*@# − . . . REMOVED???? After speed-reading more than thirty different web pages, and poring over countless diagrams with coloured arrows and text-boxes, I settled on what I was fairly sure was a rare illness called distal ureteric calculus with possible primary retroperitoneal seminoma. I wrote an email to my GP describing my diagnosis:

> I don't want to waste your time and I know this requires quite complex surgery so would you be able to push on with booking the op for me as I am in quite a lot of pain, thanks.

The GP, a charming woman called Dr Deirdre O'Gallagher, replied that it might be better if she was able to examine me first, as 'this is the way we usually work'. Reluctantly I agreed, although my diagnosis seemed unshakeable and I knew I would need a three-hour operation.

A week later, just before I was due to see Dr O'Gallagher, I had to write her the following email:

Dear Deirdre

I feel I owe you an apology for insisting that I had a complex condition called distal ureteric calculus with possible primary retroperitoneal seminoma that would require long surgery. Since using Google to diagnose myself, I have discovered that the culprit was six new pairs of pants that I was given for Christmas and which I had just started wearing. Clearly they were too tight and were squeezing my private areas all day (which is why the 'condition' eased at night), and when I Googled the situation it said my symptoms should not be ignored or 'death could result'. I have since stopped wearing the undersized pants and the pain has completely gone. My apologies for this embarrassing situation.

Yours ever, Jeremy

Now, staring at my enlarged freckle in the mirror, I brought the Xmas-pants incident to mind. I did not want to jump the gun and assume the worst. I could not think of any innocent reason for a freckle to enlarge suddenly, but I would not rush to conclusions. This was one for Dr Jarvis, and it was a time to be calm, sensible and rational.

'I'M SCARED,' I told her.

'Are you sure it's larger?' she asked.

'It's double the size. I have compared it to holiday photos.'

She said the key test was known as ABCDE: you should be alert to Asymmetry, Border irregularity, Colour that is not uniform, Diameter greater than 6mm (the size of the eraser on a pencil) and Evolving size, shape or shade. My mole seemed to have some of the ABCDE qualities, but not others. 'It is growing like Topsy,' I said, keen to keep perspective.

She reassured me. I should keep it under review, and we would talk again.

At that point I thought there could be an advantage to my programme. If it was a malignant melanoma, could we use it to educate our audience? I went to the editor and suggested a feature on the expanding freckle. 'We could have a live biopsy,' I said. A surgeon would remove the mole on air, then test it for cancer while the programme went out. Possibly the result could be announced between two records.

The crazier the idea, the more likely Phil is to agree to it. This is a man, remember, who said we could only do an item on the popularity of sheds if a builder could put one up in the studio during the programme.

'Let's do it,' he said.

I made a couple of announcements on the air.

Two days later, I stared at the freckle. To my surprise, it had now reduced in size dramatically. I stopped making the announcements on the radio and told Phil we should keep the situation under review.

By the end of the week the freckle was back to its normal, tiny size.

Here I have to swallow my pride and explain.

It turned out that the fake suntan which had been applied for the final show on *Strictly* – where there is a group dance in which all fifteen celebrities have a part – had faded rapidly from every part of my body except that freckle, where for some reason the deep brown spray mysteriously pooled in a semi-permanent island around the existing blemish. Two full weeks it had stayed there – long enough for me to nearly have the fake tan sliced out and examined under a microscope live on Radio 2, in an item which might well have been the most embarrassing in broadcast history.

* * *

Urging a doctor to act on a non-existent melanoma was a mistake. But it was not the only lesson from *Strictly*. I mentioned earlier an experience I had on the show which 'needs a bit of thoughtful unpacking'. So here we go.

The other blot on my landscape during the dancing was not one I could biopsy – it turned out that some people just didn't think a non-dancer should be in a dance contest.

Some generous souls wanted to reach out. Coincidentally, I had set up a Facebook page just before *Strictly* and one of the first comments was from a genuine fellow called Stewart who said: 'I have watched you move Jeremy and I am a Movement and Rehabilitation Specialist. I think you need some help.' It was the well-meaning tone that made me roar with laughter.

Others were not quite so friendly. Martin's photo suggested rural living. He was a viewer who expected the amateur dancers to be at a higher standard and wrote: 'Def time for Bovine to leave the show. Great for a laugh but not a natural dancer. Sorry m8 but time for you to MOVE ON.'

I remember exactly where I was when I saw that message on my phone. It was a Sunday, and I knew (because the results show is pre-recorded) that Karen and I were through for another week. Nothing, not even a nuclear strike on my local newsagent, could spoil the thrill of another seven days in the contest. So I thought I should post a friendly reply.

Lots of people would advise: *Don't feed the troll*. Apparently DFTT is a rule of modern life. But because Martin's message wasn't especially malicious, I turned my phone to video-selfie mode to reply. Sitting at the outside table of a café I taped a message without even really thinking about it. Word for word, it went like this.

'Hi there. I was looking at this message from Martin and reflecting on it, and a couple of others that have been similar – and just thinking I should reply like this [with a video message] because it's much better than typing a reply.

'And so Martin – thank you by the way for your message, Martin, I really appreciate it – said, essentially: "You shouldn't be in *Strictly* because you're no good." And I've just got two responses to that which I wanted to say, because I think it's quite important.

'One of them is that I promise that I'm taking this seriously and not doing it for comedic purposes. So I can think of some competitors in the past who have just done it for a laugh, and I know – I'm well aware – that during my dances – excuse the noise of the truck passing – during my dances there has been laughter, um, but it's not been something that I have sought. I really wanted to dance well. So I am trying to get some technique.

'I always say that Karen started dancing when she was eight, and I started dancing on August the 8th. So it's not easy but I'm trying – that's the first thing.

'And the second thing, Martin, which is actually more important and in fact crucial, is that I've got two young daughters. Martha and Anna. They're eleven and eight. And I said to them when I started this, I said: "I promise I will really really work at getting better, I am not just going to muck around here. I'm gonna really be serious about it and try to learn to dance."

'Now you might argue that hasn't gone very well. I think I have improved since the start, but regardless of that, the message I don't want them to take away is – "Once our dad thought he couldn't win, he just gave up."

'So I'm feeling like what I want them to see is that, until the very last moment in the contest, until I'm voted out, I will always work at getting better. I'll always try, I'll always be back in the gym – I'm about to go and see Karen now.

'Sometimes eight, nine hours a day. I'll always, always work. And the fact that I am not the best is not a reason to give up. And that's true of so much of life. Just because you can't win doesn't mean you stop working. So to Martin, and just a couple of others – and I'm saying this very politely, like I say I appreciate your messages – please understand I have to compete and work and work, because I don't want my daughters to see their father say: "Argh, that's it, why did I ever enter it?"

'So have a great day.'

Uploading the video took fifteen seconds. I went back to my mid-afternoon coffee and thought no more of it. I did not think of mentioning it to Karen when we next met in the gym. We had to learn something called a reverse fleckerl, which sounds more like my suspicious mole than a dance move.

In fact, I forgot all about Martin and my reply.

Until I was in the *Strictly* studios the following weekend and saw one of the make-up artists. 'Hey, I liked that post you did about your kids,' she said.

'Oh.' I was confused. 'Which one?'

'The one about dancing as a way of telling your kids something.'

I thanked her but was perplexed. How had a message sent – I thought – to a single person on Facebook been seen by anyone else? I did not yet know my way around Facebook and had assumed the selfie message was in a public place but would be of no interest to anyone but Martin, and probably not even to him.

I was wrong. By the time I took a second look at the video it had reached *more than a million people*. The figure would eventually rise to nearly two million.

That is the definition of viral. And as a broadcaster I had the obvious thought – oh, how I wished I had scripted it better, filmed it in better light, sat in a better pose and in a better place – and that bloody truck, engine roaring as it passed! But then I realised the only reason it had been viewed so many times by so many people was because it was real, and it was real because it had been done in one take, from the heart, without a script or a plan.

By complete accident, I had said something that meant far more than I expected; something universal. When I watched the video back, I could see it was the mention of my daughters, and how I felt as their father, going into a contest and wanting them not to be affected by the inevitable humiliation. I realised that there is a hunger among parents, especially the parents of girls, for a message that doesn't involve perfection. That says: you don't have to look like Taylor Swift to have the best life. Enjoying what you do is success in itself – coming first is just a bonus.

In fact coming first may not even be the point. Joy is the key. The most powerful people in life are the ones who exude joy. If you enjoy something you have boundless energy and inspiration. Too many people think joy will arrive when they have found success. Actually it is the other way round – follow joy, and success will come. And if it doesn't come, it doesn't even matter.

I only blundered onto this message. As you can tell, it's not something I thought through because I almost had to have the significance explained to me. But when, a week later, a friend said the video had been played at the morning assembly in her daughter's school and discussed by the headmistress – a story repeated in other schools as the days went by – I reflected on the strangest thing. The single broadcast which had had the greatest impact in a thirty-year career was spoken without a BBC microphone in sight, without a script or a studio or a producer. It was recorded with no forethought into a phone on a busy high street with trucks and taxis passing.

But it went viral because it was real.

8. The Elongated Lozenge

With four minutes to go, Boris Johnson ran in. I was already concerned – maybe more concerned than Boris. It was an awards ceremony at the Hilton, Park Lane. The room was packed with financial people in bow ties. It was a couple of years before Johnson became Mayor of London. At this point he was a backbench Conservative MP and newspaper columnist. Right now he was due to make a funny speech.

In four minutes.

There I was, at 9.26 p.m., sitting with a table-load of London bankers, trying to answer their questions. 'Will Boris actually arrive?' 'Is he normally this late?' 'Has he got lost?'

I answered them all as best I could – (a) I'm sorry, (b) I don't know, (c) I don't see Boris Johnson that often. You see, I explained, I am only here to hand out the awards for . . . (I consulted the sign at the back of the stage) . . . for International Securitisation, and Boris is making the after-dinner speech. So we have not coordinated at all. I don't know where he is. Yes, I'm a little worried too.

To be perfectly frank, I had not the first idea what securitisation was either. The event was named something grand like 'The International Securitisation Awards 2006' and I really did not want to ask what exactly the prizes were being handed out for, since I was the one handing them out.

Suddenly – WHOOSH. A rush of wind from an opened door, a golden mop, a heave of body and dinner jacket onto the chair next to mine, and the breathless question, at 9.28 p.m.: 'JEREMY. Where exactly AM I?'

I actually had that stress feeling – a kind of sunburn, creeping across my arms and back. So he was late and he had not prepared a speech. And he was due on stage in ninety seconds.

I said: 'It is the Securitisation Awards, Boris.'

He said: 'Right-o. And who is speaking?'

'You are.'

'Good God,' he cried. 'When?'

I looked at my watch. 'Um – pretty much now.'

By this point we had the attention of the whole table. I speak at quite a few dinners and always feel most comfortable if I do some research a couple of weeks before – what's the occasion (that helps) – who is attending, etc. – then write the speech longhand in advance. It is not that I am the school swot. It is just that under-preparedness, that dream where you are sitting your university finals in a subject you didn't know you were supposed to revise, scares the pants off me. So right now, this was an emergency.

Everyone at the table craned in to listen.

Boris said: 'Okay, first up. What IS securitisation?'

Nervous laughter. A man from one of the big Far East banks, who had the luxurious rich-person's coiffe you see on magazine covers, explained quietly in a mid-Atlantic purr. 'It is where we take your debt – your mortgage, say – '

Boris is staring at him.

' – and we split it into tiny pieces, combine each of them with other similar slivers of debt, and sell them around the world so the risk effectively disappears.'

Everyone nodded.

The words would echo back to me two years later, when all those invisible slivers of debt would suddenly return to sender, flooding back at us in one huge torrent of slurry that kept flowing until it buried banks, businesses and homes across the western world and almost stopped the cashpoints working.

For now, this guy was the expert and we were listening.

Boris asked for a sheet of paper. Someone produced a piece of A4, the reverse side of our menu for the night. He laid it on his thigh, below the tablecloth.

'Anyone got a pen?' he said. 'Quick!'

A biro slid across the table. Very quickly, taking it, the future

Mayor of London and Foreign Secretary began to write what looked like a plan for a speech. It was now past nine-thirty. One of the organisers was staring at us imploringly from the other side of the room, as if thinking: 'How much longer can we give him?' I felt that pricking of the skin again – if I could feel the stress on his behalf, what on earth was Boris feeling? This was going to be a catastrophe. He was going on stage in a minute or two with barely legible notes written on the back of a menu and no idea even of which event he was attending. An after-dinner speaker normally talks for twenty to thirty minutes. How much material did Boris have? Looking at the scrap of paper I could make out very little of what his scrawl said. There seemed to be about ten words. There was one at the very top that I could make out:

SHEEP

and then, a few inches below that, another in capitals:

SHARK

but I could not read the rest of the scrawl. Boris harrumphed and groaned, as if straining at an idea. Then his arm was tugged and I heard the announcement: 'Ladies and gentlemen, please welcome MP and journalist Boris Johnson to the stage.'

Applause.

I pressed my palms into my trouser legs, ready for the catastrophe. And then I noticed – *he had accidentally left his page of notes on the table*. Could I run up with them? It would be too obvious. He was already at the podium.

'Ladies and gentlemen – errrrrrrrr,' he began.

This could be even worse than I imagined. They might have to cut out of it early and go straight to the awards. I had a five-minute speech myself, followed by the eighteen securitisation awards. The script was in my hand. I would need to be ready.

Boris had the look of a man who had been dragged out of a well by his ankles. His blond hair seemed to spring vertically from his head as he embarked on some opening remarks, where the occasional word, not always the obvious one, was shouted at double volume.

' – errrrr, Welcome to THE International. Errrrr – '

The catastrophe had happened. He did not know, could not remember, which event he was at. This is one of the biggest fears any speaker has, forgetting where they are.

Johnson then did a crazy thing. To find out where he was, he very obviously turned around and looked at the large logo projected at the back of the stage.

' – to the International SECURITISATION Awards! YES!' he cried triumphantly, and to my amazement it brought the house down. There was a huge cheer. Everyone realised this was not going to be a normal speech. The chaos had descended on us, we were in it, and we were going to enjoy it.

'SHEEP,' he began. He started a story about his uncle's farm and how OUTRAGEOUS it was that they couldn't bury animals that had JUST died, as they used to do back in the sixties, seventies and eighties. No, he said, EU regulations meant an abattoir had to be involved. 'One died today. A SHEEP. And my uncle had to RING a fellow at an abattoir fifty MILES away. His name was Mick – no, it was Jim – no, sorry, MARGARET, that was it, yes, MARGARET . . . '

People were now not just roaring with laughter but listening. He continued.

'Which is why my political hero is the Mayor from *JAWS*.'

Laughter.

'Yes. Because he KEPT THE BEACHES OPEN.'

More guffawing around me. He spoke as if every sentence had only just occurred to him, and each new thought came as a surprise.

'Yes, he REPUDIATED, he FORSWORE and he ABROGATED all these silly regulations on health and safety and declared that the people should SWIM! SWIM!'

More uproar.

'Now, I accept,' he went on in an uncertain tone, 'that as a result some small children were eaten by a shark. But how much more pleasure did the MAJORITY get from those beaches as a result of the boldness of the Mayor in *Jaws*?'

Brilliant. The whole room is hooting and cheering. It no longer matters that Boris has no script, no plan, no idea of what event he is attending, and that he seems to be taking the whole thing off the top of his head.

I realise that I am in the presence of genius.

The speech is now about halfway through. Perhaps gaining in confidence after the disaster with the timings and his forgotten notes, Boris embarks on a story about a former Foreign Secretary, George Brown.

As soon as he starts, I know what to expect. The 'George Brown in Peru' story is so well known that most people have stopped telling it. The tale is probably untrue. George Brown was a high-ranking Labour politician in the sixties and seventies who took to drinking as a result of the pressures of high office (he famously said: 'A lot of politicians drink and womanise – I've never womanised'). He was said to have been at an official reception in South America when he saw a beautiful Peruvian in front of him and asked for the honour of waltzing with her.

The reply came in three parts.

'I cannot dance with you, Foreign Secretary, sir, firstly because you are drunk. Secondly, sir, because the band is not playing a waltz, as you imagine, but the Peruvian national anthem. And thirdly, I cannot dance with you because I am the Archbishop of Lima.'

So the story goes. Boris ploughs into it with gusto. 'And the reply came back, from this vision in red, NO, I cannot DANCE with you, firstly because you are drunk.'

He paused.

'SECONDLY because this is not a WALTZ but our national ANTHEM.'

Again, a pause. 'And – and thirdly because . . . '

Now Boris had stopped.

He looked around.

There was silence.

He looked behind him at the logo on the screen, as if 'International Securitisation Awards' was going to help.

A lone person at the back burst out laughing as we waited.

Finally, from the stage: 'I am terribly sorry, everyone, I have forgotten the third reason. Very sorry about that.'

It brought the house down. He had spent five minutes starting the story about George Brown and forgotten the punchline. I had never seen anything like it before. Something about the chaos of it – the reality, I suppose – was utterly joyful. The idea that this was the opposite of a politician, that suddenly we had an MP in front of us who was utterly real, who had come without a script or an agenda and then forgotten not just the name of the event but his whole speech and the punchline to his funniest story – I watched in awe.

Finally he said: 'Righto. Jeremy VINE is out here and he will be presenting the – ' (looks behind him again) ' – International Securitisation Awards – ' (cheering because he has said the name a second time) ' – and I ACTUALLY have some of those very trophies here.' He starts handling one of the glass awards. 'I suppose you could call this, not really an award, but a sort of elongated lozenge.'

Laughter. A wave. Cheering. Applause.

I did something I have never done before. Ditched all the funny things I had planned to say as a warm-up to the awards, because I realised what I was saying could not be even faintly amusing after that. I had been completely blown off the stage.

Later I sent Boris a postcard –

Boris. Brilliant. Inspired. Funniest speech I have ever seen.
In the presence of the master. Jaws!

He responded a week later in the scrawl I remembered from the back of the menu:

Jeremy. You were INCREDIBLE.

*   *   *

I thought about that night for a long time. During the Blair years, we got used to a way of presenting information that was so mechanically smooth, so professional, that in the end we stopped believing any of it. This mastery of the message eventually backfired completely and came to be known as spin.

You could see why Labour sharpened up. Seeking re-election in 1997, John Major's Conservatives proved they had no knack for presentation at all. During that campaign I was sent for a day to follow the MP for Chester, Gyles Brandreth, in what would surely be his unsuccessful bid to hold the seat.

The assignment was a disaster for the likeable MP (who I often see around the BBC these days, and we still laugh about my visit). Brandreth told me I could bring the *Breakfast News* film crew along when he welcomed spectators to Chester City's home game the following day. He would be the guest of honour, making a pre-match presentation on the pitch in front of all the fans. So we set off in his car – him at the wheel, my camera and sound operators in the vehicle behind – heading for the Deva Stadium. But quite quickly it became clear the MP did not know where the football ground was in his own constituency. We spent an age travelling around a ring road, passing the same leisure centre three times and crossing the canal again and again. I kept saying I wasn't sure this was the right direction, but that was no help as Brandreth was so completely lost. He did not want to admit it to me, so he kept saying: 'I know exactly where it is, don't worry, it's my local ground' and 'It's just around this corner' and 'I know it's the next turn on the right,' and so on, time and again.

A journey that should have taken ten minutes ended up lasting three quarters of an hour, during which we even lost the crew in the car behind, so I knew there would be no footage.

By the time the MP pulled up outside the football club, the film crew were already there and the first half was nearly over. He strode into the ground and several bemused Chester City executives broke away from the game to welcome him. To his credit,

Brandreth did not look even slightly ruffled, announcing loudly: 'I am now launching a campaign to overhaul road signage in Chester!' The faces of the executives told the story of a constituency that was about to fall to Tony Blair's Labour. To cap it all, in the second half of the game Gyles accidentally took a seat with the opposition fans and was engulfed in jeering from the Chester end.

Spin was the attempt, led by Labour, to professionalise the presentation of politics and stop that sort of thing. But the Blair years saw the public grow tired of smooth surfaces, feeling increasingly that political formica was being used to mask untruths. We may not have been longing for MPs who couldn't find their own football stadiums, but at least we wanted sincerity; politicians who were honest about what they didn't know and what they couldn't do. When Gordon Brown took over as Prime Minister, his first public performance was praised because his head was blocked by a pillar, meaning that the main camera was unable to get a proper shot of his face.

So after watching Boris's remarkable performance at the Securitisation Awards that night I wondered: was he part of the new wave? Was Johnson's shambles a beautiful kind of honesty?

Eighteen months after the marvellous securisation night, I arrived at an awards ceremony for a totally different industry. I cannot recall whether it was concrete or chiropractors, but once again I had dutifully done my research and brought my script. However, the organisers had asked for only five minutes of opening remarks.

'Is someone else speaking?' I asked.

'Boris Johnson,' the organiser said, a frown appearing on her brow. 'Do you know where he is?'

And here we were again. He was due to speak at nine-thirty. He arrived seven or eight minutes before the actual moment, heaving and laughing himself into the chair beside me.

'Jeremy,' he said, 'what is this?'

I told him. Others at the table helped. Did they have a pen, paper? Both were produced. A better ballpoint this time, the back of the menu again. I watched, fascinated, as Boris pulled the paper tight across his thigh and wrote a few words – yes, SHEEP was definitely one – in a barely legible scrawl.

Then he was on.

'It is wonderful, and a privilege, to be here at – oh goodness.'

Laughter.

He turns, reads it off the screen.

Shocked expression, as if – *that has honestly never happened before, my God, I am so sorry, how embarrassing to forget which awards I am at.*

Louder laughter. The hair everywhere.

Into the tirade about the uncle who is not allowed to dispose of a dead sheep on his farm and had to call the man at the abattoir. 'I can't remember his name. Mick – no, Jim. No. Hang on. It was MARGARET . . . '

Then to the Mayor from *Jaws*, who kept the beaches open.

A moment's pause. 'I do accept that some small children were eaten by a shark as a result . . . '

The hair really is all over the place now, as if rising to meet the level of the audience's appreciation, the script left on the table beside me *again*, people at the tables lapping it up.

On we go to the George Brown story. This time he will remember the first, second *and* third reason, won't he? He can't forget the punchline to this story again, can he?

'SECONDLY because this is not a WALTZ but our national ANTHEM. And – and thirdly because . . . '

I sit forward in my seat, I can't believe what I am watching.

'This is very embarrassing. I am awfully sorry, I have forgotten the third reason. Very sorry, let's move on, forget about it.'

Brings the house down.

Now he is about to introduce me and I think I know what will happen, and it does.

'I actually have some of the – er, well, I suppose you could call them AWARDS here. A sort of trophy. Well, really this looks like a kind of elongated LOZENGE . . . '

*   *   *

As he said that phrase for the second time – *elongated lozenge* – I had the Hercule Poirot moment. Having read all sixty-six of Agatha Christie's detective stories as a teenager, I came to realise the vital moment was actually not the scene where everyone assembles in the living room to hear Poirot explain how the murder happened and who did it. No, the key instant in each book comes just before the denouement as the solution suddenly falls into place in the brain of the great man. At that point the crime-busting Belgian touches the delicate ends of his moustache, winks at the air and utters the key phrase:

'Now, *mon ami, now I understand everything.*'

Watching Boris at that second event, in the middle of a crowd of dinner-jacketed business people all laughing and hooting, I was momentarily apart from the proceedings. I would have touched the ends of my moustache if I had one. People who speak after dinner don't usually get to observe each other because no one books us in pairs. So when we do accidentally come together, we watch with close fascination. Now, I thought, *now I understand everything.*

Since then we have all seen Boris's progression . . . MP, then a twice-elected Mayor, then Cabinet Minister. Very nearly Prime Minister.

And watching him from a distance I have often remembered those two speeches and wondered.

Johnson became Foreign Secretary after leading the argument for Brexit. He has had his ups and downs – before deciding that everything he does is part of a brilliant act, we should probably call as evidence his shambolic run at 10 Downing Street in the summer of 2016. His leadership campaign was kyboshed at the very press conference he had booked to launch it. MPs who turned up to support him sat with their jaws slack as he goldfished at the cameras, finally telling the world he would not be able to do the job. Surely that was a real accident? People who fake car crashes tend not to get hurt in them.

And yet.

I come back again and again to the realisation at the end of the last chapter, when I wrote about the Facebook post that went viral. The video spread to a million people because it was real.

And I realised that those two Boris speeches had made me pose the fundamental question, the one that concerns you most when you listen to a politician:

Is this guy for real?

9. What's Real

It is the main lesson I take from Radio 2: what is powerful is what's real. The backlash against conventional politics is partly driven by the sense that we have dressed a whole generation in sharp suits and put them on generous expenses, and in exchange they stopped telling us the truth. We long for that famously rare thing – authenticity. Ask yourself this question: putting aside who you wanted to become American president, which candidate was most real? Who was most raw, Trump or Clinton? Who was the least varnished? Whose campaign was a shambles? Who kept firing campaign managers and having to apologise? Who was the least professional? Who was the least political?

And who won?

In May 2016 I had a peculiar message on my phone. 'Please ring Ed Balls about a private matter.'

I knew Balls only from the studio. We had jousted across a desk full of radio lights and wires. It was the usual thing: 'Why will you not take responsibility, while you were in government with Gordon Brown, for spending money like a drunken sailor?'

'Jeremy, come on. The sub-prime crisis in the USA was not caused by Labour spending on hospitals in Britain.' Our interviews were like the electrified banana the monkeys cannot unclench their paws from. I had to ask the same question, he had to give the same answer. Round and round we paced as the voltage cracked above our knuckles.

Balls was now out of politics, of course, beaten by a challenger in his own constituency in the 2015 election. Dimbleby had called on me for some graphics the instant it happened. I remember thinking how painful that moment of ejection is for a politician, especially in Britain, where you are stripped of your status under the unblinking stare of the TV cameras and as the ex-MP you must stand there, smiling good-naturedly, and soak up the full humiliation while your opponents go crazy.

So why would he be calling?

'I have been asked to do *Strictly Come Dancing*,' he explained quietly down the line. 'Yvette [Cooper, Labour MP and his wife] says I should do it because she loves the show. But I need your advice. I'm worried it may affect my – '

I filled in the blank. 'Seriousness?'

'Exactly. But we all saw how much you enjoyed it. What's it like?'

I described the full joy and madness. My ongoing friendship with Karen. The assault on the nerves that is the live dance moment.

'Do you think I should do it?'

I didn't even pause. 'Yes. Definitely! Don't worry what others think. You're out of politics at the moment. Do it for yourself, do it for Yvette and the kids, do it to see inside the most successful show in the BBC's history.'

I offered only two pieces of advice. 'Start working on the Charleston now. It is a horrific step. And go for it. Don't hold back.'

Back at home I told Rachel about the conversation and my advice. 'Oh, God, Jeremy, did you really tell him that?' she exclaimed. 'It's fine for you to dress up as a cowboy and ride in on a giant horse but he is different, he is a politician, he has to preserve his serious image. He might want to be Governor of the Bank of England one day.'

Rachel has always been able to see when something is sensible and when it is not. In 2000, soon after she told her parents that we were romantically involved, I suffered a diary malfunction (code for: I messed up my attempt to write down a date she had made me promise to keep free). Her family were celebrating forty years since her grandfather's ordination as a Church of England vicar. There would be a special lunch at the Deer Park Hotel near Honiton, East Devon. For some reason I made a note of the event under the wrong month in my diary, meaning that when a friend asked me to approve a time and place for the christening of my godson, his child, I said the grandpa-date worked fine and I would definitely be there.

When the clash emerged, Rachel was mortified and I was in a terrible position. The lunch in Devon would have been her family's first sight of me. A table plan had been drawn up and my cancellation would make me look thoughtless, graceless and rude. The christening was two hundred miles away in Bedford, and could not be changed.

There was a single ray of light. The church service for my godson would end at approximately half past twelve. Lunch in Devon was set for one o'clock.

Desperate, I contacted a firm offering helicopter rides for business people. Yes, they could whisk me between events, they said. The pricetag was in four figures but there was no other way. It helped that the MD of the company lived in Bedfordshire and had a house in Devon, so he knew the Deer Park Hotel and said he would fly me personally. It would take a little over an hour, but we would be able to land in the hotel gardens, just yards from where the lunch was being held. Problem solved!

Feeling pleased with myself, I gave Rachel the news.

'I will arrive after the starter, by helicopter, and the pilot will touch down about fifty feet from the dining room.'

Her reaction was an understated explosion.

'I am not having my new boyfriend, who none of my family have met, appearing late for this lunch in a helicopter which lands in the garden outside the window. My grandfather is a gentle, modest pensioner who is partially sighted. What sort of impression is it going to create when he is sitting at lunch, they've had the soup, there is suddenly a deafening noise, everything stops, and people have to shout at him, "That's Rachel's new boyfriend just touching down in a chopper"?'

'Would it help if I didn't wear sunglasses?'

'NO!'

I cancelled the helicopter and sent Devon my apologies.

It left me with the certainty that in matters involving fine judgement, I should always defer to my wife. So as the 2016 unveiling of *Strictly* celebrities approached, I thought Rachel might well be right about my advice to Ed Balls. I got more and more nervous on his behalf.

I had only ever known the former Cabinet Minister as a suit-and-tie man, a Westminster insider who had publicly struggled with a stammer and, in the heyday of New Labour, operated as the second brain on Gordon Brown's economic strategy. Balls was the turbo-nerd who coined the phrase 'post neoclassical endogenous growth theory'. To his credit, he had helped Brown wreck Tony Blair's attempts to take Britain into the euro, which would surely have been a disaster. This was different territory; this was a dance floor.

Ed's first televised outing made me even more worried I had advised him badly. On a night when there were no eliminations – and the standard of dancing by the others was frighteningly high – he wore a dark politician's suit (he had reportedly requested 'no sequins') and did a clunky waltz, compounding the viewers' discomfort by telling the judges it was 'better in rehearsal' and 'had gone wrong halfway through'. He looked like he had turned up for BBC *Question Time* and been led to the wrong studio. Now I feared he might suffer the ultimate blow to his pride, going out first the following week. How I wished I had told him to spare his dignity and stay clear.

The crunch show was clearly going to be the next one. Episode 2 of *Strictly* sees the first elimination. Balls was odds-on to go. I had sent him only one text since the waltz: 'Remember, the judges look at your feet, but the audience look at your face. Just enjoy it!'

But Ed's second dance was the dreaded Charleston. I was at a Devon book festival and due to attend the organisers' drinks party. They agreed I could hang back until I had seen the critical *Strictly* moment.

When it happened, it was just astonishing. The former Shadow Chancellor appeared in cowboy jeans and braces and a checked shirt and did a series of highly aerobic lifts and leg-swings to the song 'The Banjo's Back in Town'. I sat in my hotel room laughing and whooping loudly enough to stop people in the street outside. The Balls Charleston with *Strictly* newcomer Katya Jones (plainly a genius choreographer) became the standout moment of the TV year . . . until his next dance . . . and the one after that, and all the ones that followed. Balls got to Blackpool and beyond.

Most people at bus stops on Mondays that November were asking each other, 'Did you see it?', and they never needed to explain what they were talking about. After the awkwardness of the first waltz, Balls had evidently decided to abandon all attempts to preserve dignity and play safe. He put body and soul into every single second that followed. During one dance Katya reportedly shouted: 'GIVE THEM MORE!' He drenched himself in sequins and fake tan. Then paraded as a mad professor. Balls seemed to veer madly between successful stunts and cardiac arrest. He descended from the ceiling with a flaming piano ('Great Balls of Fire' in Blackpool) and did a Gangnam Style routine where he galloped astride his partner like a horse. The only time I have ever heard a *Strictly* audience gasp in horror – like spectators do at a circus when the trapeze artist misses a catch – was during a Balls-Jones lift. Ed was supposed to elevate Katya into a position like Kate Winslet in *Titanic*, but somehow her foot slid off his thigh and he had to grab her chest to stop her falling. It all added to the spectacle.

Former prime ministers David Cameron and Gordon Brown publicly congratulated him. Thousands of members of the public uploaded supportive comments online, people who might have disagreed with his every political utterance or perhaps not listened to a single word from any of his speeches. They might not even have clocked him at Westminster at all. When Ed Balls was finally knocked out of the competition, every commentator, even those in right-wing newspapers who had been sworn enemies of the Westminster Ed, agreed: this middle-aged man, fresh from a public drubbing in the 2015 election and possibly deep in a midlife crisis, had danced his way into a nation's heart.

The day after his exit I was invited on to *BBC Breakfast* to speak about the significance. Balls had talked publicly about that first conversation we had had, so people knew of our connection, and I had rooted for him on Twitter throughout (becoming gradually more certain that, in the age of Trump–Brexit, he was actually going to win the entire contest). The *Breakfast* presenter asked what I thought of his performance. I said it was stupendous. We had probably just seen 'the most profound reinvention of a politician, ever'.

I then added, without any prior thought and almost as an aside: 'It is very interesting that we saw fifteen per cent of Ed Balls through his work at Westminster. It took a dance show to reveal the other eighty-five per cent. When you think about it, that is a terrible indictment of our politics.'

MPs who heard that will feel the unfairness and kick out at the nearest table leg, but I think it is true. I sense in my listeners a desperate hunger for the politician who dispenses with all the silly on-message stuff and really shows us who they are.

I noticed this phenomenon with Jeremy Corbyn soon after he became Labour leader. The whole episode was predicted to be an electoral disaster for his party but the main shock of the 2017 election was that Labour were anything but finished. From the moment Corbyn took over as leader, my audience seemed allergic to his leftward tilt. But my goodness, when he first appeared in my studio, placed his cycle helmet on the table between us, paused mid-answer to think and sip his coffee, seeming utterly uninterested in crafting any sort of soundbite that could be picked up and used in the 1 p.m. news . . . listeners responded with positivity that gushed like an oil-strike. Whatever you think of Corbyn, he is not one of the robo-politicians we have come to hate.

I heard an account of the Labour leader speaking to a huge crowd in Trafalgar Square and coming to the climax – 'I tell you now and I tell you again, brothers and sisters, the war in Iraq was an absolutely APPALLING, DISGRACEFUL, EVIL ACT OF –' when someone handed him a slip of paper and he broke off without even thinking about what it would do to the flow of his speech. 'I'm sorry. Would the owner of car registration number GL85 6RL please move it as you are double-parked near an access point.'

Somehow the fact that Corbyn voted against Tony Blair more than four hundred times in Parliament is not taken as disloyalty, but as truth.

The election of Donald Trump confirmed that voters are now prepared to insist their politicians are not political. During one of the presidential debates Hillary Clinton reminded Trump he was the first candidate in forty years to refuse to publish his tax returns:

Clinton: 'Maybe he doesn't want the American people, all of you watching tonight, to know that he's paid nothing in federal taxes, because the only years that anybody's ever seen were a couple of years when he had to turn them over to state authorities when he was trying to get a casino licence, and they showed he didn't pay any federal income tax.'

Trump: 'That makes me smart.'

That makes me smart! Up until that instant, there had been a rule: *You will not get elected if you boast about how you avoid paying tax.* Trump broke all the rules and still won. *You will not be elected if you boast about how you grab women 'by the pussy', call Mexicans 'rapists and murderers', do an impression of a disabled reporter, or say this of the presenter Megyn Kelly:* 'You could see there was blood coming out of her eyes. Blood coming out of her wherever.'

It is not that Trump tore up the rule book. It is that he was the lucky candidate to discover it had already been thrown on the fire. When he won and immediately abandoned his promises to put Clinton in jail and build a 'beautiful wall' along the Mexican border – it seems long stretches will be a fence – one shrewd commentator summarised: 'The media took Trump literally but not seriously. The voters took him seriously but not literally.'

One thing we can surely agree on. Trump was the opposite of political. If he had been political, he would not in a single twenty-four hours have blurted out that he was considering prosecuting women who have abortions, and that he could not rule out using nuclear weapons in Europe. Yes, he actually said both things *on the same day*. Both had to be retracted.

Put on air themselves, my listeners confirm that they are also the opposite of political. If the definition of being a politician is avoiding saying what you think people don't want to hear, then the definition of an audience is saying whatever the hell you like. Politicians speak with calculation – listeners speak with conviction. Calculation is the opposite of conviction.

There is a reason that the word 'political' is almost the same as 'polite'. In the first hundred adjectives you might choose for my show, 'polite' would struggle for a place. When it sounds angry, it's because the listeners feel angry on a particular day. If it sounds sad then it is because they feel sad. Funny, then funny. An audience cannot hide how it feels. Listeners are so real I can hear them breathing.

A pensioner rang when British Home Stores were closing down. She was tearful. Diana explained that she 'used to go into BHS for an item which I can only buy from the men's department'.

There was a pause. In a microsecond I had to decide, should I ask her? Finally I did. 'What item was that?'

'Men's trousers,' she said. 'I really do sympathise with the staff. I am crying.'

The next caller was less tender-hearted. 'I would cry if I had to buy men's trousers from BHS.'

Okay, impolite. But the kind of conversation you overhear in a shop queue, somehow conducted just as intimately in front of millions of radio listeners.

Real can be gritty. Discussing the sudden surge in red kite numbers in Buckinghamshire, apparently caused by an over-successful operation to stop the birds of prey dying out, we heard from a young mum who told us she was 'just giving my little girl a muffin to eat in the playground, when a red kite suddenly swooped and took it away. It used her head as a ledge.' The kites, she argued, should now be culled.

The first email in reply was not really broadcastable.

'Sorry but oh we now have hundreds of these birds so let's have a cull of them, just because it ate some poor little fat girl's cake. That stupid woman.'

Not exactly how a politician would react. Yet other interactions are magical. During an item about rekindling a failed romance, Ann rang to say she had decided to remarry the man she divorced ten years earlier. There followed a glorious exchange with our relationships expert, Barbara Want.

Expert: 'What was the problem in your relationship?'

Ann: 'We weren't communicating.'

Expert: 'And what's changed?'

Ann: 'We are communicating.'

The simplicity of that – so truthful, so open. And as we found out from the viral Facebook video, all that matters is what's real.

We did an item on circumcision which got coverage for the wrong reason. I misheard a woman tell me she had had her son circumcised 'after what I saw my brother go through when he was younger. He had his foreskin caught in a lziigffipt.'

In a what? The quality of the line was not perfect and I was sure she had said his foreskin was caught *in a lift*. I pictured a set of elevator doors closing and – and what? It raised a whole host of questions, not least about the size of the foreskin and the speed of the doors. When I gasped, 'IN A LIFT?' she replied patiently, 'No, in a zip', and I knew we would splash on all the media websites, as indeed we did.

sport   football   opinion   culture   business   lifestyle   fashion   environment   tech

society   law   scotland   wales   northern ireland   education

Jeremy Vine floored by foreskin 'stuck in lift' cock-up

Radio 2 presenter mishears caller in phone-in about circumcision

BBC Radio 2's Jeremy Vine Photograph: Linda Nylind for the Guardian

But in a way the best part of the discussion came later. Maurice, a Nigerian man with a strong accent, shouted down the phone line that he had been circumcised and all men should have the same procedure 'because it has been medically proven'. The last words were delivered with a flourish, at particularly high volume, as if that should be the end of the matter.

'But what exactly is the medical evidence?' I asked.

He sighed as if it hardly needed explaining.

'The medical evidence is that if you are circumcised, a woman will be all over you.'

During the summer of 2016, I noticed a list pinned to the office noticeboard by producer Tim Johns inviting people to note *Recent Good Items On The Show* and couldn't help celebrating the memory of every single one that had been written down:

- A man describes getting an infection on his genitals after touching a fish . . . 20/7/15
- Caller describes being arrested for being naked and why he is annoyed about it . . . 4/9/15
- Fight over reduced-price duck breast in supermarket . . . 17/6/15
- Futuristic robot comes into studio and is completely and utterly useless, won't even turn on . . . 14/9/15
- Man cooks and eats dolphin live on air . . . 9/12/15
- George, 75, describes his sex life . . . 12/1/16
- Caller admits to having shot and killed several cats . . . 3/2/16
- Item about the murder of a village goose, possibly by sniper . . . 27/2/16
- Caller not happy about cows living outside a nightclub in Bristol . . . 22/4/16
- Caller's defence of circumcision . . . 19/4/16

As I read the list I remember thinking, 'This is a very long way from *Newsnight*', where every night I would have to announce the names of senior politicians as the curtains opened and hope viewers would stay to watch them argue with each other, when often the only real difference was the colour of their ties. I often used to wonder, presenting Newsnight: *Where is the audience in all of this?*

The 'murder of a village goose, possibly by sniper' was an example of where audience interaction gets complicated. The goose – actually a gander, as it was male – had become so much a part of village life that his image featured on the welcome sign to Sandon in Hertfordshire. The bird had been right at the centre of the community for a decade, and was especially popular with local children who were, of course, distraught about the murder. In happier days the goose had been celebrated for chaperoning ducklings and scaring off foxes. To widespread amusement, it treated the traditional red village phone box as home. Villagers told us none of the four hundred residents could be considered a suspect. The goose was so popular it would even take part in keep-fit lessons at the village hall and be welcomed.

Then one day, according to an eyewitness, a car drew up, an air rifle was pointed out of the window and the goose was fatally shot above the eye. Eyewitnesses said the shooter 'leaned out of the passenger side of a dark four-by-four', which then screeched off. A man gave us an interview about how he had heard the bang and screech of tyres. The old phone box was now a temporary shrine, filled with flowers and sympathy cards, many in the felt-tip scrawl of the village kids.

But there were murmurs. Reporters despatched to the town after the goose died heard one resident recall how 'the goose was cursed at by some, as you couldn't post a letter without a stick', and the animal would grow angry during the mating season 'because he could see his own reflection which he believed was another bird'. This was a proper murder mystery, and it needed solving.

There is a vibrancy with animal stories, as if you can feel the air in the studio bend. Cruelty to humans is somehow seen as a thing we have brought upon ourselves, but with animals there is outrage.

We have occasionally tried to argue against our own audience. When a man returned drunk from the pub in Wolverhampton and killed the family parrot in front of his wife, he was jailed. 'The parrot had no chance of fleeing,' said the district judge, sending Paul Pugh to prison for five and a half months.

Let's pause and reflect on that: *Five and a half months. For killing a parrot.*

We constructed an item suggesting the judge had been over-sentimental. Prison was too harsh when the only victim was a small bird and someone guilty of assaulting a pensioner might well walk free. We called as evidence a police news conference held in a different part of the country after four louts threw a dog off a bridge. The police officer at the news conference called the youngsters 'beyond evil' as he appealed for anyone with information to come forward. Sorry: *Beyond evil?* The phrase is the kind we reserve for child-killers or genocidal tyrants. Had we lost all perspective when it came to animals?

No, definitely not, responded every single listener who called in. All of them, without exception, seemed to think the jail sentence on Pugh was grotesquely light. Some even called for the individuals involved to face the death penalty.

I learnt from that. Just as they say in business that the customer is king, in radio the audience is right. It is not my job to lead them towards daylight or anything silly like that. They are perfectly capable of leading themselves.

So when the story about the Sandon goose was broadcast, we had given up resisting the listener reaction. If anything, they were even more furious than we expected. Quite a few rang in offering a reward for information that led to the capture of the gunman. Then a caller said he would 'give the perpetrators two hundred thousand pounds if they give themselves up'. This was quite sensational. At the time, seeing the notes of what he would say on a scrap of paper brought in by a producer, I did not grasp the problem. It seemed like a novel solution. Others must have thought the same, because they added their own amounts to the sum. By the time the show was halfway through, we seemed to have become the unwitting facilitators of a huge national whip-round. Almost £275,000 was now being offered to the goose-shooters 'if they do the right thing and hand themselves in'.

The tone then changed.

Sensing they could collect hundreds of thousands of pounds simply by *not* having an alibi for the day in question, a number of people began to contact us with credible-sounding claims that they had killed the Sandon goose. I AM THE SHOOTER, read one comment, NOW GIVE ME THREE HUNDRED GRAND.

I felt we might be running into trouble. And events suggested we certainly had. Into our email box dropped a serious complaint, and several others like it, accusing us of effectively putting a bounty on the head of every goose in the country.

'The Vine Show today broadcast statements by people who are mentally ill offering to reward a goose killer with huge sums of money. I think it stood at £275,000 by the end of the show. As Vine himself said, this is actually providing an incentive for people to shoot birds and animals (and possibly even people) and by allowing the broadcast the BBC is promoting the principle that crime pays. Someone failed in their responsibility and they should be dismissed with immediate effect.'

Oh well. Lesson learnt.

Sometimes the thing you remember is not what the interviewee intended at all. When *Panorama* was brought back to its old Monday slot with a huge fanfare in 2007, I was appointed its sole presenter. For one diamond-studded second, I felt I had got where I wanted professionally. Aged 42, I would be sitting in a chair only ever occupied by the holy trinity of television news – Richard Dimbleby, David Dimbleby and Robin Day. Even Paxman had not done it. Nothing could ever take that away from me.

But every mountain in the BBC is made of ice cream. This one swiftly melted. The Beeb went from deciding the show really needed a presenter to deciding it didn't really need one – something it signals to you in the most deliciously passive-aggressive way. 'We cannot afford your make-up lady any more,' the editor told me. 'You will have to buy your own make-up.' Dutifully I went into a branch of Boots to ask about foundation. The lady behind the counter recognised me: 'Don't you have someone to do this for you?' Three years after I was appointed, a manager earning £350,000 a year let me know I would have to leave the show to save the BBC money.

I could have borne her a grudge, but then she became embroiled in one of the most torrential BBC crises ever and ended up half-broken herself – and I saw how the two of us were both hostages in the same hijack. Like the children on the slaloming school bus in *Dirty Harry*, managers and staff in the BBC have to keep singing 'Row, row, row the boat' as loudly and as lustily as we can or the crazed hijacker will smash our heads and throw us through a window. Now, when I see that manager, we hug and chat like old friends.

During this slightly painful time, the thing that gave me solace was the audience. Presenting – standing outside the BBC in a coat and grandly announcing to a camera what is on the programme – felt empty. Reporting felt like joy.

With a film crew I took the train to Romford to find victims of the financial crash in 2008. Romford is on the way out of London, with a slightly tatty high street sixteen miles east of the centre. There I met a young woman I will call Megan who worked part-time for a travel agent. I felt sorry for her. She had a sincere manner and wore make-up that had been industriously applied. Megan explained how determined she was to try to make a career out of high street travel. However, her rental costs were high and she lived miles from Romford.

'What's the commute like?' I asked, conscious that we had a boom microphone suspended in the air over our heads and a TV camera nosing in towards her, which never helps a conversation feel real.

'Not easy. Expensive.'

She described her daily route in the post-cockney accent I now hear everywhere, which people call Jafaican.

'And do you buy a ticket every day?'

'Nah,' she replied. 'I've got an anal pass.'

Home. The Radio 2 studio at eleven minutes to twelve on an ordinary day in 2017. Finger on the fader. Are we ready?

And this was the team on day one: 6 January 2003. The champagne was only handed over when I hit the correct button to play 'Thunder Road' by Bruce Springsteen. Three of us remain in 2017.

They should make teenage pregnancies an Olympic sport then we would get another medal.

Ed

One of many classic comments. We used to stick the best ones to the office wall, but we ran out of Sellotape.

Below Some of the guests in my studio. Let's turn this into an *Eggheads* question: can you name all sixteen?

With Taylor Swift, just before I embarrassed myself.

Hillary Clinton had arrived half an hour before my show and, incredibly, was alone. At the time she seemed certain to be the next President. Behind her, out of view, the coffee machine is recreating World War One.

The inspirational Terry Walton with his beautiful family on Radio 2's 'official allotment' in the Rhondda. At least one listener believes all Terry's crazy fruit and veg sound effects are played off a tape in an attic somewhere.

When Paul Simon appeared on Ken Bruce's show, I asked if I could join the photo of them both. This was supposed to be a picture of all three of us. Ken never ceases to remind me that the camera suffered a fatal leftwards drift that cut him out.

In 2001 I was told to drive a campervan around the country for *Newsnight*'s on-the-road election coverage. Our promise of a 'rapid response to breaking stories' was slightly undermined when the van broke down in Hartlepool.

With Tony Blair for a *Newsnight* special in 2001. How young we both look. He was about to win a second landslide. But now the Radio 2 switchboard is deluged with abuse when his name is mentioned, the audience as furious as a lover who was cheated on.

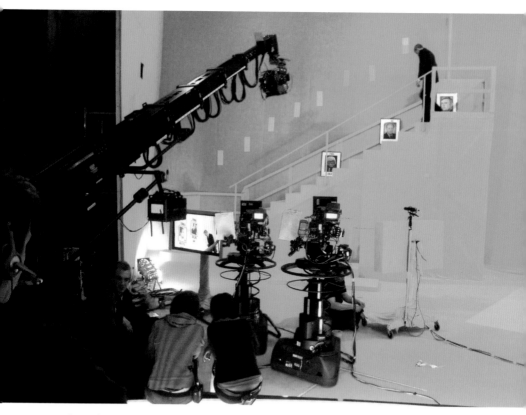

How I love the election graphics. Here they have rigged a 'Downing Street staircase' (in reality chipboard painted a brutal CGI green) which enables me to point out past Prime Ministers on an imaginary wall . . .

. . . and this is what the viewer sees on TV.

By 2015 the graphics set was enormous, just like the election result itself. That's me in the middle of the floor. For 2017 we dusted off the same rig.

The early morning I spent with David Cameron recording his 3D image for our 2015 election graphic. The Prime Minister was kind to my daughter Martha, despite my disastrous attempt to persuade him to ban Maplin from selling drones.

Taking a radio show on the road seems to elevate the general madness. Here we are in Mumbai. Editor Phil Jones discusses sockets and cables with technical whizz Steve Bridges. My job is to pray we stay on air, and we just about did.

One former presenter of *Newsnight* . . . and Jeremy Paxman. If the legendary frontman looked a little grey at the gills it might be because his programme was being engulfed in the BBC's biggest scandal at the time. He left *Newsnight* soon after, apparently unimpressed when it was accused of wilfully canning its Jimmy Savile investigation.

I spent a couple of seconds working out how an anal pass would help a person move around Romford, and the camera started shaking, but apart from that we got through it. More than that – Megan, bless her, took me out of my world and into hers. That is the journey every broadcaster needs to make.

A different train took me to West Sussex to meet Kay Gilderdale and hear about her daughter. Kay was a charming, softly spoken 55-year-old mum who gladly opened up her house to invasion by our film crew of five. She did not look like the sort to commit murder.

'Oh, Lynn was very popular,' she said, when the lights were up and we were shooting. 'She'd come home from school bursting to tell you everything that was going on. She loved sailing, she loved swimming. She loved music and dancing. She was interested in everything really.'

But Lynn was dead. A catastrophic reaction to a routine immunisation saw her young life drain away. Two days after receiving a BCG injection she fell ill. She would never see the inside of a classroom again and was bedridden, unable even to lift her head from the pillow, for a full seventeen years. Eventually Kay helped Lynn die.

Now the former auxiliary nurse was – bewilderingly – being charged with the killing. She described the final hours to me. Lynn had written a note describing her own wish to leave this world. She wanted to inject herself with a fatal dose of morphine. But it was Kay who offered the syringes.

'Lynn took the last two syringes that I gave her, and she wouldn't let me go near them. She obviously knew that she had to do it herself. And she pressed the plungers. And as she did, the lights went out in the house. One of the electrical circuits had blown.'

I was conscious of the silence in the room as she spoke, as if the circuits had blown again. Every single member of the *Panorama* crew was listening to her every word.

'I said, "Wait", because my heart was wanting her to stay. And Lynn said "No", and continued to push the plunger.'

It wasn't an interview any more, but a conversation. What were Lynn's last words to her mother?

'That she's frightened,' said Kay. 'And I thought she meant she was frightened of the unknown. And I said: "Why are you frightened?" And she said: "I'm frightened for you, and frightened that it won't work."'

Kay was eventually cleared of murder, as everyone knew she would be. It was crazy she was ever charged, but maybe someone had decided the law needed clarifying without thinking about the effect on the loved ones left behind. I remember the encounter so well – the bedroom left exactly as it had been when Lynn was alive, bed positioned so she could see through the French windows to the garden; the sandwiches Kay made us. And above all, the incredible power of that connection – your life with another person's, perhaps just for an afternoon.

That was a rare TV interview, because most are not that personal. Radio is usually far more intimate than television – a great advantage. Make-up and spotlights kill intimacy, and intimacy is truth. Television also suffers from the capacity to cause immense distraction: no reporter's words will ever be as interesting as the cravat they are wearing or the comb-over that suddenly lifts in the wind as if on a hinge. When an American politician was interviewed on *Newsnight* wearing a green neon bicycle on his lapel, so many viewers asked 'What IS the badge for?' that Jeremy Paxman was forced to ask him live on air, thereby ensuring the entire conversation was drowned out by the green bike. Because it had no deeper meaning other than that the Congressman was a cyclist, the interview was destroyed and no one now remembers anything about it except that he wore a bike on his jacket.

To record the Kay Gilderdale encounter we needed lights, microphones, a chap with sound-recording equipment, cables, a tripod and heaven knows what else. For radio you only need a 1970s telephone and the person can be live from their home in a dripping bathrobe.

I often think the Radio 2 listener speaks as if I am the only one on the line. A lady caller in her seventies quietly said she had been raped at the age of twelve. 'Who else have you told about this?' I asked into the silence. 'You are the first,' she replied.

But the saddest stories can also bring surprising joy. Reporting on an international survey which said British hospices were the best in the world, we had a call from Keith in Matlock about his mother, aged 101. The record was just starting to fade when I heard him crying.

JV: 'That was Orchestral Manoeuvres in the Dark. Let's talk to Keith in Matlock. How are you doing?'

Keith (*in tears*): 'Hi Jeremy.'

JV: 'Tough time I know.'

Keith: 'Yeah.'

JV: 'So your mum is 101. She has had a good innings?'

Keith: 'She has seen a lot, she has outlived two husbands. She will be 102 in December.'

JV: 'Can you bear to tell us how she is?'

Keith: 'Well the incredible thing is, there's absolutely nothing wrong with her. She's just old. Her body is gradually folding in, I guess [*he sighs*] . . . She stopped eating a week last Friday so now she's on liquids but she is just fading away. I have to say she is just in an ordinary residential care home but the staff have been absolutely fantastic. They turn her every two hours so she doesn't get bed sores, they wet her mouth and give her liquids if she can have them. They wash her all over and sit with her in the evenings when my brother and I can't be there. She's comfortable. She's warm and she's peaceful.'

JV: 'The last thing you want is her being shuttled backwards and forwards in an ambulance.'

Keith: 'Oh, we've done all that. She came back last time and she wasn't sure where she'd been – so she thanked the ambulance crew for a wonderful trip out.' (*He laughs*)

Part of the reason radio survives is the intimacy it makes possible. The internet is a billion; television is a million; radio is one.

The fact that, while taking those 25,000 calls, my audience has grown from 5.75 million a week to 7.2 million[2] is something I find incomprehensible, given the choice now available via Spotify, podcasting, iTunes, Periscope, YouTube, etc. – and of course the way digital has opened up the spectrum to even more radio stations. The proliferation of choice has killed newspapers and wounded television, but somehow radio has danced through the battlefield like Julie Andrews and the Von Trapp singers.

The 7.2 million figure is incomprehensible in other ways. When I sit in the studio chair I never think: 'There are seven million people who will hear what I say when I touch the red fader.' That way lies madness. Instead I remember Sir Terry Wogan, whom I admired so much, being asked how many listeners his breakfast show had. He gave the immortal reply: 'Only one.'

Of course it was not me who increased the audience to my show. It was the audience that increased the audience. The show is the audience, the audience is the show. I am just a passenger on their train. They shovel coal into the furnace and check the tickets. They operate the signals and change the points. I am the lucky traveller admiring the view. They drive it.

Ann Hamilton, 61, rang from Flitwick. We were asking whether violent video games made society itself more dangerous. Ann was a retired primary schoolteacher so I had an idea of what to expect from her.

She completely confounded me.

'I play *Call of Duty* with my brother who lives in Leeds, and

---

[2] Figures from RAJAR. They measure total listening per week. Broadcasters constantly joke about how inaccurate the system must be given that it asks sampled listeners to keep a written diary of what they've heard. But the trend over time – rises and falls – is the key thing we focus on. I should add that Radio 2's audience is rising across the board, so I should be very grateful to Ken Bruce.

my son who plays in Milton Keynes. I'm rubbish really but I do enjoy it. I know there's been a lot of bad press about these games, but I was a primary schoolteacher and the children in my class loved the idea that I played *Call of Duty*. We do group texting. You can form what they call a Clan . . . The other day I was trying to do a challenge where we had to get headshots, and we got split up, and I was in the opposing team, and my son told me where he was and he said "Come on mum, you can come and shoot me in the head," but I couldn't do it.'

Unforgettable. The retired teacher who spends weekends with headphones on, blasting enemy players in a shoot-em-up game? The joy of radio is that people say stuff they wouldn't say elsewhere. After Jeremy Clarkson was sacked for punching his producer we heard from Angela Starkey in Liverpool. Had you made an appointment and pointed a camera and spotlight in her face with me sat in front of her, I doubt you would have got this spur-of-the-moment tirade:

'Clarkson should not have been sacked. The real fault here is on men. *Top Gear* is the only totally male programme left. Jeremy Clarkson is the icon of that and they want to neuter him. For daring to be a man, warts and all. Maybe they'd reinstate him if he got in touch with his feminine side. I think it's awful.'

'He is too politically incorrect for the BBC?' I put in.

'Yeah. We are all being raised on a diet of cultural Marxism. Why didn't that producer just hit him back? He probably was terrified of hitting him back because of the implications.'

I tried pointing out: 'There are some people who have never hit anyone because it's not the way they operate.'

'Well,' she snorted, 'they don't operate like that now, do they? What have men turned into? That producer ran to A&E like a wet lettuce with a thick lip. *He ran to the state, Jeremy*. Male-dominated societies used to be able to happen – men used to be able to have skirmishes and scuffles and the odd fight and they shook hands and got on with it. But we have had to make women out of men and now they say, "Oh, we've got to have investigations, you must get to hospital, you've got to call the head of the BBC, the police − ." It's a sad state of affairs because I think men can't have anything. Every male industry has been shut down or adulterated with women. *Top Gear* was *Loose Women* for men . . . What has happened to men? Why didn't the producer hit him back?'

I replied with the only thing I could think of. 'Angela, thank you very much.' And felt like a wet lettuce myself. Some calls make you flinch − ouch.

I have written a lot about the listeners who ring us, because their appearances are unscheduled and punky and they give the show an element of surprise. You may find what Angela said abrasive, even offensive, but she was not larking around or speaking for effect. We didn't air the red kite 'poor little fat girl' comment because it would have hurt the mum it was aimed at. But Angela's target was wider. I love being on a show where the default setting is − *put it on air*. We set a premium on what is genuinely meant and felt, even if, listening to Angela, I had a second wave of sympathy for the producer with the fat lip.

But I should mention guests, too. Most items are booked on the day itself. I cycle in for the programme meeting at 8.10 a.m. and we all sit in a circle and discuss what is happening in the world. We schedule one or two people for each item who can shed light before the arguments start. Often they are sat across the desk from me as I introduce them.

Sometimes we use − oh, how I hate to admit this − a *diary*. The diary is necessary because a good number of people are never free on the day itself. So on a particular Tuesday we will look on the wall (the diary is really a calendar) and see that we have a guest today who we invited several weeks ago, and this was the only day they could come, and what was it they were talking about?

Today it was Tony Long, known as 'the Met's serial killer' because as a police marksman he had shot and killed three people. He described one shooting in chilling detail: 'I shot him through the side window of the car, and because it was safety glass it frosted over, so I couldn't see him. There was just a hole the size of a dinner plate, so I kept firing through the hole.'

People think of Radio 2 as a music station, and my programme as a moment of semi-seriousness, or quite often silliness, in the schedule. But the gap between entertainment and tragedy is narrower than tracing paper. Walking into the Radio 2 elevator, I found myself squashed into the armpit of a burly music industry person and closer than I had ever been to the gothically inspiring Nick Cave, one of the greatest indie rockers of all time.

It was a strange way to meet a hero. A decade earlier I had seen him in my local high street, playing a game with his young son whom he clearly adored. Back then I would never have troubled him with a stranger's hello. The contrast between that sweet father-and-son scene and my teenage memory – his snarling breakthrough track was 'Release the Bats', with the lyric 'Sex horror bat bite' – was striking. I thought for a second how fatherhood can unpunk a person.

Now, in this enclosed space, Cave was the goth indie rocker again. Tall, dark, dressed in black. As we all edged upward in our metal box he looked at me like a hanging judge in the Wild West, with the black-eyed stare I had seen in countless music videos.

I reckoned he was thinking: 'Here's that serious bloke off the news. Non-person.'

Because we were less than six inches from each other I thought I should say something.

All that would come was the single line: 'Release the bats.'

His face broke into the warmest smile. 'They don't write them like that any more.'

'I love that song. Nineteen-eighty. I was fifteen.'

He grinned. 'Thank you.' Not so much gothic horror as Edwardian gent.

A couple of years later I saw the tragic news. The child I had seen him embracing in the high street had become a schoolboy. He took some LSD and stumbled off a cliff in Brighton. Arthur Cave fell onto the underpass of Ovingdean Gap and died in hospital. All I could remember was my momentary conversation with his father, and whether he would ever smile like that again.

*   *   *

A life may change in an instant. Sometimes the single instant changes many lives in less than a blink. A radio programme can try to share the instant and the lives changed, but once in a while its circuitry is simply overwhelmed. That was the case with the parents of April Jones, a five-year-old girl murdered in Wales by a paedophile.

Her disappearance had triggered the biggest search in British police history. The mum and dad were Coral and Paul and I don't think what they said will ever leave me or the audience. To me these exchanges sum up the power of personal truth.

JV: 'Did you think about whether you could attend the trial?'

Paul: 'I've always said I don't want to do some things like that. Coral said "I want to do it". We had a split opinion on it. So I went, and I'll always be glad I did it. The organisation of it all, to watch the kids and everything was a bit complicated, but we had lots of friends and family round.'

JV: 'Coral, I know that when the trial started you then had to tell Harley [April's brother] exactly what had happened.'

Coral: 'Yes.'

JV: 'And that was really hard.'

Coral: 'It was really hard. I took Harley upstairs to our bedroom. He knew stuff had gone on – some stuff. He knew more than we thought he knew. But I had to tell him – sorry – that she's not coming home.'

Paul: 'You could hear him squeal.'

Coral: 'The scream just pierced your – I got hold of him and hugged him – and the scream just ripped you to pieces. And it was something I will never forget.'

JV: 'And I know you talked in your victim impact statement about how much harm had been done, yes to April, but to your whole family. Part of that was in that scream.'

Paul: 'That shriek is something you will never forget. You will never hear anything like it and I hope no one hears anything like it. The damage he [the murderer, Mark Bridger] has done to us as a family is immense. But we are a strong family and we did hold it together.'

Coral: 'A lot of us are stronger than we were before. But he wrecked us. The town he wrecked as well, in some ways. And the other families he's hurt as well.'

JV: 'But you decided you would go into the courtroom? You were ten feet from him? How did you manage that?'

Coral: 'It's hard. I felt – I wanted him to know that we were there. And I wanted him to know he wasn't going to get away with stuff. I felt if I had laser eyes, I could burn him from top to toe with the anger I had.

'I said to the police, if I had a nail gun, I would have nailed him to the floor so he could not get away and not do anything else . . .'

JV: 'You have been to the house which doesn't exist any more . . . I was amazed you did it. I don't know how you had the strength to do that, but for you, you had to see it, I guess, Coral, did you?'

Coral: 'I had to. You see all the pictures that the police give you. And the evidence. For some reason I had to go into the house. It was horrible to see the . . . the evidence was still on the floor. They had a pool of blood in front of the fireplace. Where the blood was, you could see the knife marks that were on the floor in it, and you could see the bloodspots on the walls where the arrows pointed to – on the washing machine, on the toilet where all these little arrows were.'

Paul: 'It's a bit like a weight on your mind. It's one of them things you've got to get it out of the way. If you don't, it just sits on you for the rest of your life. We face everything we can.'

That shriek from Harley. The bravery from April's mum and dad. The pool of blood on the floor and the ruined lives. I realised as they spoke to me – no one could understand their words unless they had lived them. They were as close to reality as you can ever get.

10. i-Power

On 23 June 2016, the governing class were hit by a different reality. The realisation came slaloming at them like a runaway truck in the early hours of the morning – most people in the UK wanted to get out of the European Union. Once again I was on graphics duty in the election studio, and I can't imagine ever doing a bigger show. As I rushed around my green swimming pool, David Dimbleby was back behind the desk.

Dimbleby. The name is the broadcast news equivalent of Windsor. The king of current affairs presenters – perhaps I should say 'prince', his late father Richard being the original BBC monarch – had hosted the first EU Referendum results programme in 1975 when I was a ten-year-old running along a beach in trunks.

I got my mum to email me a black-and-white snap of the young Jeremy in 1975. 'In case you were wondering what I was up to last time you did this,' I said, showing David.

'Do you have to remind me of my advanced age?' he laughed.

I asked: 'Can you remember any of the highlights of the 1975 programme?'

His answer surprised me. 'No, none of them.'

Speaking to Dimbleby, I recalled a fragment of a poem by an obscure American, Hyam Plutzik. He dreamed that Shakespeare was living near him in a manor house in a forest, sitting behind a curtained window – but is devastated to find he can't wake himself quickly enough and run to the house. Had he got there, Plutzik writes: 'I would have met him as he lived!'

Well here I was, presenting with the undisputed number one. I met him as he lived.

Incredibly, Dimbleby would go on to front Theresa May's snap election in 2017, despite the BBC's firm announcement that 2015 had been his last. Huw Edwards, first promised the succession in the previous century, would have to wait until 2022 – although it is quite possible that David will present that too. With an unsurpassable ten general elections under his belt, Dimbleby has written the playbook for presenter survival.

For me, the EU Referendum results show was bigger than anything else staged in our election thunderdome. Bigger than the 2010 election, which sensationally brought in a coalition government. Bigger than 2015, with the shock Cameron victory and that twelve-foot hologram of him looking fed up with my drone monologue. When I co-presented the EU Referendum I had that thing a person rarely gets in broadcasting – the sense that history is spooling off the reel you are holding.

That night, the Prime Minister had settled down to dinner in Downing Street in the certainty that Britain had voted to remain in the EU. Number Ten insiders were quoted saying Cameron was 'totally convinced' his side had won, and when he turned on the BBC at 10 p.m. to watch our programme it would have reassured him. Pundits were predicting a 52 per cent–48 per cent victory for Remain and the bookies had shut up shop with odds of 3:1 against Brexit.

So infectious was the optimism of the Remainers that Nigel Farage and Boris Johnson, the two most high-profile Brexiteers, appeared to concede immediately. Having spoken to contacts in the City who had conducted their own private polls, Farage said with a disconsolate shrug: 'It looks like Remain will edge it.' The Leave victory party was cancelled.

So the very first results from Sunderland and Newcastle were electrifying. My battleground graphic – which measured actual results against expectations in nearly 400 counting areas – showed Eurosceptic Sunderland more gung-ho for Brexit than anyone expected. Meanwhile Newcastle, expected to vote decisively for Remain, was closely balanced.

The studio air fizzed with expectation.

Were all the pundits wrong? The whole country was watching.

Had we decided to leave the EU in defiance of nearly all the experts?

Yes we had.

Twenty feet from me, Dimbleby shuffled his papers at 4.42 a.m. and announced: 'The British people have spoken, and the answer is, we're out.'

So would there now be recriminations about why people chose to ignore so many experts begging them not to vote Leave?

Yes there would.

And would I then wonder . . . this is the key question for me now . . . would I wonder if my show was partly to blame for debagging every voice of authority who came near the studio, in favour of our precious listener-wisdom?

Yes, indeed I would.

In the last chapter I gave some examples of the beauty of what comes to us spontaneously from the audience. I explained how, to me, their reality is the programme's foundation stone. An expert in ladders is someone who's fallen off one. A specialist in Lyme disease is a person with all the symptoms. An authority on road safety is a trucker with a clean licence. And why speak to a historian about the Falklands War when there's a veteran on the line?

The next paragraph is the most important in the book, so I am giving it a whole page to itself.

People divide into astronomers and astronauts – those who look at the moon, and those who walk on it. The media are full of astronomers because there are more of them; but most astronomers have never left their attics. Really we want to hear from astronauts, because astronauts have actually been to the moon. The same with listeners. Listeners do the walking. They are not experiencing life through a telescope, they are actually living it.

When Professor Rory Collins arrived in the studio in September 2016 to tell us how his massive study of 10,000 patients showed statins were almost completely safe, with relatively few side effects, he set the minds of many older listeners to rest – for about three minutes. The impact of the first caller was like a truck hitting a bicycle.

'My mother took statins. She became suicidal and lost control of her bowels.' The two worst symptoms imaginable. In thirteen words Keith from Caerphilly had destroyed the professor's entire five-year study.

The real-life experience of listeners will outclass anyone else's expertise. *Listeners are astronauts.*

Or so I had always thought.

We had a delicious confrontation between an expert and a listener – I nearly said astronaut – during the build-up to the EU Referendum. Royal commentator Richard Fitzwilliams gave his view after the *Sun* ran an explosive front page saying the Queen was backing Brexit. Fitzwilliams disagreed, saying Her Majesty would never disclose an opinion on such a matter, and anyway, because she had lived through the Second World War it was far more likely that the Queen thought the EU was a good thing.

At this point a listener, Phyllis Capstick from Sheffield, appeared on the line. If we had been in the theatre she would have come with a loud flash and a puff of smoke, such was the force of her intervention.

'Jeremy. We need to be brave and lead the way to set a precedent for the other countries who would dearly love to leave.'

I began: 'But – the royal expert was guessing the other way because –'

She cut in indignantly. 'I don't care about the royal expert.'

Phyllis said nothing further, so I added: 'No.'

'These are people who have common sense,' she said.

I didn't know who she was referring to, so I tried: 'I was just going to say that the – '

She cut in again. 'The experts – '

Silence. Me again: 'Yes – '

'THE EXPERTS BUILT THE *TITANIC*.'

That was it. That was what she had been warming to. 'Yeah, that's true,' I agreed.

'And what about the people who built the Ark?' Phyllis asked.

'They were experts as well?'

'No, they weren't,' she said abruptly.

'They were amateurs?'

'Yes, they were.'

It didn't really matter that her argument tailed off. She had dropped the T&A-bomb. *The Titanic, built by experts, sank. The Ark, built by amateurs, floated.* It was one moment among many on the road to the EU vote – on which, by the way, I stayed (and still stay!) impartial. But actually the Phyllis call was more than a moment. It echoed beyond the programme.

When the leading Brexiteer Michael Gove was asked on a Sky News Q&A if he could name any economists who wanted Britain out of the EU, instead of admitting he couldn't he retorted: 'People in this country have had enough of experts.'

A number of newspaper articles touched on the Phyllis call in articles about Gove's retort, which both satisfied and disturbed me. Was something big happening here? The *Telegraph*'s Group Business Editor Ben Wright delivered a powerful reply. The Gove moment had been 'one of the most depressing' in the campaign, he said, in a country that so loves 'nerd-bashing' that its people even use the ridiculous phrase 'too clever by half'. He cited several facts he said were being totally ignored in the Brexit debate – the UK has the second-lightest regulatory burden in the OECD, the UK has become more prosperous since joining the EU, migrants in the UK contribute more than they extract – and argued that if we don't listen to experts, 'we leave ourselves open to the tyranny of the anecdote'.

That gave me pause.

Was my show prey to the tyranny of the anecdote?

I wish I had been in Saint Lawrence Park in Canada in June 2016. Then I would have witnessed a truly rare event in the twenty-first century – a fight breaking out over whether the earth was flat. In a campsite near Brockville, Ontario, a 56-year-old man, his son and the son's girlfriend were sitting around a campfire. The girlfriend mentioned that she was of the firm view that the earth was flat. It had an edge and you could fall off it. The father, older and wiser, said she was wrong. The earth was round. It is not clear whether he qualified his words by saying that, strictly speaking, the earth is an oblate spheroid because of the way it bulges around the equator. But anyway, things got nasty. The girl was unwilling to concede the earth was not flat. The argument escalated.

Finally, in a fury, the father started throwing things into the fire, including a propane gas cylinder. At that point he fled the scene. Fire engines were called. He was later arrested. The police department said that, despite their intervention: 'Neither party would change their views about the shape of the earth.'

NP National Post @
@nationalpost

Flat or round? Intense dispute over the shape of the Earth ends in a fire in Brockville, Ont
natpo.st/1S4dTEB

This is remarkable, given that Eratosthenes of Cyrene, two hundred years before Christ, first established the earth was a sphere by measuring the angle of the sun's shadow in two places thousands of miles apart. After him came Galileo, Giordano Bruno, Marco

Polo. Yet here we are, hundreds of years on, finding that the issue is not settled. The roundness of the earth is merely a fact. And a fact is just a point of view said in a slightly louder voice.

Some bright spark – not an expert, surely – has already found a name for this. We are living, they say, in a *post-truth world*. In this world every single fact is up for debate. A fact is an opinion disguised as a certainty; in fact, there are no facts. There is only emotion. The argument is won by the loudest voice, a voice at Spinal Tap volume eleven or Trump volume twelve, won by the most indignant denial or by the first person to cry. Experts are derided because they are just people who own a telescope and a Velux window. If you use the phrase 'a panel of experts' these days you can actually make people break into uncontrolled laughter. Try it.

When we reported that Britain's murder rate had fallen close to its lowest in recorded history, a furious caller rang from the Midlands: 'These figures are wrong, plain and simple. There was a murder near my village only last year.'

I am regularly amazed by the power of the first-person account. The mass carnage in *Schindler's List* makes no sense until we see the girl in the red coat. My programme is a mass of red coats – one first-person story after another. But what if someone says the earth is flat? It is not impossible a caller could say that. We once had a man tell us the world was being run by an underground network of reptiles. Could we not bring in an expert to prove them wrong?

The problem is that experts seem to infuriate people. And along with a distaste for facts comes an absolute rage at statistics.

I was struck by news about children climbing trees. In a classic example of the power of the first-person account on Radio 2, we covered the story of the public park where trees with low branches, which kids could use for climbing, had been cordoned off to ensure no one climbed one and fell out. And this was not a one-off, but part of a worrying trend – in 2014 Bristol Council proposed tightening the rules in 207 of its 430 open spaces.

Among their thirty-nine new regulations was this one: 'No

person shall without reasonable excuse climb any wall or fence in or enclosing the ground, or any tree, or any barrier, railing, post or other structure.'

The words 'or any tree' caused national exasperation and the regulations were withdrawn within hours. A ban on tree climbing? What is left of childhood if you put an end to that? When the story aired on my show, scores of listeners lined up to vent their fury. It turned out that the regulations of nine Royal Parks – including Richmond and Hyde Park in London – banned the climbing of trees too. Listeners were furious. To me their arguments were bang on. One after the other, they denounced the risk-averse councils, pointing out that risk avoided is risk deferred. A child who is not regularly exposed to minor risks like falling out of a tree may not be able to process bigger risks later in life. Road safety figures bear this out, by the way – the most dangerous time to be a pedestrian in the UK is the age of twelve, because at that point a child's overprotective parents withdraw and the lone youngster simply has no idea how to cross a road.

In fact, we could add, just about *everyone* agrees with the idea that children should be allowed to climb trees, experts included. In 2008 a major study by Play England, part of the National Children's Bureau, found that half of all children have been stopped by parents or teachers from going up trees, a fifth have been banned from playing conkers and 17 per cent have been told they cannot take part in games that involve chasing each other, like 'it'. Apparently some parents even say their children must not play hide-and-seek because of the dangers.

The director of Play England, Adrian Voce, an expert if ever there was one, said: 'Children are not being allowed many of the freedoms that were taken for granted when we were children.' He pointed out that it is now a 'social norm' for younger children only to go out when accompanied by an adult, which he said led to many of them spending great chunks of their lives on computers, presumably drinking three-litre bottles of Coke as they forage online (I added that last bit). And the situation makes no sense in logic anyway – the year before, Play England pointed out, 'almost three times as many children were admitted to hospital after falling out of bed as those who had fallen from a tree'.

The National Trust agree. Mollycoddling parents and interfering councils are doing children real harm, they said, after a two-month inquiry in 2012. The Trust urged parents to send kids outdoors to build dens, make mud pies, go bug-hunting and, yes, climb trees. As a result of current attitudes children are spending huge amounts of time seated in front of a screen. And we already know where that leads. In England, 10 per cent of five-year-olds are obese. By the age of eleven, the figure doubles to 20 per cent. In 2014 nearly a third of children aged between two and fifteen were classified overweight or obese.

At this point I am guessing nothing I have said surprises you. You won't be surprised, sadly, that councils think it is even part-way sensible to ban the climbing of trees. You won't be surprised that a battalion of Radio 2 listeners mounted the studio ramparts to denounce them for it because, as astronauts, they see childhood obesity all around them. And you won't be surprised that experts, real experts like the estimable Mr Voce, take into account all the various pros and cons and tell us firmly that a ban on scaling oaks and sycamores does nothing to make a child safer. You would avoid more injuries if you stopped children climbing out of bed.

It is what happened next that made me think.

Just before the news came the last caller. She was not a spokesman for anyone, just a middle-aged mum. She spoke quietly and persuasively, her voice breaking at times. And she came from a different angle entirely.

The councils were doing something that was in the best interests of kids, she said. She knew this because of what had happened in her family.

Her nephew, a boy of ten, had been climbing a tree in his local park. He had reached the upper branches when he slipped and fell, head first. The fall broke his neck. This was four years ago. He had been confined to a wheelchair ever since, would never walk again, and could now only communicate by blinking.

I thanked her and said how genuinely sorry I was. The item had overrun because her story was so compelling, so there was no time for a last record and we went straight to the news. I frowned and stared at my desk. I looked across at the editor, who was also frowning. 'Did that just happen?' I asked.

'I think it did,' he said.

The listener – take nothing away from her or from her story – had successfully double-aced every single other person who had contributed. The expert, the listeners, every other voice . . . all were roadkill in the wake of her first-person account. The facts of the story – those percentages, the numbers, the inquiries and the reports, the road safety comparison, everything – were gone like grains of sand blown from the palm of your hand. The facts were cancelled by her emotion. A single anecdote trumped all the statistics.

The answer to 'Isn't it crazy that a council banned tree climbing?' was now: 'Not at all. Tree climbing left a small child in a wheelchair.'

That is all anyone will remember of the item. A wheelchair is a fact.

*   *   *

The split between opinion and fact has been with us for ever. The Greek philosopher Plato drew a distinction between *doxa*, what the general public think and believe, and *episteme*, what is true. *Doxa* is from the ancient Greek meaning 'to think' – *episteme* from 'to know'. The division could not be clearer. But the line seems not to be holding. The centuries-old idea that you cannot 'know' something which is untrue seems to have collapsed in the internet age.

During the Brexit debate, the Vote Leave campaigners rode around the country on big red buses with the slogan, 'We send the EU £350m a week', and followed it up with posters which urged:

'Let's give our NHS the £350m the EU takes every week.'

Nearly everyone who looked closely at it found this figure

was untrue. The total bill from the EU to the UK is around that sum, yes, but the UK doesn't 'send' it and the EU doesn't 'take' it because there is an immediate rebate which Margaret Thatcher negotiated.

Let's quickly run the numbers. In 2015, the total bill of £17.8bn (£342m a week) becomes £12.9bn (£248m a week) after the Thatcher auto-rebate is applied. This would mean the £350m on those buses was about £100m out. The figure was false.

But the gulf between the slogan and the reality is actually wider. The Treasury estimated Brussels returned about £4.4bn to the UK in 2015. Some is spent in the private sector and some is distributed by public bodies to farmers and poorer parts of the country like Cornwall and South Wales. Let's call that grant money.

Subtract the auto-rebate and the grant money, and the starting figure of £17.8bn drops to a net annual figure of £7.1bn. That would be £136m a week, less than half the figure in the slogan: 'We send the EU £350m a week.'

Now, if you supported Brexit, you are probably thinking: 'Typical BBC guy, favours the statist approach, wanted us to stay.' If so, please pause before you throw this book out of the window! The £350m fib was probably the most lurid example in a campaign where truth was murdered on both sides. There were fantastic reasons to leave the EU, not least the promise of actually writing our own laws or not paying to be represented by an MEP nobody anywhere can name who shuttles between two Parliaments in Brussels and Strasbourg because the EU cannot decide on a single location. High on the list of campaign disgraces was the taxpayer-funded government leaflet that told us all why we should vote to Remain, and the threat by the Chancellor George Osborne that a Leave vote would be swiftly followed by an emergency budget in which he would put up taxes (it was actually swiftly followed by his resignation).

As I have said, I'm impartial. But might that be the problem? How do I deal impartially with the £350m figure? Should the BBC send reporters to lie in front of the bus? Should our camera operators refuse to film the slogan on the side of it because we say it's not true? Who are 'we', anyway? What right have 'we' got to do that? Were we elected?

Or do I announce: 'A lot of people say that figure is a blatant lie, but now I'm joined by someone who says it's not'? – and treat them equally? The figure is either true or false, surely. Or is every fact just the starting point for an argument? If so, do we not all end up at that campsite in Brockville, throwing our propane cylinders into the fire to make sure we are right?

To illustrate this madness, see what happened when Nigel Farage came to my studio during the campaign. I had intended to raise the £350m slogan with him, but a listener got there before me.

Helen Thompson in Dudley asked Farage: 'Why does the Leave campaign insist on telling us the EU costs us £350m a week? It feels like we are being lied to.' I read her comment to him and this is the exchange that followed.

JV: 'I have got the figures here – it isn't £350m.'

Farage: 'No. It's £385m a week, that is the actual figure.'

JV: 'What about the rebate?'

Farage: 'Hang on. Hang on. I tell you what I'm going to do, Jeremy – I'm going to make this very simple, right?'

JV (*laughs*): 'I've got the figures here.'

Farage: 'No, no.'

JV: 'Yes.'

Farage: 'Well you've got the *Treasury* figures which have been twisted. Let me give you – come on – let me give you the Office of National Statistics figures, which are double-checked, by the way, with the EU. These are the figures for 2014 and I will put it in terms I hope people can understand. We pay a membership fee of £55m a day.'

JV: 'Oh, you're going to do "a day". I've got the figure per year – we're going to get very confused here, aren't we?'

Farage: 'No! Because if we do it by day it's easier I think to get hold of. Billions confuse everybody.'

JV: 'Well, you're going to say it's a lot of money. And I'm going to say it's slightly less than you say – '

Farage: 'Please hear me out. So we pay £55m a day. There's a big rebate, albeit one that's being crumbled away every year. We get money back in terms of agricultural support, bits of regional aid, research projects. So effectively we get £21m a day back. Our net membership fee is £34m a day. That is £10bn every single year. And that is a fact.'

JV: 'Okay. You say £10bn a year. I've got £9bn a year, and I make that between £150m and £200m a week, so it's *not* £350m a week.'

Farage: 'It's £385m a week.'

JV: (*Laughs*)

Farage: 'But let's not argue.'

I have now read that exchange back a dozen times. It is like a card trick where you miss the whole pack disappearing up his sleeve and dropping down his trouser leg. The £350m is wrong . . . then it's right . . . then it's wrong again. I have always got on personally with Farage and think he is probably one of the most effective communicators British politics has ever seen (he changed history with only one MP – a guy he didn't even get along with. When does anyone do that?). But even I was discombobulated when, as he left the studio, with the microphones off and a record playing, he told me: 'I wish they hadn't chosen that bloody £350m figure. It's caused no end of trouble. It wasn't me who chose it.'

His words were repeated more publicly when the campaign ended. The pledge to take the £350m and give it to the NHS had been 'a mistake', Farage told Susanna Reid on ITV only hours after the sensational result came through. There was understandable outrage at this retraction, because polls showed nearly half of all voters had believed those critical two sentences: *We send £350m a week to the EU; when we leave, the cash will go to the NHS*. The second statement could not be true because the first was false. It was a double-decker whopper, driven around the country on a big red bus and sold to every passenger as God's honest truth.

I have already protested that I had no dog in the fight – in the sense that I didn't desire a particular outcome to the Referendum myself. Professionally I am forced to be impartial, and personally I was totally stuck making a decision. But where I do have a dog, a great big barking one with shaggy wet hair, is in working out what is true and what is not. If journalists decide that lies and truth are the same, it's over for us.

Thus I was fascinated at the way the £350m 'fact' moved around and the way it proved impossible to kill. The UK Statistics Authority, the Institute for Fiscal Studies, several professors at the London School of Economics . . . every expert you can think of stabbed the £350m with daggers, kitchen knives, all the sharp objects they could lay their hands on. But instead of dying, the figure took wing and spread. The words of the experts seemed to count for nothing – for as we know: 'Experts built the *Titanic*.' The view of an expert is of no more weight than the view of a random punter wandering down the street after a couple of pints of Hoegaarden.

In a post-truth world, we can invent our own realities. The earth can be flat and that £350m-a-week is as real as rock. If someone tells me it is not real, I will just raise my voice and throw my propane gas cylinder on the fire.

At the end of a momentous 2016 the following letter appeared in the *Financial Times*, a newspaper that had already used gallons of ink to decry the way world-changing decisions were being made not on facts but emotion. Keith wanted to differ.

> Sir, Your pages overflow with predictions of disaster brought on by the Brexit/Trump axis. Leaving aside the depressing and repetitive pointlessness of this mass guesswork, its underlying assumption — that things were better when People Like Us were in charge — is at best dubious, at worst delusional. Under PLU rule, we have two failed wars and the Middle East in flames, China expansionist, Europe enfeebled, America ineffective and Russia resurgent. At home, we have banking crises, stagnant median incomes, uncontrolled borders, record indebtedness, profiteering by the "professional" classes, and general social polarisation. This is the Eden from which the rude and licentious electorates have expelled us?
>
> Face it. We FT readers had our decades in charge and we blew it for everyone but us. Time for us to do what we've been telling the rest of them to do for years, and suck it up. Or go forth and earn the respect that regains power.
>
> **Keith Craig**
>
> *London SW7, UK*

I accept my show may be partly responsible for this turn of events. The 'tyranny of the anecdote' – the power of that wheelchair – is a bone-rattling force. A so-called 'ordinary person' can bring down a Cabinet Minister and still have the afternoon free. One of my listeners, Gillian Duffy, famously derailed Gordon Brown's entire 2010 election campaign as she made a trip to buy a loaf of bread. They ran into each other and she politely complained about immigration. He called her a bigot when he thought no one was listening. The resulting image of him with his head in his hands – while hearing the tape for the first time on my show – was the defining moment in New Labour's crash after thirteen years in power. Mrs Duffy was the instrument. On that day her status equalled the Prime Minister's. Deference means tipping the kind of hat no one wears any more. Deference actually meant *Mr Brown returning to Mrs Duffy's front room* to apologise in person – yes, he did that, the most powerful person in the country going on bended knee before a voter and publicly declaring himself a 'penitent sinner'! Imagine!

When Harold Wilson was Prime Minister he was hit by multiple rumours of plots in the run-up to the 1970 general election. His answer was straight out of the top drawer.

'May I say, for the benefit of those who have been carried away by the gossip of the last few days, that I know what's going on. *I'm going on.*'

Listeners who recognise me and stop me in the street to talk about the show nearly always ask versions of the same question. They roll their eyes at the chaos in the world around them – Brexit, Trump, Labour, Leicester City – then throw out their arms and ask: 'Jeremy, what is going on?'

And I want to give Harold Wilson's answer. '*You're going on!* That's what's happening! You're doing this! You have the power at last!'

We can call it i-Power. It is a word I made up, but it'll do: i-Power is the main event in this new world of ours. The motivation of individual listeners in the international insurgency against the PLU is awesome. Politicians, experts, commentators, professors, researchers . . . all are stripped of their status and paraded in rags in this world without facts.

Not everyone listens to my show, so it cannot be completely to blame; we only have eighty listeners in Canada and it is very unlikely the flat-earthers in Brockville are among them. No, there are two broader developments that have caused the situation. One is the internet, which gives everyone with a computer an equal voice in a way that is both democratic and terrifying. The other is the experts themselves.

This will seem unfair, but I blame one expert in particular. This is the story of that person.

11. Three Is Murder

In August 1964 in Devizes, Wiltshire, a hairdresser and a police officer had their first and only child. Sally Lockyer – like me, born under Elvis and the Beatles into a Britain that was having a party with itself – would have a happy childhood and be much loved by her hard-working parents. Her father Frank Lockyer rose to become Chief of Police in Salisbury.

At South Wilts Grammar School for Girls, the headmaster said Sally was 'not the brightest pupil, but what she lacks in natural talent she makes up for in hard work'. From there she went to Southampton University to study industrial geography and – proving her old headmaster wrong, or perhaps showing he was right – she came first out of 108 candidates, with the highest score ever recorded in the subject. On graduation Sally became a management trainee with Lloyds Bank and then at Citibank. Her life was set fair.

Having a senior police officer for a father can scare off young suitors, and Sally's romantic entanglements seem to have been a little transient before she met and fell deeply in love with a solicitor named Steve Clark. He is not the flashy City lawyer her friends half-expected would win her heart, but an unshowy individual with a strong Derbyshire accent. One of Sally's circle calls him 'a private man, stoical. He does not show his emotions.'

After they marry in 1990, Sally resolves to become a lawyer too. She leaves her job in London to sit a course at City University, then trains at a city law firm. Steve and Sally's shared journey takes them to the law firm Addleshaw Booth & Co. in Manchester in 1994. They settle in Wilmslow, Cheshire, and are delighted when their first baby arrives. Christopher Clark is born on 22 September 1996.

* * *

In the seventies, when Sally Lockyer was still in her early teens, a middle-aged GP from Banbury was starting to make a name for himself. Roy Meadow had a paper published in 1977 by *The Lancet*, the respected medical journal, in which he named a particular set of symptoms 'Munchausen Syndrome by Proxy'.

The original Munchausen's is a condition where a person hurts themself or fakes illness to attract attention. Meadow said there was a similar condition where, by extension, the subject hurts someone else.

Among real-life examples he claimed to have come across – I say 'claimed' because there would be some questions later about the cases he cited – was a mother who slowly poisoned her child with salt to gain the attention and sympathy of medical staff. Meadow listed particular markers for MSbP, including one he called 'doctor-shopping', where the worried mother sees lots of different doctors to maximise the attention she is given.

Despite initial criticism Meadow's study came to be seen as valuable work, which led to him being knighted. The concept of MSbP caught on among doctors and social workers.

There the story should have stayed. But it seems Sir Roy was not content for other specialists to know him as the doctor who first spotted MSbP. He wanted wider recognition. Wider recognition – another word is *fame* – is something the media grant a small coterie of experts who break out of their specialisms and communicate effectively with us all. The key phrase you hear broadcasters use is: 'We need to take the jargon out.' Scientists and other specialists who come jargon-free are celebrated.

But sometimes science needs jargon, because it is complex. Becoming a famous expert requires simplification, often grotesque simplification, of your area of expertise. In medicine, this can be dangerous.

Sir Roy Meadow published a book whose title, *ABC of Child Abuse*, suggests he wanted to do the risky thing – make his theories accessible. I have never met him and I cannot blame him for that. It is quite possible he wanted to be famous, because he confused fame with greatness. As I say, I simply do not know.

But part of the dangerous simplification of Sir Roy's ideas came in a maxim known as Meadow's Law, a sentence stated with such bald certainty in his book that it takes your breath away: 'One sudden infant death is a tragedy, two is suspicious and three is murder, until proved otherwise.'

Professor Sir Roy Meadow may have been a well-meaning person who got carried away. Or perhaps he was a rather stupid man, whom people trusted because of his medical title and a tendency to bluster. There are suggestions that he was a little narcissistic – for example, he claimed to have been 'as a junior, brought up by Anna Freud, who was a great figure in child psychology, and I used to sit at her feet at Maresfield Gardens in Hampstead. She used to teach us that a child needs mothering and not a mother.' The Anna Freud Centre subsequently denied any record of him attending these classes and says his comments totally misrepresent Ms Freud's philosophy.

These clues are important as we try to understand what followed. At this point no tragedy has happened. Sir Roy has done that thing clever people dream of – put his name to a new theory. Not just a theory, but a *law*! He is appointed Chair in Paediatrics and Child Health at St James's University Hospital, Leeds. He will soon be president of the British Paediatric Association. His career is the definition of illustrious. As part of his professional duties Sir Roy will lecture judges on how to handle evidence from expert witnesses, almost as if he is the only one in the land whose word is beyond doubt.

Meadow's Law would turn out to be utterly wrong, but we would not know that for several years.

*   *   *

Sally and Steve Clark suffered a tragedy. Aged only eleven weeks, Christopher Clark was found dead in his Moses basket in December 1996. Death was certified as being from 'natural causes'.

147

Doctors believed respiratory problems were to blame. Sally struggled with depression for a time. She also, by her own admission, drank more than was healthy. The two lawyers decided the best therapy after their bereavement was to have another baby.

Their second, Harry Clark, was born on 29 November 1997. But lightning struck twice. He collapsed without warning in his bouncy chair at eight weeks. Steve was in the kitchen, preparing a feed for the child. His wife screamed from the upstairs bedroom. Steve found Harry slumped forward and turning blue. An ambulance arrived nine minutes after their emergency call. Steve was desperately attempting resuscitation. Harry did not respond. He was taken to Macclesfield Hospital and pronounced dead at 10.41 p.m. The Clarks' first child had become unresponsive and died at the same time of day.

The chain of events that would bring Sally Clark and Sir Roy Meadow together was now in place.

The 'cause of death' in Christopher's case was revisited by suspicious pathologists and altered. Despite conflicting evidence from a number of medical specialists, Sally Clark was charged with murder. In 1998, she was committed for trial at Macclesfield Magistrates' Court.

There was a strange moment during a break in the committal proceedings. The man whose testimony would prove fatal to Sally Clark's defence approached her and her team where they sat. In a crass breach of protocol, Professor Sir Roy Meadow said: 'This is terrible for me – it must be awful for you.' He was instructed by the defence barrister, Michael Mackey, to 'go away'.

The trial of Sally Clark was held at Chester Crown Court in 1999. The most devastating testimony was from Professor Meadow. In court he not only stood by his famous law, 'Three cot deaths is murder', he actually told the court that the chance of the *two* Clark children having died from natural causes was one in 73,000,000.

This statistic is worth us examining.

The renowned expert had got to the 73 million figure simply by taking the chance of a single cot death in an affluent, non-smoking family – a little over 8,500 to one – and multiplying it by itself.

Here I confess a fascination, as I have a layperson's love of statistics and the way they work. This may well be because my dad, Dr Guy Vine, was a maths and civil engineering lecturer who still talks endlessly about the beauty of maths at the breakfast table and on holidays. It is also because good and bad statistics come up all the time in news, and journalists have to work out which are helpful and which are misleading.

Sir Roy's were in the second category.

Yes, it might be true that if the chance of one cot death is 8,500 to one, the chance of two becomes 73 million to one. But it only works in practice if you start like this:

Randomly select two healthy babies in different parts of the country, with no connection to each other. The chance of them both suffering cot death is $8,543^2$ to one, which is 73 million to one.

Sir Roy's faulty calculation went in reverse:

Exclude all healthy babies and find two cot deaths which have already happened. Now announce that because the chance of this occurring is 73 million to one, it looks like murder.

In statistics this is known as 'drawing the target after the arrows have been shot'. You can see how meaningless it is. Based on his maths, Sir Roy could have argued equally powerfully that two unrelated cot deaths in two different places were probably murder.

But there is a crucial rider which makes the statistic even more misleading. Families where one cot death has happened may actually be much more likely to suffer a second, not because the mother is a murderer, but because of an environmental or genetic factor. Some studies suggest *the chance of a second cot death in the same family may be as low as one in 100.* Anyway, even if the chance of two innocent cot deaths in an affluent home was millions to one, should we not weigh that against the chance of a middle-class mother murdering two or three of her own babies? How many times has that happened? Isn't the rarity of murder – especially double or triple murder – a statistic too?

Unfortunately Professor Meadow dramatised his 73 million further in court, telling the jury that two cot deaths in the same family where murder was not the explanation would happen 'once every hundred years in England, Wales and Scotland', and saying it was an event as likely as backing the eighty-to-one outsider in the Grand National four years running, and winning every time.

Steve Clark would later talk about the immense impact these statements had on the jury. But they carried great traction in newspapers too. They made headlines. Watching the case from a distance, I saw the way the numbers jumped out, and, without looking more closely, understood the clear implication. Christopher and Harry must have been murdered. The mother must have done it.

Tragically for Sally, for her family, for her campaigning father and husband and friends, and for her surviving son – the third child she had now given birth to – the jurors believed the expert view. Why would they not?

Sally Clark was duly convicted on a majority 10–2 verdict.

On her way to prison she heard someone shout: 'DIE WOMAN DIE.'

The innocent mother was given two life sentences. But now Sir Roy was in the spotlight, and as people started to look more closely at his claims and ideas they saw how sloppily built the edifice of his expertise actually was.

Dr James Le Fanu, writing in *The Lancet*, noted that Meadow had claimed that eighty-one infant deaths originally thought to be natural had turned out to be murder – a claim which could not be checked, because the professor said he had shredded the data – but Le Fanu pointed out that the parents Meadow referred to lost their court cases as a result of his own evidence, so how exactly did that prove his theories? Meadow's original paper, he added devastatingly, 'on careful scrutiny, exemplifies the sort of false logic and spurious argument that could only too readily have resulted in wrongful accusations against innocent parents'.

Professor Peter Green, of the Royal Statistical Society, wrote an indignant letter to the Lord Chancellor about Meadow's '73 million' figure – calling it an 'example of a medical expert witness making a serious statistical error' and suggesting the RSS should be called on to examine the credentials of so-called experts using statistics in future trials.

Stephen Watkins, vice president of the Medical Practitioners' Union, wrote in the *British Medical Journal* that the observation by Sir Roy that, murder aside, there would be a double-cot-death family once every hundred years in the whole country was completely wrong, since a study in Sheffield had found two innocent double-cot-death families in that one city in only twenty years. Sir Roy's evidence 'seriously misunderstands probability theory', he wrote.

So Meadow's Law was completely wrong. But by the time it had been debunked, Sally Clark had spent three years in prison. Her face had been glassed and she was a shadow of her former self. Gaunt, haunted, she was freed on appeal in 2003. The judge who quashed her conviction said the 73 million figure 'grossly overstates the chance of two sudden deaths within the same family from unexplained but natural causes'. Other experts in the original trial were also criticised by the judges. One had kept from the defence vital evidence which would have helped to clear Sally.

Very sadly, the trauma of losing two babies and then being blamed for killing them is not something a person easily recovers from. The website run by Sally Clark's supporters during her imprisonment now carries on its homepage a brief account of what led to her death in 2007.

Having suffered what was acknowledged by the Court of
Appeal to be one of the worst miscarriages of justice of recent

years, it is hardly surprising that her ordeal over ten years culminated in the diagnosis of 'Enduring Personality Change after Catastrophic Experience', 'Protracted Grief Reaction' and 'Alcohol Dependency Syndrome', and that she was never able to return to being the happy, kind and generous person we all knew and loved.

Sally Clark was forty-two when she died. Sir Roy Meadow has never properly apologised. He was never struck off, because he successfully appealed against a ruling by the General Medical Council that he was not fit to practise. After the first appeal by the Clark family failed in 2000, he wrote a crowing article in the *BMJ* suggesting he had been right all along and further time spent on the case would be 'wasted'.

In June 2003, Meadow was an expert witness in the case of Trupti Patel, a pharmacist from Berkshire. All three of her children had died. Again she was charged with murder. By this stage it seems juries were not inclined to believe Meadow, and Ms Patel was acquitted in less than ninety minutes.

In December of the same year, another mother wrongly jailed after Meadow gave evidence against her was freed on appeal. I have interviewed Angela Cannings, and remember feeling desperately sorry for her when she sat opposite me in the studio and told her story. She had lost two of her children and was wrongly convicted for murdering them. Jill Chambers, her friend and supporter, said: 'Not only has Meadow put Angela in prison, but he has put other ladies in prison and there are still ladies in prison. He has taken children away from families as well.'

Donna Anthony, whose infant daughter and son died suddenly, spent six years in jail before her conviction was also quashed because of the many questions about Sir Roy Meadow's expert testimony.

In the House of Commons a queue of MPs wanted answers. Anne Campbell asked ministers whether the case threw up 'disturbing indications that expert witnesses are not always as expert as they should be'. And Sally Clark's own MP – an upwardly mobile man called George Osborne, at the time on the opposition benches – stood up to put this point to the Solicitor-General Harriet Harman:

> Professor Meadow's flawed evidence was instrumental in two massive miscarriages of justice, in the case of my constituent, Sally Clark, and in the Angela Cannings case, and was also instrumental in the collapse of the conviction of Trupti Patel. All those cases aroused massive public interest. Will the Solicitor-General confirm that she has still not actually started to review criminal cases where Professor Meadow's evidence was instrumental, and will she also confirm, perhaps on behalf of the Minister for Children, that there has as yet been no attempt to review all the family court cases? In those cases, too, there may have been great miscarriages of justice — children may have been taken away from parents and families broken apart — because of the same kind of evidence from Professor Meadow.

The point was vital. There were more than two hundred family court cases in which Professor Meadow had played a part, sometimes a decisive one. All would have to be looked at again. In some of the cases, parents had already seen their children removed and adopted, which could not be reversed.

The chaos and ruin spread by a single inexpert expert was complete.

*　　*　　*

Something changed when the Roy Meadow story broke. I heard in listeners' voices . . . not just the outrage I expected, but another tone that surprised me. A kind of resignation. As if this sort of travesty was bound to happen because we had made experts the new gods. As if it was our fault to have listened to them.

The media trusted them too much. The courts called on them

too often. Society slavered over them. Why did we never consider they could be wrong?

There were other signs in the 2000s that we might have reached Peak Expert. John Ioannidis, professor of medicine at Stanford, published a paper in 2005 that opened with the knock-out line, 'There is increasing concern that most current published research findings are false', and went on to show how apparently rock-solid research is fatally undermined by bias and sampling errors. He was then the target of attacks by fellow scientists who said his own findings might be wrong for the very same reasons.

The Ioannidis paper was echoed ten years later by Dr Richard Horton, editor of *The Lancet*, who lunged out like this:

> The case against science is straightforward. Much of the scientific literature, perhaps half, *may simply be untrue.* Afflicted by studies with small sample sizes, tiny effects, invalid exploratory analyses, and flagrant conflicts of interest, together with an obsession for pursuing fashionable trends of dubious importance, science has taken a turn towards darkness.

Then came the financial crash, a power cut caused by electricians. It fell at the end of a decade the Governor of the Bank of England had idiotically complimented as 'NICE: no inflation, constant expansion'. At around the same time, growing numbers of medical people were speaking out against dietary advice we had been given for years – challenging the orthodoxy that 'fat makes you fat' and that eating cholesterol dangerously raises the level of cholesterol inside a person's body. For decades your GP would inform you that official medical advice in the UK was to eat a maximum of two eggs a week because they contained cholesterol. This has turned out to be completely wrong. The case against eggs was further undermined in April 2017, when obituaries of an Italian pensioner, Emma Moran, told how she had eaten three a day since the age of twenty: one cooked and two raw. She was thought to be the world's oldest woman when she died, living to 117 years and 137 days.

It turns out the enemy we missed was sugar, and the kind of processed carbs you find in pastries, bread and crisps. The 'low fat yoghurt' we bought to stay healthy was packed with an insidious kind of poison. In 2014 tests on popular fizzy drinks found that Old Jamaica ginger beer had the equivalent of thirteen teaspoons of sugar in one 330ml can. In comparison, single cans of Coca Cola and Pepsi had nine.

This mistake – still not fully unravelled – is probably the biggest failure by experts in human history. Dr Dwight Lundell, a heart surgeon in Arizona who has performed more than five thousand open heart operations, wrote in 2017: 'We physicians with all our training, knowledge and authority often acquire a rather large ego that tends to make it difficult to admit we are wrong. So, here it is. I freely admit to being wrong.'

He went on: 'The long-established dietary recommendations have created epidemics of obesity and diabetes, the consequence of which dwarf any historical plague in terms of mortality, human suffering and dire economic consequences.' He explained that the target should never have been naturally fatty foods like meat, but 'simple highly processed carbohydrates (sugar, flour and all the products made from them) and the excess consumption of omega-6 vegetable oils like soybean, corn and sunflower that are found in many processed foods.'

Next, Brexit – and the battle of astronomers and astronauts broke into the open. Suddenly we could see just how far experts had fallen. In a telling exchange on the BBC's *Question Time* during the EU Referendum campaign, David Cameron said: 'If we are about to get into a car and drive our children on a motorway, and a mechanic says, "The brakes don't work, the petrol gauge is faulty, the steering isn't working", we wouldn't get in the car.'

An audience member, Stephen Waller, 61, retorted: 'We'll be better off without the EU. There's no doubt about it. I'm not worried about nothing. Experts have their opinion. But I think we'll be better off.'

Waller won the argument without using a single fact. He basically got the Prime Minister sacked. I felt a bit sorry for Mr Cameron that night. No wonder the man from the *Telegraph* was left asking why experts were being ignored and claiming we were living under 'the tyranny of the anecdote'. Ordinary people, with life experience but no formal qualifications, were having the final say on issues where, ideally, an expert could have given us the benefit of years of study. The astronauts were running riot.

People laugh when Phyllis Capstick rings me from Sheffield and says, 'Experts built the *Titanic*', but she would surely have been one of the heroic pair of jurors who held out in the 10–2 verdict that gave Sally Clark two life sentences. I would love to be able to say that I would have held out like one of those two: wouldn't we all? The Brexit result was caused by the entire country behaving like them.

I guess I should be pleased. Ordinary people outrank the titled and the entitled. My listeners not only outvote the astronomers, they outrank them as well. The terms 'research', 'study' and 'survey' are used as much by PR firms as scientists. Debased, they all fall together.

But this is a mess, and somewhere in the middle of the discussion we need to agree that there is such a thing as a fact. A fact is not just half an argument. Data is not the plural of anecdote. I don't want a bus driver to give me a vaccination, nor will I board a double-decker with an immunologist at the wheel. For that matter, I probably shouldn't be the one to commission surgery for the pain in my underpants (see Chapter 7 if you are baffled by this reference).

One of the wildest calls we ever had on Radio 2 was from a supremely well intentioned mum. She told me we needed to 'stop paedophiles abducting and killing so many children in this country. It is a scar on our national life.' It certainly is, but as horrendous as that crime is, it remains very rare – there may be no more than four or five cases annually. Yet when I asked the listener how many children she thought were snatched and murdered by strangers in Britain every year, she replied: 'Sixty thousand?'

It may be the horror of a complete free-for-all in opinions – the tyranny of the anecdote – that led to the Royal College of Paediatrics and Child Health declaring that their large portrait of Sir Roy Meadow would remain on public display, even though Sally Clark's release from jail had brought the roof down on the entire profession.

Professor Meadow did indeed invent a new law – 'The more certain an expert sounds, the more likely they are to be wrong' – and probably contributed as much to this difficult situation as anyone. Perhaps it is right that his portrait continues to hang on a wall somewhere. He may have done more than any other single individual outside politics to take us out of the European Union.

But that's just my opinion. Not a fact.

Part Two

12. . . . about Being a Father

It's the maddening thing about life. You never learn the important stuff second-hand. You have to find it out for yourself. When I was a teenager I was inspired by a scene in James Bond to try lighting the jet from an aerosol to turn it into a flamethrower. Roger Moore did it to kill a dangerous spider. I struck a match and hissed deodorant at the flame. *Whooooooooosh* – the effect was every bit as lively as it was for Bond, flames licking yellow around the room. The canister became a portable Bunsen burner, and for a moment I was a secret agent on a mission. No one could have told me that a small amount of flame sucked back into the can would have blown off my hand.

In the mid-2000s I was about to become a dad. Everyone said: 'Jeremy, this will change your life.' I did not think it would, but of course it did. The aerosol would have taken my fingers off. The kids blew my whole life away. Imagine – 25,000 phone calls from adult listeners, yet the biggest life lesson came from two little girls.

Blokes often fail to grasp the simple stuff. One friend said to me: 'Having a baby was easy. The trouble came at six months, when it started moving about.' My brother has a mate who became a father after an exceptionally long labour in hospital. 'That must have been exhausting,' Tim said to him. 'Oh, horrendous,' replied the friend. 'I had one arm around my wife, and by the end it was really aching.'

Martha, the oldest, was born in 2004. Anna rolled up in 2006. I remember during an early run of new-dad sleepless nights being a little impatient with a studio guest. The guy was with us to talk about how to buy a second-hand car. At some point, early on in the interview, he had said: 'Jeremy, I think you and I will go on

161

later to talk about a different issue, which is when the milometer on cars gets tampered with.'

I didn't know my impatience had been noticed. But during a break he asked: 'Out of interest, why did you roll your eyes when I said that?'

Apologetically I replied: 'Sleepless nights caused by new daughter making me grumpy. I'm so sorry. But if you really want to know, it's because – in broadcasting – there is no "later". There is only now.'

'I'll remember that,' he laughed.

'When you come to be interviewed you need to take all your best things and say them first,' I added. 'If you think, "I'll say that later", and save it, I guarantee the presenter will thank you and wrap the whole thing up before you say your key thing and you'll be fed up you lost the chance. Store nothing up.'

'There is no later,' he repeated. 'Lesson learned.' I did worry slightly I had caused offence, and mentally pleaded in mitigation the broken sleep of the night before. We went back to the discussion after a moment, and yes, he had time to clock the milometer.

There is no later – there is only now.

I was thinking about that on a visit to my parents at the start of the whole fatherhood adventure. At their home in Cheam they keep dozens of family photo albums. At some point the albums stood in bulging columns reaching from floor to light-switch height. But in slow motion the piles slumped sideways and stayed like that, so they now look like a modern art installation. Feeling a little like the naughty boy I used to be, I fished in one of the half-collapsed piles for my childhood.

From a seventies album, I found the photo on the next page.

I knew every detail of the image before I saw it. For decades the snap was pressed down like a crushed flower beneath the weight of hundreds of other perfect squares of Kodak paper with faded processing codes on the back. My childhood years, painstakingly labelled, frame by frame.

I found this in the 1973 album – they have an album for every year.

So what can we tell from it? That the Vines, a family of five in Cheam, had a treehouse.

The picture says a little more. It tells you our garden in suburban south London was a modest one, which did not matter as it backed onto an underused playing field. That it snowed sometimes. That we had good neighbours; bad ones would not have tolerated the eyesore at the centre of this photo. And that my father loved me.

Look closely at the photo if you can. I just spent ten minutes looking, and forty years melted away. I was eight when it was taken. You see the distant rugby posts. Nearer, those solitary diagonal footprints – child-sized? Heading towards what? And the tree house, which looks for an instant like a living thing reaching out its arms and embracing the trees on the left, forcing them to join in the fun. The over-eager boss at the office party.

Had the lens been wider, my dad's garden shed would have shown up on the right. How ignored it must have felt. The treehouse is what he spent his time on.

It started as a couple of short planks fixed in the hollow of a modest birch. Somewhere for the young me, and my very young brother Tim, to have adventures. Our sister was not yet born.

But it is not easy for young brothers to have big adventures on small planks, so my father went to work.

He was thirty. Athletic. Slender build, thick brown hair. A Cambridge blue at fives – I should know what that is, but I still don't. Not the blue or the fives. Or Cambridge, come to think of it. At this point in his life, Dad was a civil-engineering lecturer at the local college, Ewell Tech. But mostly he just civilly engineered the treehouse, because that was the most important thing in the world.

After the two-plank platform came a ladder, a smaller trunk with battens screwed into it. Then a narrow passage made from six-inch timber and hardboard. A cabin floated above the tree on stilts. It even had a sliding window. First floor, second level, roof tilted just enough to let the rain run off. The slide you can see. Chipboard, paint and nails all converged to build a childhood home that was more home to us than the real one at the other end of the garden.

By now I was nine. Tim was seven. Sonya four. We had spent our summers hammering and lifting, painting and sweeping, gluing and sanding. My dad gave me work to do. One day we had the neighbours' children round to pull a big hunk of tree-trunk vertical using a ramshackle rope-and-ratchet system. Of course I realise now that dad could have done the job in a minute, but the complicated operation was his way of ensuring that us boys could battle to elevate the trunk for a whole week. That way we owned the final result.

We have photos of the trunk at every angle as it approached the vertical. You see it there at the back of the photo, visible above the treehouse roof.

I learnt some of the big lessons of life in that treehouse, which by now was so elaborate it could have been called a tree-complex or even a modern living system. For example, I discovered gravity. Newton thought he did that with the apple, but actually it was me and a hammer. I dropped it from the top roof on a sunny afternoon, just to see how the earth's pull would snatch at it. A high-pitched cry from below informed me that the hammer had narrowly missed my brother's head. A polite lecture from my father informed me that:

- A hammer is a heavy object

- A heavy object dropped from a height will damage what it hits
- Your brother's head would have been damaged if the hammer had hit it, and
- If your brother's head is damaged he may not go on to be a famous comedian and publish a book containing his one thousand funniest jokes

I am looking at the photo again. Oh, it reminds me: I had a childhood in black-and-white. This is the key dividing line in the modern era. What colour was your childhood?

Those born after 1975 never had the pre-colour phase. The world, we are told, now divides into digital natives and digital immigrants. The second group are the older generations who learnt how computers worked by ringing helplines and getting angry. We had instruction manuals and we read them before plugging anything in. The natives, by contrast, are simply born into it. I remember watching the five-year-old friend of my daughter try to change our TV channel by swishing her finger across the screen. A professor I know said students now ring his doorbell with their thumbs, not with their forefingers as they used to. When an undergraduate protested that he should be allowed to use a laptop in an exam because 'the desks are designed with a hole in them to feed cables through', my professor friend patiently explained the desks were older than him and the hole was actually for an inkwell.

A female comic joked on TV that the best way to hide an affair from her husband was to save all the incriminating messages from her lover in a folder with the title INSTRUCTION MANUALS, because no man would ever dream of clicking on it.

A black-and-white childhood dates you. In the early days my parents took photographs sparingly, because each time the shutter moved they were fined 18p by Boots. In the first picture of me I am fully nineteen days old. My dad says he turned to my mum and said: 'Hey, what about getting a photo of him?'

By contrast I had taken twenty snaps of my first child before she had been on this earth a minute. Being able to take unlimited numbers of photos free of charge turns out to have an unforeseen downside – the world is filling up with bad pictures of other people's holidays.

In 1974 the television in Cheam was monochrome too. I actually watched the famous snooker moment when the commentator, 'Whispering' Ted Lowe, said: 'Steve is going for the pink ball. For those of you watching in black-and-white, the pink is next to the green.'

An analogue upbringing has certain advantages. There were only four dimensions, as there had been since dinosaurs roamed the high streets – width, depth, height and time – but those four were enough. The fifth dimension, the online world, was not a place anyone had the option of disappearing to. So we had to spend a lot of time drawing things and colouring them in. Our games made clanking and scraping sounds and there was glue on our fingers.

One day I dug a hole in the garden. The next day I climbed into it, and on the third day, after a rather officious friend of my father told him the hole posed a safety hazard to burglars, I filled it in. Then there was the aeroplane I tried to build to escape Cheam using paper and masking tape. My parents encouraged me even as the fuselage came together with foolscap. Next, building a maze in the garden, I cut my hand on discarded timber.

Things had texture. I stroked the neighbours' cat in a cardigan knitted by my mum.

Because we were analogue, there was less choice. Three TV channels and four types of biscuit. Boredom was not an option; it was compulsory. Our lives were spent resisting boredom, and great things resulted. The treehouse was one of them.

So this photo speaks powerfully of the physical world that held sway until the computer screen took us away. When we covered a story on Radio 2 about an online game called *Second Life*, I was fascinated. It is not even a game; it is more serious than that. Second Life offers space on the web where listeners live out alternative existences as film stars or beach beauties or even armed robbers. You simply design your own avatar and join in.

Are the relationships formed on Second Life real? If a balding fifty-year-old man becomes a young dude with Harry Styles hair and hooks up with a teenage cheerleader without realising that she, too, is a balding fifty-year-old man, is that real?

We want to say no. Yet by the time we did the item on Radio 2, there had been a property boom on Second Life where people made and lost real money, and relationships between avatars were being cited in true-life divorce cases ('He fell in love with Cindy Kruger, a slut he met in a pool hall, and I caught them having sex in the desert when I walked into the study').

The reason Second Life appeared on my radio show was that now, incredibly, there was concern that a group of paedophiles had found a private spot behind some apartments – all online, remember – where they were abusing children. The problem for those who wanted the participants prosecuted was that the 'children' were actually avatars controlled by other paedophiles. Does the law stop paedophiles abusing each other in cartoon form? What was to be done?

Linda, one of our 25,000 callers, rang me with the answer.

'I am a policewoman on Second Life. We are racing round there now to see if we can break this up. I will shoot on sight.' Her real job was running a nail salon in Hull.

Afterwards we all shook our heads in the studio, then shook with laughter. And I recalled the line from the brilliant sixties movie *In the Heat of the Night*, where a dumbfounded Mrs Colbert asks the police chief: 'What kind of place *is* this?'

A different place, for sure. Different to the one in the photo. Never mind Second Life. The treehouse was my first. Because I now possess every piece of new-fangled digital kit available, iPhones and mp3 players and e-readers and set-top boxes and yes, even a digital watch . . . (I am reminded of the Arthur Smith joke: 'I'm so old I remember when they brought in cordless pyjamas'), I can hardly complain about the passing of the old order. I am not a Luddite, I am not anti-technology, I am not one of the

Humphrys who protest 'I've never had a mobile phone, never needed one' before boring the pants off you about missing apostrophes in road signs. I like having six thousand songs in my breast pocket, many of them sung by Elvis Costello. But quite by chance, one of the Elvis tracks I was listening to yesterday nailed the issue. The song 'Black and White World' contains a line that hints at the indefinable sadness we feel about the way our world has altered: 'There'll never be days like that again.'

Before we leave the treehouse, I should explain why it changed my life. It is not because you could get a splinter from swishing your finger across it. Nor even because of the hours of analogue joy spent clambering around it and even spending nights in that floating cabin. It is simply because it tells me an unquestionable truth of my life. My father loved me.

This photo shows me that my father gave time. Later, when I attended a school where a lot of my fellow pupils were boarders who only saw their parents once or twice a term – while I used to go home each night – I noticed an interesting thing. The boarders all had better stereos than those of us who came and left each day. We piled into their bedrooms to listen to what would now be called sick gear. These people also had suspiciously large cassette collections. Their parents could not be physically present, so they gave them surround sound instead. There seemed to be a simple back-of-an-envelope formula:

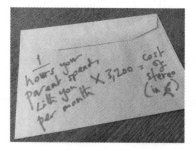

Thus, a pupil whose parents only spared them four hours per month would have a huge sound system worth eight hundred pounds.

By contrast, the Cheam treehouse was not purchased and dropped off in a box. It had to be built. The building took time. The time was my father's. He spent it with me because he loved me.

Not long ago we did an item on treehouses on the radio. The starting point was an item in the *Telegraph* about the world's most successful writer:

The Harry Potter author J. K. Rowling has won permission to build two luxurious Hogwarts-style treehouses in her garden, despite protests from local residents.

The writer applied to have the 40ft high structures erected, at an estimated cost of £250,000, as part of a programme of major renovations at her home in Edinburgh.

The two-storey structures on stilts are for her nine-year-old son and seven-year-old daughter and feature secret tunnels, a rope bridge and turreted roofs.

Residents living nearby lodged objections with Edinburgh City Council, claiming the size of the treehouses meant they would be seen from the road and would blight the conservation area.

For our studio discussion we booked the founder of a luxury treehouse company. Yep, they exist. His glossy brochure offered treehouses in all shapes and sizes, priced anywhere between £2,000 and £100,000. You order, they build. The man bowled in. Full of infectious enthusiasm. I could not fault him for that.

The curse of journalism is that we never do happy-clappy. No one is allowed just to roll up in the studio, promote their product and take the applause. An objection must be sought. We thought about it. Tricky . . . how do you start an argument with someone else's garden furniture? The producers drew a blank. If a parent wants to shell out for a set of turrets, who could mind? Leaving aside JK Rowling's neighbours?

I reflected on everything I have written in this chapter, and decided that I definitely objected.

My question, 'Isn't your brochure just a way of allowing absent fathers to spend even less time with their children?', triggered the faintest flash of panic in the interviewee's eyes.

Rather thoughtlessly, I pressed on.

'I mean, if you love your kid, you build the treehouse yourself, don't you?'

'Well —' he began.

'How can it be right for a dad to pay you to be the father they're not?'

'Um —'

I had gone too far. You can't have a man in to talk about treehouses and give him the full Robin Day.

Afterwards, the editor laughed.

'Blimey, Jeremy, you really can start an argument with anyone.'

'I'm sorry,' I grimaced.

'Don't be! It was great.'

Even so, I now offer long-distance apologies to the treehouse entrepreneur. Sometimes a presenter gets it wrong, lays a bit too much of their own *Weltanschauung* on the table, and I certainly don't want to put any other guests off arriving in my studio wearing khaki shorts.

In a strange, maybe even a wonderful way, Treehouse Man really was acting as the dad to children whose own fathers couldn't spare the time. He launched a business doing something fun and succeeded beyond his wildest dreams because it turns out every parent wants their child to have a photo in their pocket just like mine.

So when I look at this wintry scene from 1973, it is not the treehouse I see at all. I see my father's time.

Time is a measure of love. The photo tells me that my father loved me.

* * *

When I rolled my eyes at the studio guest who told me we would talk about mileage-tampering 'later', and then politely informed him there was no such thing as later on the radio, I was touching a great truth about fatherhood without even realising.

When you're a father, *there is only now*.

Typing this chapter, face glued to the laptop screen, I heard two cries of 'Come out here, dad, we're swimming!'

We are on holiday in France and our rented home has a pool at the back. The temperature is 34°C and the sun is blinding-bright outside so I have angled the shutters against the glare and as a result am in darkness so complete I can barely see my keyboard. Because adult minds work differently, I mistakenly thought there was a spare hour after lunch to type. I dived into my paragraphs while Martha and Anna jumped into the pool. The next thing – of course – is that they decided I should join them.

The gigantic fib we were told in our childhoods that 'you can't swim for twenty minutes after lunch, you might drown' is up there with the famous announcement on planes that passengers must 'stop using all electronic equipment because it can interfere with the navigation systems'. The first instruction seems to have been based, not on any kind of science, but on mums and dads in the seventies understandably wanting half an hour to themselves after eating.

So I shouted from behind the shutters: 'Later, girls! Let your food settle!'

'Come on, dad! We're out here now!' they replied.

'Girls, I will come to the pool and swim with you *later*.'

But there is no later on the radio, and there is no later for a child; there is only now. More fool me – I never listened to the advice I gave my second-hand car guest when my girls were tiny.

Somewhere on my shelves is a book about being a dad. It is very thin, but I have never read it. A well-intentioned person gave it to me. I skimmed the first page, and it said something like: 'You're a busy guy. That's why you've got this book. But you've also got kids. So the chances are, you're not going to read the book. If you *are* too busy to read it, just turn to page 68 and read the single line there. That's all you need to remember.'

I turned to page 68 and there was one sentence on the page:

The slower day will never arrive.

That single line! KAPOW! So insightful. And it reminds me of the unusual song released in 1974 by Harry Chapin, which we play on Radio 2, perhaps not fully understanding the tragedy it disguises as pop:

> My son turned ten just the other day
> He said 'Thanks for the ball, Dad, come on let's play
> Can you teach me to throw?' I said 'Not today
> I got a lot to do.' He said, 'That's ok'
> And he walked away but his smile never dimmed
> And said 'I'm gonna be like him, yeah
> You know I'm gonna be like him' . . .
> . . . I've long since retired, my son's moved away
> I called him up just the other day
> I said 'I'd like to see you if you don't mind'
> He said 'I'd love to Dad, if I can find the time
> You see my new job's a hassle and the kids have the flu
> But it's sure nice talking to you Dad
> It's been sure nice talking to you'
> And as I hung up the phone it occurred to me
> He'd grown up just like me, my boy was just like me
> And the cat's in the cradle and the silver spoon
> Little boy blue and the man in the moon
> 'When you comin' home son?'
> 'I don't know when, but we'll get together then, Dad
> We're gonna have a good time then.'

Sandra Gaston, who married Chapin, first wrote the lyric as a poem. It was inspired by the troubled relationship between her first husband James Cashmore and his father John, who had been a super-energetic New York politician and businessman. Harry Chapin called the song 'Cat's in the Cradle' and said the words offered insights into his own relationship with his son Josh: 'Frankly, this song scares me to death.'

It scares every dad to death. I didn't always tell my girls 'later' — my routine at Radio 2 has given me many lucky afternoons where I am back home by the time their school is out. And, by the way, their stereos are quite small. But how strange it is that I could lecture the milometer man without realising the same lesson applied to me.

We do indeed have to discover stuff for ourselves. Through the faces of our children we understand that *later* sounds too much like *never*. If the treehouse showed us that time is a unit of love, then the opposite of love is 'not now'.

So I am off to the pool. I will unplug this laptop and run for my trunks. I am going now. There is no later.

13. Uncontrollable Music

In the nineties, when I started on *Newsnight*, there was a gentle-man in the technical team called Loz. I think 'Loz' might have been short for Lawrence or possibly . . . no, Lawrence. He was a handsome guy in his late twenties, stubbled, usually dressed in saggy black T-shirts and bottoms. Loz was – I mean no disrespect when I say this – extremely large. I would guess he weighed thirty stone. Nevertheless, he did his job efficiently and was always courteous.

One day a courier arrived to hand-deliver a parcel with the name 'loz' scrawled in black marker on the padded envelope.

'Excuse me everyone!' he called. The *Newsnight* office fell silent. Kirsty Wark, Mark Urban and all the producers turned to listen. The courier peered at the envelope.

'Is there someone called "ONE OUNCE" in this office?'

I often think of that incident when the music computer at Radio 2 throws up the one record that should not be played after the one story we should not play it after. The music computer is preloaded by a responsible and knowledgeable human being before each programme, but the machine then sequences the discs in a way that suggests it has been hacked by pro-Putin Russian agents who believe they can launch the destruction of western Europe starting with the lunchtime show on Radio 2. We want Loz, and we get One Ounce. We get *the opposite* of what we asked for, without even trying.

Just yesterday – the day before I started this chapter – we covered the awful story of a serial killer who targeted victims through his work as a taxi driver in Bristol. The song scheduled to start the programme was 'Love Is a Stranger' by the Euryth-mics. Researcher Mark Payne thought he should check the lyrics and immediately realised it would be a disastrous choice: 'Love is a stranger /In an open car /To tempt you in /And drive you far away'.

The record was pulled. The number of near-misses – songs that almost get played, but one of us sees the danger and changes them – makes me think the computer actually has a malign personality. When we did an item on the soaring cost of funerals, it lined up a song called 'Work This Body'. I was not sure who the band were or how the song went. But after calls from listeners who had struggled to pay for the burial of loved ones it would be outrageous to put on a disco song with that title. After an item on Vladimir Putin's bombardment of Syrian cities, the computer lined up 'Party Like a Russian' by Robbie Williams. That one was easy to spot and save. But an item about a cure for paralysis which had been trialled on paraplegic monkeys was followed – really – by the ZZ Top song 'Legs'.

It happens constantly, and we need to be on our guard.

A year ago I handed to the newsreader for the 1 p.m. bulletin and he began to read a story about how hospitals had recorded increased death rates the previous winter. Health reporter Adam Brimelow started giving details of this serious story. 'Experts say flu played a major part. Older people were particularly susceptible to last year's strain – '

At this point I made a mistake with the mixing desk. Trying to choose the song to play directly after the bulletin, and needing to preview 'Straight Ahead' by Kool & The Gang, I pressed the start button while the fader was up – a schoolboy error in a radio studio. The song launched at full volume during the flu deaths story.

'Straight Ahead' is not any old song. It heaves like a farewell do in a flared jeans factory. So just as Brimelow finished reading the sentence, 'Older people were particularly susceptible to last year's strain', there was a sudden cascade of drums. *Boof-Boooooof-Bam*. A guitar came in with a funky disco rhythm and the Kool singer JT Taylor shouted 'WOOOOOOOOOOOOO!' over news that 'the vaccine was less effective than usual'. When the

175

reporter added the important line, 'Winter deaths also increased in Scotland last year', JT Taylor screeched 'LET'S GO!'

At this point I realised my error, swore, grabbed at the fader and closed it.

When the newsreader came back after the report had finished, he did that little sigh newsreaders do, which means: *My bulletin was just blown away by the musical equivalent of a drone strike.*

After every musical balls-up, we have an inquiry. Procedures are tightened so it can never happen again, and then it does. An item about a Leicester doctor accused of perversion after he asked a female patient seeing him for a heart examination to do squat thrusts while topless was followed by Tiffany singing 'I Think We're Alone Now'. A serious medical feature about recognising the first symptoms of a stroke, which can include one-sided facial paralysis, was followed by Sia singing 'You're Never Fully Dressed Without a Smile'. An intriguing story about the medicinal benefits of drinking your own urine was derailed when the computer – how does it do this? – selected a song by Christie called 'Yellow River' to follow the item. When we discussed a man who was working on his camper van and rubbed the fuel on his hands onto his fleece, causing a flash of static which turned him into a fireball, the computer gave me a record by Sparks. We spent so much time checking the lyrics that we played it, not realising the name of the band was the problem.

Among the worst was the record which came on after a dreadful story about the zoo in South Africa which tried to transport two giraffes on the motorway out of Pretoria, forgetting that there were a series of low bridges on the route.

An engineer using the same highway snapped this picture seconds before the disaster. Incredibly, while the foolish driver ploughed down the road blissfully unaware, the giraffes successfully ducked and weaved to avoid several bridges. But then one of the animals was caught unawares by the oncoming concrete span and killed by the impact.

The computer chose 'Bits and Pieces' by the Dave Clark Five.

It really does take a twisted kind of genius to do that.

So I keep looking at the playout device and wondering. On the face of it, our music machine is nothing special. It is basically a hard drive with a touchscreen. The gismo is so easy to operate that even the techno-sceptic Terry Wogan, God rest his beautiful soul, learnt to use it in a day and never uttered one word of complaint when it took the place of the clunky CD player we shared and loved. But could there be a malicious Russian midget hidden inside it? Before we decide that is impossible, consider the subtlety of some of the choices.

Jennie Hurst from Southampton was a charming guest with a terrible story. No one had told her, or me for that matter, that you should never swim with contact lenses in. Apparently a microscopic bug can slip between the lens and your eyeball. The same for running your lens under tap water – never do that. Not knowing the danger of mixing lenses and swimming, Jennie, twenty-eight, climbed into a hotel pool in the West Country to do a few laps while wearing her monthly contacts.

A parasite, *Acanthamoeba*, which is usually found in fresh water and sea water, somehow crept behind the lens in her left eye. Three days later the eye was so sensitive to light she could not even look at her smartphone or observe the moon at night. The surface of the eyeball was red and Jennie suffered a continuous burning sensation. She had to retreat to a dark room, she told me. Doctors tried to purge the parasite by scraping the eyeball and administering eye drops, but as the poor lady explained: 'I have now lost nearly all the sight in my left eye. I don't even like swimming.' Uneven pavements and crowds were now especially difficult.

Before the item, aware of the dangers, I asked the producer: 'Can we please check the next record is okay?' He came back and said he couldn't see a problem. So I played 'Disconnected' by Keane, with the lines:

> Something's crept in under our door
> Silence soaking through the floor
> Pinching like a stone in my shoe
> Some chemical is breaking down the glue
> That's been binding me to you
> Oooh ooh ooh.

I relaxed at this point. 'Chemical breaking down the glue' was not ideal, but no damage had been done. Then –

> I feel like I just don't know you anymore
> But I've been burned and I've been wrong so many times
> We walk in circles
> The blind leading the b-lind.

'HOW THE F*****G HELL DOES THAT HAPPEN?!' I shouted at the studio wall.

* * *

I adore music. My job is describing things, but I am not sure I can even begin to describe how much I love listening to a good song. If we leave aside those abject moments when a news story clashes with the music on my show – which we should probably blame on the news story anyway – I can't think of any time in my life when music hasn't been there for me.

When the BBC unearthed Lou Reed's 'Perfect Day', wheeled on an orchestra and transformed the song from an obscure 1972 album track and B-side into a corporate anthem delivered by thirty megastars that spent weeks at number one, I was appalled. Foolishly, I had thought the song was there purely for my own private joy – for me it was torn jeans, not dripping jewellery. But then music fans are like that. Possessive and a bit opinionated. When I see those qualities in myself I know they are not attractive, but I'm really not a rock-snob . . . honestly. I am open to everything, so long as it's not a cover version. The other day, listening at home, I put on 'I Can't Feel My Face When I'm With You', appalling my children who said I had 'stolen' their music. Then it was 'Living Next Door To Alice' and I decided it was the best pop song in history. I quietly told my wife that those famous Smokie lines, 'Just for a moment I caught her eye /As the big limousine pulled slowly /Out of Alice's drive', were probably the most filthy in pop history.

Three years ago I was on a train heading north and saw one of my heroes.

'Glenn,' I said. 'Really sorry to bother you – I'm Jeremy Vine.'

'I know who you are,' the man kindly smiled, probably thinking: *There goes my peaceful rail journey.*

Suddenly it was 1978 and I was thirteen. A show called *Hullabaloo*, hosted by Maggie Norden on London's Capital Radio, introduced a new band called Squeeze as I listened in my teenage bedroom in Cheam. The band members, including a keyboardist named Jools Holland, laughed and joked with Norden. Then they played a song called 'Take Me I'm Yours' and I was instantly struck by the peculiar opening lines – 'I've come across the desert /To greet you with a smile /My camel looks so tired /It's hardly worth my while' – and the very peculiar, escalating series of notes in the guitar riff, which had the exotic minor-chord feel of a James Bond theme. Plus, although the vocalists sang the same tune, they were pitched differently. Chris Difford's voice was low. Matching him syllable-for-syllable, but one octave higher, was Glenn Tilbrook.

There and then the 12-year-old Jeremy decided there was no better band in the world than Squeeze. They were pure pop but also part of the post-punk, anti-corporate 'new wave' that had caused creaky stadium rockers like Genesis and Rush to have an identity crisis of life-threatening proportions. Squeeze had coolness, cutting edge and ties as narrow as watch-straps. They sounded like great-grandsons of the Kinks and first cousins of The Jam.

Actually seeing them play live on stage would have been too much of an adventure for this prepubescent square whose mum still dressed him in corduroy shirts, but after listening to their first album a hundred times I joined the Squeeze fan club. The membership card came back, confirming I had got in early:

Mr Jeremy Vine
OFFICIAL SQUEEZE FAN CLUB MEMBER No. 25

Sara Cox still makes jokes about this now. 'And tomorrow, at noon, Squeeze Fan Club Member 25 presents the lunchtime show!'

Anyway, I loved the band as they grew. From 'Take Me I'm Yours' through 'Cool for Cats' to the moving 'Up the Junction', which is somewhere between a cartoon and a novel and simply one of the greatest British pop songs ever written. I guess you never forget the first band you fall in love with.

Now, as the train rumbled around us, I asked Glenn Tilbrook: 'Where are you coming back from?'

'Scarborough,' he said, hanging on to a seat corner. 'A fiftieth. A guy wanted me to play there. Good fun.'

'Gosh,' I said, 'I'm forty-seven. That gives me an idea.'

He laughed. I could see he thought it was a 'Let's have lunch sometime' kind of line.

For my fiftieth I had a family meal – the one where my mum made a speech and burst into tears – and then a slightly bigger moment with friends and relatives in a London hotel skybar that somehow managed to overlook St Paul's Cathedral. Eventually my wife hushed everyone and said some generous, funny words about what a passionate person I was but how I didn't really like long walks or looking at ancient buildings, probably because I was one. Then I had to speak.

'Friends and family,' I started nervously, as they all stared, 'one of my favourite bands in the world is Squeeze, who as you know are led by the great Chris Difford and Glenn Tilbrook. If you had told me, aged twelve, that one day I'd turn fifty – well, I wouldn't have believed that for a start.'

I looked into the faces of my friends, most born in the sixties like me, all equally appalled about how old we have become.

'And if you'd told me that when I turned fifty, the man who brought us all those Squeeze songs, Glenn Tilbrook, the man who co-wrote and sang them, would be in the same room, I wouldn't have believed that either.'

My friends now started darting glances around.

'And if you'd told me that Glenn would be in the room *with his guitar*, and would play some of the songs that are the soundtrack to our lives – '

Aaaaaaah! The penny dropped. A big cheer. Out comes Glenn Tilbrook with his guitar. He launches straight in – 'They do it down at Camber Sands /They do it at Waikiki' – which is the start to 'Pulling Mussels From the Shell'. Then comes 'Another Nail in My Heart' and the classic opening line of 'Up the Junction': 'I never thought it would happen /with me and a girl from Clapham'.

Standing to the side, resolutely not using my phone to take pictures but instead just trying to ensure I remembered this moment properly, I saw two of my friends wipe tears from their eyes. And it did feel very powerful, for sure. The intensity of music, I guess, stirring memories like perfume. Suddenly we were all back in our teenage bedrooms.

Talking to Glenn before the night started, I had said: 'Could you finish with "Cool for Cats?" Everyone loves that so much.'

'Ah, there's a little issue with that. It fits the lower voice, so Chris sings it. It's not my register.'

'Oh,' I said, hiding my disappointment.

'Unless you have someone at the party who wants to try to do the lead vocal for me?'

I spent a long time wondering who could do it, at least half a second. Now the moment arrived. Glenn had done 'Pulling Mussels', 'Another Nail', 'Take Me I'm Yours', 'Tempted', 'Up the Junction', 'Labelled with Love' and the peerless 'Goodbye Girl'. Then he announced: 'I've asked for a guest vocalist on this last one. It's "Cool for Cats" and it's Jeremy Vine himself singing!'

Which I really, really hadn't foreseen when I sat by my record player in 1980 and played the song over and over again. I remembered going up to London to get Squeeze's second album on the day of its release. So here we were in 2015 – thirty-five years on – and here was Glenn playing guitar right next to me, and I had the microphone. Oh, and my two gorgeous daughters, aged eight and eleven, stood beside me and supplied the female backing on the chorus: 'Coooooool . . . for cats . . . coooooool . . . for caaaaaats'.

A big roar and the night was over. I never took a single photo but the picture in my mind is as sharp and clear as any slip of paper in a frame. I am not sure there will ever be a birthday party moment as good for me, even if I live to be four hundred and twenty.

*　　*　　*

I started with Squeeze then discovered Elvis Costello. If someone says to me, 'Hey, I'm a Costello fan too, "Oliver's Army" is my favourite', I have to put at least two knuckles into my mouth and chew them. If you love Elvis Costello, your favourite record is not going to be his only big hit. Sorry. It's like saying, 'Van Morrison – Brown-Eyed Girl'. It can be anything, but not that.

Mind you, I always embarrass myself with Costello. I have now met him three times and always start by telling him how often I have seen him play live. It's a reflex, I guess. Probably triggered by the natural shock when an ordinary mortal meets the divine. The first time Elvis and I were in the same room – okay, the lobby of a concert venue – was 1985.

'I have seen you live four times.'

The second time was 2006.

'Seventeen times. That's how many of your gigs I've been to.'
The last time was 2016.

'I have seen you in concert twenty-three times.'

Each time he looks politely surprised. When I was on *Strictly Come Dancing*, knowing my adoration of this truly exceptional songwriter, the production team got Elvis to record me a personal good luck message. 'Jeremy,' he told the camera through those heavy spectacles, 'take no unnecessary risks.' This was truly bizarre advice from a man whose first album combined country music with punk. Still, believing that Elvis was watching, I trembled all the way through my waltz.

Why do I love Elvis Costello, real name Declan MacManus? Because he took pop music and filled it with personal quirks. He writes hooks and riffs that take you where you are not expecting – the chorus of his first and finest love song, 'Alison', uses a strange chord sequence which grows and grows with every fresh listen. Yet he also gives his music extraordinary emotional precision. 'Alison,' he sings of the lover who rejected him, 'I know this world is killing you /Oh, Alison, my aim is true.'

Or from 'Hand in Hand': 'I don't like you walking round with physical jerks.'

Costello's announcement that he would never play a guitar solo only added to the adoration I felt in my mid-teens, bored to death by long-haired prog-rockers who didn't realise a double-necked guitar was a comedy prop. Elvis drew on feelings which I had never heard anyone express in a song – a burning desire for revenge, acute self-loathing, sexual inferiority – but included humour and wordplay too. And he ranged far beyond boy/girl relationships for his material. 'There's a smart young woman on a light blue screen /Who comes into my house every night', he sang bitterly, 'She takes all the red, yellow, orange and green / And she turns them into black and white.'

Isn't this a TV newsreader Elvis is singing about? Isn't he condemning the way we journalists take the four dimensions of every story and crush them down to one? Isn't that the most efficient takedown of a profession you have ever heard?

Isn't it – here comes the most important thing – *true*?

During the very first edition of my show on Radio 2, on 6 January 2003, I announced: 'Next – the King.' Then I deliberately played Costello instead of Presley. Childish, I guess, but I was a bumptious thirty-something. A listener called to complain. 'Vine made so many mistakes it was unbelievable. He even confused Elvis Presley with someone totally different.'

Yep, *someone totally different* is exactly right.

*　　*　　*

A stranger on Twitter has the same love of music as me. She summed up the joy of my show in 139 characters. Sam Fawcett tweeted: 'What I love about the Jeremy Vine Show is that he can have an in-depth discussion about select committees and then break for Destiny's Child.'

And it's true. I lope around Radio 2 (thank you Ken Bruce for that verb) knowing I'm the square guy who chats current affairs while all around me are these foxy, funked-up presenters whose lives are nothing but music. When our worlds intersect I feel a joy I can't describe, but I am not sure anyone can see how deep it is.

I passed my studio on the sixth floor one morning and saw the BBC 6 Music presenter Shaun Keaveny recording an interview. He waved me in. I had an American guest with me and we watched two members of a band called Temper Trap play an acoustic version of a beautiful song called 'Sweet Disposition'. I bought it, listened to it non-stop and then went to see them live. Three years later my friend Anita Rani and Gleb Savchenko pulled off the most incredible tango to the same song on *Strictly* and I found myself almost overcome, standing there on the balcony and joining the dots right back to that welcoming wave from Shaun. But I guess a journalist should never admit a song and dance made him cry.

Something similar happened with Ken Bruce. My team were prepping with me on the second floor when I happened to catch a stray phrase from a radio on the desk: ' . . . King, here, later . . . '

Eh? That guy with the big hair who sang 'Love and Pride'? No. It turned out that 'King' was Carole King herself. She would be sitting at the piano upstairs in less than half an hour. 'This,' I declared portentously to the team, 'is a major moment. It is bigger than the news. Forget our programme.'

Carole King wrote 'Will You Love Me Tomorrow?' and with her subsequent album *Tapestry* did that rare thing – wrote a one-off disc that turned out to be a greatest hits album. Who else has done that? Maybe Oasis with (*What's the Story*) *Morning Glory?* or Michael Jackson with *Off the Wall*?

I led as many of the team up to the sixth floor as I could without torpedoing my own show. We stood and watched Carole play 'It's Too Late', which she seemed to choose on the spot. Shivers down every spine. I want to shout out to Radio 2 – 'I know you think I eat, drink, sleep, breathe the stuff between the records! But it's music that I love!'

They would never believe me.

Still, the differences in the weave are what make a radio station. Just this morning I texted Sara Cox because I opened a newspaper and saw a story describing her as 'the Radio 2 DJ and former hellraiser' and thought, *That's what I want to be! I want to be a former hellraiser!* But no, I am a former political correspondent and *Today* programme reporter and former Africa correspondent and *Newsnight* and *Panorama* . . . oh, as Tim in *The Office* sighs: 'I'm even boring myself.'

But you see the point. I am not a muso. I have never hung out with Paloma Faith or smoked something unusual with Bob Marley. Come to think of it, I haven't even smoked anything usual. *I am not a former hellraiser.* We had a news item on my show announcing that a flypast celebrating the hundredth birthday of Vera Lynn had been cancelled by poor weather, and dozens of listeners misheard and asked why Paul Weller would want to do that; and I thought, in a rather pathetic way, that it was the closest I had come to getting Weller into the news, and how it should happen far more often.

Occasionally the radio station reminds me where I am in the musical pecking order. When Radio 2 produced its 'Festival in a Day – Live in Hyde Park' programme for 2016, a lot of people were impressed by the list of bands. Madness. Status Quo. Elton John. LeAnn Rimes. Jamie Lawson. The big names went on and on.

At that point presenters are contacted and asked if they will introduce the musicians. There is a very definite sense of seniority. Ideally you want to be introducing an act after the sun goes down. The process shows where your star is in the firmament. Bob Harris and Johnnie Walker, for example, would both get big bands. Jo Whiley was asked to go on stage to welcome Elton himself.

I met a producer three weeks before the event. 'We want you to introduce The Map, Jeremy.'

'Okay –' I immediately agreed. But this was tricky. I do know my music, but I wasn't sure I had heard anything by The Map. They had to be an indie band. Not well known, that much was obvious, but clearly cutting edge. I was going to embrace this experience. Meanwhile, I needed to bluff it.

'Great first album,' I said.

The producer looked puzzled.

'Sorry – to be clear – we want you to introduce *the map of Hyde Park*. This is right at the beginning before the concert starts. You go on stage, you say hello, and we put a big map on the screen behind you with arrows showing where the toilets are.'

I did it with as much positive energy as I could. If you were in Hyde Park on the day, you will have seen me bound on stage and point at the map of the toilets as if I was introducing Rod Stewart.

* * *

Towards the end of my birthday party, a friend said they had joined an amiable conversation between Glenn Tilbrook and my dad.

'I remember taking Jeremy up to London one day,' the friend

heard my dad telling the singer. 'He was fifteen, and he was most insistent that he needed to get to this particular record shop on this particular day because it would have your album the morning it came out. I never understood any of that, really. I couldn't see the point of it.'

Then my father added: 'Tonight, I understood.'

If you're reading this, dad – I love you. Always have. Just never said it enough, and had to write a book to make sure you knew.

14. Coatman

In the mid-nineties, on a warm summer evening in London, a man walked into a bar.

It sounds like the start of a joke. But it wasn't for the man. John wore an expensive leather jacket made by Belstaff, costing more than £500. The 25-year-old was overdressed for the warm evening, so he unzipped the jacket and threw it across a chair, asking his friends what he could get them to drink.

Five minutes later he came back to their table carrying a tray loaded with beer and wine.

'Hey – where's my jacket?' he said.

They all looked around. No one could remember John putting the Belstaff down, and no one could remember seeing it being taken. The valuable jacket had vanished. John spent the night drinking with his friends but his eyes kept darting around the pub. Had one of the drinkers, the people he could see, stolen and hidden his jacket? Would one of them go home with it tonight? Had someone taken it and left the pub immediately? Would he ever see it again?

Many people would grump for a day, curse humanity a little, then write off the lost jacket to experience. When John told me his story, I remembered my own. At the Edinburgh Fringe in 1984, drinking in a packed pub after putting on another edition of our slightly shaky Durham University Revue with fellow students – audience: twelve – I turned my back for an instant and my coat was gone. The innocence of a 20-year-old. The garment itself would not have mattered. It was a lightweight grey fabric, not a patch on the Belstaff, not even high enough quality to wipe a window. But unfortunately my car keys were in a side pocket. My memory of that festival is constantly trying to ring the factory where the 1979 Mini Clubman was made to see if they could print me a new ignition key.

(The manufacturers, British Leyland at Longbridge, needed the code from the car's log book to print the key. To get the log book I had to break into my own car. I took the book to a local dealership so they could make sure I was who I said I was, but then the staff challenged me to prove that the car's owner – my father – was actually my father. He had to fax them a photo of himself. The staff checked my face against the fax to see whether we looked like close relatives. When they were satisfied, a man at the dealership laboriously photocopied pages from the book. He sent them to Longbridge who made the new key and posted it back to Edinburgh. The entire process took three weeks. The other students used to demand daily updates. By the end I had made more than forty calls from the phone box outside our flat, at a total cost of more than two pounds. Incredibly, I never minded the inconvenience.)

John did mind. He was made of sterner stuff. For a person in their mid-twenties to lose a £500 jacket is life-changing – so he told me. He could not forgive the person who took it. Neither could he understand them. Rather than shaking it off, John set out on a course of action that would serve as revenge while also giving him an insight into the mind of the thief. He started stealing coats himself.

*　　*　　*

My first contact with 'John' – the name we gave him – was ten years later. He rang the show from Yorkshire during an item about people compelled to steal. When the conversation started, I knew nothing of the background.

'Hello,' I started.

'Hi, Jeremy, hi.'

'Are you stealing now?'

'I am, yeah, I've been stealing coats and jackets out of pubs for about ten years. I steal about two a week.'

'Coats and jackets from pubs?' I was incredulous, remembering my own.

'Yeah, it's really easy.'

'Er, right.' I sounded uncertain, to say the least. 'Why do you do that?'

'I lived in London years and years ago, and I bought an expensive jacket, and it got stolen, and I just started stealing back. As revenge, sort of. The problem is, I came from a very poor background and it took me a long time to save up the money for this jacket, and it really, really hit me hard. The problem is that it has really got out of control. I've rented two lock-up garages to store them in.'

The call was one of half a dozen in a busy hour. The expert guest was counselling each listener who rang, condemning some, and John did not get much of his time or energy. The item swished by and we moved on quickly. Only later, discussing John's comments with the team, did I find we were all desperate to know more. If he had been stealing coats for ten years, how many did he have in the lock-up garage? What did he feel about his victims, people who must be as devastated as he was when he lost his own jacket?

So we followed up. Two weeks later, on 10 March 2006, we announced we had recorded a longer interview with a man in the Yorkshire studio 'whom we will call John, and who has spent ten years stealing other people's coats'.

I was unsure. The guy was a criminal, and there are rules about any interview which makes it sound like crime pays. We called David Jordan, in charge of BBC editorial matters, who advised caution. But the producer who spoke to John said this was a genuine cry for help. The coat-stealer had hundreds in his rented garage and was now suffering a crisis of conscience over his terrible behaviour. The interview would be his way of making a clean breast of his crimes. Possibly a first step to getting the coats back to their owners.

Here is the conversation we had.

JV: 'How many coats do you think you've got?'

John: 'I think there's about one thousand. Rough estimate, there's about a thousand, yes.'

JV: 'ONE THOUSAND? And you have catalogued them meticulously?'

John: 'Yeah. Well, when I took the first one, I felt so bad I was physically sick. I went home and was sick – er – I couldn't eat, I couldn't sleep for a week, and I wrote a note and I stuck it on the jacket saying where I got it from and when – and I was going to take it back. But I didn't. The reason I didn't was because, as the week went by, I had a change of heart and I wanted to get into the mind of the person who had taken my coat.'

JV: 'Because that's how it started?'

John: 'Exactly. Yeah. it was a Belstaff jacket. It was an expensive jacket. The only expensive thing I ever bought. I wanted to get into the mind of this person and I wanted to feel like the person that took my coat . . . I guess it got out of hand and I just kept taking more and more . . . I guess I was playing the game of averages and thinking, if I took enough jackets, eventually I would take the person's that had taken mine.

'As well, the day after, I went in the pub, and there was a group of people laughing, and it seemed to go quiet as I went past, and I felt really paranoid, I felt they were laughing at me . . . I can't describe the feeling. Those were the events that set me on this path.'

In an interview which made us gag for air from start to finish, surely that was the line that fully took your breath away: *If I took enough jackets, eventually I would take the person's that had taken mine.* Assuming John is not stealing coats from children, and each of the fifty million British adults has three coats, there would be 150 million coats to target. If he and the man who stole his Belstaff were in the same town or village, you could change the parameters. But his original coat was stolen in London and John is launching his reprisal from a base in Yorkshire. So without meaning to sound like a stato-wonk – even stealing at his current rate of a hundred coats per year, to have a 50–50 chance of lifting a coat from the original thief he would have to keep stealing for 750,000 years.

I did mention this to him as he sat there in our Yorkshire studio.

'Yeah, it is just ridiculous to think like that,' he admitted, voice as clear as a bell down the high-quality line. 'But I guess it just became an obsession. I know inside that it's wrong. I know inside I am never going to get the person's coat.'

He then changed tack. His reason for breaking his silence on Radio 2 was because he was no longer able to afford the rent on his lock-ups – apparently he now had two of them – and needed a way out.

John: 'I visit the coats to see if everything's okay. These two lock-ups are big lock-ups, they are the sort you could pack a Jaguar in. They're high, they've got high roofs, and I've got all these racks I bought from Argos. I mean, the rent I've got on the lock-ups is £100 a month, and I've had them for over five years, so you can imagine it's a lot of money and it's just got out of hand.

'The only reason I have two is because the chap next door, he was giving his up, and I carried on renting it in his name. So I ended up with two and I shifted the coats I had from my house to his lock-up, and, er, I've got them on racks, they're all covered in plastic, they're all catalogued, they're all immaculate. I've not been through the pockets, I've not done anything with them, I've not tried to sell them.

'I tried to get help years ago, Jeremy. I went to a doctor because I was so freaked out by it all. I felt so badly . . . and the doctor told me just to stop stealing. And I said I've got this problem . . . it's ruining my life, I can't cope with it.

'He asked me how bad it had got. And I told him, "I have gone to buy a rope because I didn't want to live any more, it was horrible." And I didn't go through with it, obviously, but the tow rope wasn't a waste of money because my van broke down.

'Now I told this to the psychiatrist and – this is how funny the truth is – he told me not to joke about it. I said: "I am not joking, I am telling you the truth."'

Many of the calls to my show are tragedy disguised as comedy.

This one seemed to be comedy disguised as tragedy. A psychiatrist takes exception to John finding wry amusement in the fact that he found an alternative use for the rope he bought to hang himself with?

The interview went on for a full ten minutes. It is probably one of the most memorable I have ever done. John said he felt his first, fleeting, appearance on the theft phone-in had been 'an opportunity to confess . . . I saw this item you were doing as a confessional, and when I did, it was like the weight was lifted off my shoulders . . . I was buzzing, I was on a high, and I decided to start returning the coats.'

I wondered out loud how he could possibly do that. He explained that each of the thousand coats was tagged so carefully that he could take it back to the same pub. He had not looked for wallets in the garments when he stole them because at the time he had felt that it would not be right.

'I have taken five back since I confessed to you on your show, Jeremy . . . I took them to the pub, two pubs actually, I had an overcoat on, I took them in the pub, and I deposited them on seats in the pubs.'

'How did you do that without being seen?'

'I took my coat off,' he explained, 'rested that on a coat, went to the toilet, came back, took another coat off, put my coat back on, walked out. The second pub that I went in to leave a jacket, the doorman came after me and he grabbed me by the shoulder. And he said to me, "Is this your coat? I think you've left your coat", and I said: "No I haven't, it was a coat that was on the chair next to me." I really thought that was it, I thought my number was up and it was all going to come crashing down but I got away with that . . . I want to return them. It will be difficult because I've taken them from the Isle of Skye, Glasgow, Cardiff, places I've worked, er, but I'm going to return them, that's what I'm going to do.'

The man we called John finished speaking. The producers had his real name and number, I was told. Might the police arrive at the studio in Yorkshire and arrest him on the way out? It seems they had not. Listeners were captivated. They responded with a strange, contradictory mix of anger and appreciation. 'More joy in heaven over one sinner who repenteth than over ninety-nine just men', captured the tone of several.

Afterwards I wondered how he could hope to return the coats without being caught. Details of the peculiar conversation came back to me . . . the first jacket, which had been a Belstaff . . . the towrope he had planned to hang himself with . . . and the hard-to-miss aside: 'Actually I took a couple of jackets in a bar in California. Returning them will be difficult, so I will give those to a charity shop.'

Then the next item was suddenly upon us, as it always is on a talk show, and Coatman was swept away in the tide of other stories.

Sadly, he was to enter our lives again more than a year later.

*   *   *

If Goldfinger strapped me to his trolley and shouted, 'Tell me the best thirty stories on your show or feel the heat of this laser!', I would probably be wishing I had signed up for that trial of asbestos underpants. It is in the nature of the events that swirl around us that every story you cover is the most exciting one you have ever heard. The most important show we have ever done was the one we did yesterday; the most memorable call was the last one. But that approach interferes with the brain's cataloguing system. After a day, most stories fade to grey. It is why I keep notes of great moments – so if Goldfinger was really serious about getting my all-time top thirty, I would need permission to consult the notebook. If he replied that my memory was all I had, then I would have to surrender. Tell him to crank the laser to max and wave goodbye to my gonads.

Yet some contributions never go grey. Coatman was one. Another came barely six months later. The item was on pest control. Most people with problems for our pest expert spoke of moths, wasps and flies. A young woman troubled by bees droned just like them. But then Steven Field phoned from his home near Scarborough with the most extraordinary story of infestation.

The Field family had a problem with bats. A few had nested in their barn. Steven had left them where they were – aware, vaguely, that you can't simply wander into a barn and swat a bat. The animals are protected under draconian laws. They cannot be shooed or disturbed in any way.

However, Mr Field did not realise that the bats had found a way of moving from the roof space in the barn into the attic at the top of his home. His second mistake was to believe the bats had remained small in number, when actually the animals were using the barn as a muster point before the journey to the attic. The small number hanging out in the barn were not a reliable guide to the true situation. One night Steven left his house and was shocked to see a swarm of hundreds of bats gush from a gap below his roof.

'It was a big black cloud. They dive-bombed me,' he explained.

It was almost as if the bats, having lodged in his home, were now trying to drive the Field family away. The ominous noise upstairs increased. Steven's wife became panicky and went to see her doctor about anxiety. The homeowner knew he should go into his attic to see what was happening there, but his wife was beginning to be fearful of what he would find.

When he called us, Steven Field was in a crisis. There were so many bats in the attic he had had to bring in students from a college in Scarborough to count them as part of a project. 'I thought there were hundreds.'

'How many were there?'

'The students counted more than five thousand.'

He described the shocking situation his family were now in. The attic was now almost impossible to access because bats were teeming inside it, a solid mass of fur. Their accumulated droppings were so heavy the house was creaking under the strain, possibly close to collapse.

Worse was to come. From the attic, the bats had now penetrated the main bedroom.

JV: 'This is like a Hammer Horror film.'

Steven: 'So what do I do with them?'

JV (*to the expert*): 'Oliver?'

Oliver: 'Bats are actually protected, so there is little that you can physically do to them.'

Steven: 'Yes, I've been told this.'

Oliver: 'Probably the best advice that I can say is contact one of the bat protection leagues and they will be able to give you advice.'

JV: 'There's more than one bat protection league, is there?'

Oliver: 'Yes.'

Steven: 'What's happened is, I live on a smallholding between Malton and Scarborough, and originally they went in a barn, but they've broken through into the main house, and they've actually taken over the loft in the main house, then they've broken through into the main bedroom, and I've had to weld one of these steel doors on that you'd keep squatters out with on the bedroom door – my wife and daughter have gone to live with the mother-in-law in Scarborough, my wife has nearly had a breakdown because of this.'

JV: 'This is an incredible story.'

Steven: 'Five thousand bats.'

JV: 'They are moving in, these bats.'

Steven: 'Well, what do I do? I know they're protected, but they are going to take over the house. And I've got to be there for my animals. I have a little bit of cattle and have to be there. They actually come out at dusk and they dive-bomb you when you're going out to the barn.'

JV: 'Well, you say the bats go out – can't you, when they go out, shut the door behind them?'

Steven: 'I asked them about blocking the hole but you're not allowed to.'

JV: 'Really? Is that right, Oliver?'

Oliver: 'Yeah, you're not allowed to disrupt their roosting or their habitat in any way at all. Fines have actually been imposed of up to five thousand pounds per bat.'

Per bat? The expert was not helping. In a flash of gallows humour, Steven said his ambition was to put all the bats in a large container 'and take them to the House of Commons to meet all the people who made these laws'. His wife was now 'on valium, in Scarborough'. He believed that because the house was old it might soon collapse, 'starting with the floors'. He had to stay there because 'I have got to feed the animals'.

He finished: 'The noise is incredible and the dirt, the droppings, which they produce, it looks like someone's run in my loft and sprayed it with one of those foam insulation things. I think the weight of the droppings is going to crush the house.'

So it ended. Steven Field went back to his creaking home and his crumbling marriage.

Perhaps it is the power of the image that made his words so memorable. You picture the swarm of bats, grouped with not an inch of air between them, angled in the close twilight sky like a question mark, shaping and reshaping before a vicious dive. The metal plate. The trembling wife. You hear the noise.

Some months later came another call I will not forget. We were discussing benefit fraud. A man left a message with the researcher in the office, which I read out to my listeners:

'I used to work in social care. My job for a time was to be day care for a man with a lot of health problems. He had round-the-clock assistance in his home. He was deaf, mute and blind and in a wheelchair. It was very hard work. For example, he could not use the toilet on his own and there was a lot to clear up because he was doubly incontinent. I had to develop a tapping system to communicate with him. I would tap out messages on his bare forearm. But he was totally imprisoned by his disabilities, which were the worst I ever saw as a care worker.'

While reading this comment I wondered how it related to benefit fraud. Sure enough, there was a sting in the tail.

'After a while I left the industry and changed my career. Three years later I was sitting on a busy beach in Spain. I looked out to sea and saw a man racing along the waves on a very fast jet ski. He looked very good at it but when he dismounted right in front of me I immediately recognised him as the person I had looked after in that wheelchair. I said hello and he saw it was me and he just laughed. Clearly all of his disabilities had been faked in order to gain state benefits. I was absolutely disgusted.'

Remembering reading the comment now, I can recall how my own disgust stung like a physical thing. The idea that someone would pretend to be that severely disabled to gain money and assistance, taking money from genuine cases . . . it was shocking, appalling, disgraceful.

But Phil Jones, the editor, was listening at home on a day off. He came in the next day with a rather different reaction.

'I am not sure we should have read that comment out.'

'Oh?' I said. 'Why not?'

'I don't think it was real. I think it might have been a . . . '

He tailed off, unwilling to use the worst word in journalism: *hoax*. But the caller had given us his name and his number and the mobile would certainly have been checked before he went on air.

'It just seems to me that the story is just too amazing,' Phil went on. 'Leave aside the jet ski, what about the idea that this guy would have faked a condition where he needed someone to wipe his bum in the loo? How likely is that?'

'Good point,' I said. And *tapping* as a way of communicating with a deaf-mute person – how exactly would you establish that system? How would a person tap out the words SHOPPING or HARRY REDKNAPP for example? The more I thought about it, the more I worried Phil might be right. It is often the smallest detail that gives away a lie. For me, the way the fraudster 'raced along the waves on a jet ski' and then 'dismounted right in front of me' did not, on reflection, stack up. I just couldn't imagine how that would work on a busy beach.

We pulled the original comment out of our filing system – straight after the show we shove all the paperwork into a thick document wallet, just like Sir Jimmy Young's team did in the 1970s. The name of the caller did not look familiar. But what about the number?

It was a mobile. We typed it into the contacts computer to see if the guest had called before.

'Ah!' said a researcher. 'Yes, he has been on before. On the pest special.'

'What was he talking about?' asked Phil.

'How his home had been invaded by bats.'

'Oh no,' I said. 'That's not good. Is that it?'

We all began to move towards the computer.

Some tapping on the keys, then –

'One other,' said the researcher. 'The tenth of March 2006. He was Coatman.'

*   *   *

Once or twice you cover a story that seems too amazing to be true. A farmer in Suffolk appeared in every newspaper after declaring quite openly that for ten years he had been exporting gallows for public hangmen in countries with some of the most odious regimes. David Lucas of Mildenhall, a burly, bearded, red-faced man who looked like he had been booked for the part by a casting agency, posed proudly for photos in front of a huge scaffold with a noose hanging from it, arms contentedly folded across his chest as if to say: 'Bully for me.' Lucas told how he had been making a little money selling animal bedding, garden sheds and outhouses, but much more when he began exporting execution equipment.

The gallows behind him had been made to order, the farmer explained. He told how he had been able to work around UK law on the export of execution equipment by labelling his gallows 'other small buildings'.

There was fury from Westminster and human rights campaigners across the country.

Lucas inflamed the situation, retorting that 'business is business' and insisting 'some people deserve the death penalty'. He described various sizes of scaffold – he would be happy to sell you a single gallows for £12,000, or could supply one of his

'Multi-Hanging Execution Systems' for mounting on the trailer of a lorry, allowing multiple executions in remote areas. The MHES would cost £100,000.

Amnesty International UK director Kate Allen said: 'It's appalling that a British man is apparently attempting to sell gallows to President Mugabe's government in Zimbabwe.' She urged the EU to act. 'It makes a mockery of the UK's efforts to oppose the death penalty around the world if right under its nose a British company is sending hanging equipment abroad.'

A spokeswoman for the Department of Trade and Industry said a new EU directive would soon make it unlawful to export gallows.

I can't be 100 per cent sure, but I don't think the story was ever true. I think this enterprising individual realised there was a great opportunity – but it wasn't in the field of gallows exporting. It was in appearing on the news. He built one enormous gallows and posed for interviews with it framed against the charcoal clouds above him and the story went round the world.

Lucas appeared on TV as far away as Australia. The issue was covered on my show: *Is there anything wrong with selling gallows to repressive regimes? Do give us a call!*

Because everyone fell for the hangman story simultaneously – assuming there was a hoax to fall for – I look back on the farmer-selling-gallows as the typical kind of incident which can momentarily hobble the entire news world before it straightens itself out and gets back on the move.

Coatman was different.

He had targeted us directly. He was not interested in being on any other programme. He was our own personal problem.

After the jet ski phone number threw up a match with Coatman and Batman, we quietly launched an inquiry into every single contact the person had made with the programme.

He was clearly a kind of genius – albeit a twisted one. I had never met him, because the only time he came into a BBC studio it had been down the line from Yorkshire. Coatman knew exactly the kind of story that would grip an audience, and he cleverly spoke in a way that suggested he was underplaying the drama; almost as if the key facts were only coming out as an accident of the conversation. Interviewers love that, I have to confess, because afterwards people say 'Great interview' and you know the story would not have emerged without your questions. What made him so intensely believable was his seeming inability to understand how dramatic his own stories were. Except of course he understood completely. He made the famous 25,000th caller, the man who just shouted 'SPERM BANK' and hung up, look like a raging amateur. In life, the people who tend not to be trusted are the shameless exaggerators. This man was the opposite – a cool liar. Arrogant, creative, but always controlled, he was the Salvador Dalí of spoof callers, twirling his waxed moustache-ends at us in a show of contemptuous superiority.

Looking back at the coat interview, I thought there were tiny clues. The fact that he was trying to return multiple jackets by walking back into pubs *wearing all of them* – and then discreetly taking them off one at a time – well, that sounded improbable. And he had a thousand coats, all tagged and logged, but had never taken out wallets and purses and peered into them?

There was some good news for us. Our own cataloguing system suggested he had only spoken on the show twice – having listened to the Coatman and Batman tapes side-by-side for these chapters, I can now tell it is the same person – but he had made multiple attempts to have comments read out by me, of which the jet ski story was only one. When we had gathered all of his contact details we did our best to find what he had sent in, but we are not experts in truffling through IP addresses and metadata. We did take a long look at the source of the email below, apparently from a man called Eric Sutton.

```
[mailto:          @hotmail.co.uk]<BR><B>Sent:</B> Wed 18/10/2006
22:25<BR><B>To:</B> Jeremy Vine<BR><B>Cc:</B> Jeremy Vine
Show<BR><B>Subject:</B> house exchange<BR></FONT><BR></DIV>
<DIV><BR>
<P><FONT size=2>hello<BR><BR>i am using my wifes email to tell you a story about
a holiday house swap we<BR>did two year ago.<BR>I swear I saw the advert in the
'Hull Daily Mail' but my wife reckons it<BR>were it the Lady Magazine or one of
them type glossys.<BR>We contacted a couple in California who wanted to spend
two weeks in<BR>Yorkshire. I made contact and through discussion agreed to do a
house swap<BR>for two weeks in july 04.<BR>The wife and I flew to LAX and made
our way to the house, we had a great<BR>time. The house we stayed at was huge
and had a tennis court and a pool and<BR>a hot tub, it was a new place and was
so well designed and the views over<BR>the hills were fantastic<BR>The couple
who stayed at our place in Swanland in Yorkshireloved our home<BR>and the
surrounding countryside and they seemed to have had  a great time.<BR>you
can imagine our surprise when we were sent a promotional copy of a
film<BR>called 'Jack and Rory's Big adventure'<BR>basically a porn film had been
made at our house whilst we were over in the<BR>states. jack was a donkey and
Rory was a ferret and they had filmed them in<BR>my lounge with  girls
actually making contact with them. My wife was sick on<BR>the carpet and we have
since put house up for sale as we cannot ever feel<BR>the same again.<BR>if you
want to call me and I will happily tell you about the whole
sordid<BR>episode.<BR>It was filthy and I urge people considering a
house/holiday swap to do some<BR>research before making a
commitment.<BR><BR>beryl<BR><BR>my number              ask for
william<BR><BR>                                                        <BR>
```

It was Coatman. It had been sent during his busiest period, in 2006, before we caught him. The email address seemed to be linked to another he had sent, and the text also contained references to Yorkshire and California, which previous incidents suggest was his calling card (remember the 'two coats I stole in a bar in California'?). The clincher was that the mobile number I have blacked out at the foot of the email was his.

The message had arrived during a brilliant item about the joys and dangers of arranging a house swap, the new craze made possible by the internet. You sign up to an intermediary's site and then stay at the home of a family you have never met, often based abroad, while they come to the UK and stay at your place. We had been deluged with stories and the switchboard was jammed. House-swapping is a tremendous subject because people divide sharply down the middle, each side as certain as the other that they are right. One half says, 'What a fabulous idea!' and the other half cry: 'No way are strangers sleeping in my bed!'

Here is the Eric Sutton email, with all the original typos included:

From: Eric Sutton
To: Jeremy Vine Show
>Subject: house exchange<
hello i am using my wifes email to tell you a story about
a holiday house swap we did two year ago.I swear I saw
the advert in the 'Hull Daily Mail' but my wife reckons it
were the Lady Magazine or one of them type glossys. We
contacted a couple in California who wanted to spend two
weeks in Yorkshire. I made contact and through discussion
agreed to do a house swap for two weeks in july 04. The
wife and I flew to LA and made our way to the house, we
had a great time. The house we stayed at was huge and had
a tennis court and a pool and a hot tub, it was a new place
and was so well designed and the views over the hillls were
fantastic The couple who stayed at our place in Swanland in
Yorkshireloved our home and the surrounding countryside
and they seemed to have had a great time. you can imagine
our surprise when we were sent a promotional copy of a film
called 'Jack and Rory's Big adventure' basically a porn film
had been made at our house whilst we were over in the states.
jack was a donkey and Rory was a ferret and they had filmed
them in my lounge with girls actually making contact with
them. My wife was sick on the carpet and we have since put
house up for sale as we cannot ever feel the same again. if you
want to call me and I will happily tell you about the whole
sordid episode. It was filthy and I urge people considering
a house/holiday swap to do some research before making a
commitment. beryl my number [XXXXX XXXXXX] ask for
william

The email was passed to me in the studio and I did not look at
it before starting to read it on the air. You can imagine what
it felt like when I started to hear the story through my own
mouth.

Doubtless some listeners were shocked. Many others would
have roared with laughter at the combination of the indignant

tone and sordid details. When I got to the bit, 'Jack was a donkey and Rory was a ferret', do you think I had to suppress laughter? Actually I lost all conviction. Tailing off, I said: 'Hmm. I am sorry but I don't think this story sounds true.'

In the end, truth matters to us.

It can't be any other way.

Now I see the email again, it looks so fake I am amazed any of us were taken in. The way the sender goes from Eric to William via Beryl. The notion that someone with a palace in California wants to swap it for the Suttons' home in Swanland. Or that they would mail a 'promotional copy' of a porn film . . .

Perhaps Coatman was losing his touch. Having second album syndrome. There was only one other contact with him that we could find, during an item about litter.

'I told a group of kids off for dropping litter and in response they verbally abused me and then vandalised my car. I'm in a wheelchair as I don't have any legs, and on politely telling them not to drop litter, they let rip, calling me "spazzy" and "cripple". They then poured a five litre bucket of gloss paint over my car. My car is specially adapted for me because of my disability, and is the only way I get out. It cost £2,000.'

We had begun to see a theme. He would not catch us again. In the ten years since, I do not think he has. But I was reminded of Coatman recently when a producer who had joined us in the mid-2000s told me, 'I remember all these notices on the office wall. DO NOT PUT THROUGH CALLS FROM ANYONE CALLED STEVEN FIELD, ERIC SUTTON, OR ASSUMED NAME "JOHN", IF SUBJECT INVOLVES YORKSHIRE, DISABILITY OR BATS.'

Doubtless Coatman is now in his mid-forties and reminiscing in pubs about the majestic graffiti he aerosoled across our shop window before he was exposed. And what did I learn? Well, I was left ruing our failure to listen to David Jordan. The experienced journalist who advises programmes on complex editorial matters — and is, by the way, brilliant — was played a tape of the longer Coatman interview before we aired it.

'Well, there is no problem putting this out from a crime-doesn't-pay perspective,' he said, 'because this guy is making a clean breast of what he has done and he wants to put it right. But there is one thing you should be aware of. It could be a hoax.'

We had ignored him.

15. It's All Kicking Off in East Grinstead

I was thinking about the bat story just the other day. Had it been true, at some point the homeowner would presumably have seen his house collapse under the weight of the five thousand bats and their droppings. There would have been an explosion of brick dust and bat dung, and a local newspaper reporter would have been sent to the scene to describe the crater. What would her headline say?

The reason I ask is because I love local newspapers and have been avidly building a collection of their headlines – with a special interest in what they put on those sandwich boards you see in the street. Who can resist this Hampshire classic?

I started my career on one of those local papers, the *Coventry Evening Telegraph*. Although I became a BBC foreign correspondent and had my share of situations that were exotic and dangerous, a lot of people are more fascinated by those days in Coventry because talking about them is like describing the lost island of

Atlantis. The newspaper was all manual typewriters and hot-metal presses, and my memories are perfumed by ribbons inked red and black. Telling students recently about the suction tube that whooshed our copy from one side of the building to another, where the print-setters worked, was like showing them pictures of a UFO and assuring them I really had been abducted by the crew. They could not believe the ribbons existed. Or the suction tube.

They are gone now, for sure. Those days are gone.

When I joined the newspaper straight from Durham University, thrilled to have a job where you got paid to write interesting things into a notepad, there were eighty-five journalists in a grand newsroom overlooking the city centre. We were in command of the agenda and we had a monopoly on the information. Readers paid us to find stuff out about what they were doing and then tell them – a strange arrangement when you think about it. We sat there yanking manual carriage returns in a room as noisy as a Panzer factory. Computers were supposed to help the paper print in colour, but actually they gave its readers the power to go elsewhere. They told their stories to each other without us getting in the way, and the results were literally devastating. The building I proudly stepped into as a trainee in 1986 is about to be knocked down. At least sixty of the staff have gone.

The power of those readers – psychologists use the word *agency*, meaning a person's ability to change the world around them – is only a different expression of the elbow that my 25,000 callers now feel they have. No question, i-Power is forcing the old world to claw and scratch for attention. Local papers are in a very tough place. But gloriously, they are showing what they are made of with some of the greatest billboards – in local newsrooms they are known as 'bills' – that we have ever seen.

The *South London Press* offered 'STREATHAM: SPANISH-SPEAKING PARROT ON THE LOOSE', which follows the rule, *For extra impact, mention an animal*. The same law was put to great effect by the *Cambridge News*.

After seeing one of these billboards a few years ago – it was, if I remember rightly, the *Croydon Advertiser*'s 'POLICE STORM PUB IN MORRIS DANCERS ROW', I appealed on Twitter for people to take photos of bills in their own high streets and send them to me so I could share them. I now get half a dozen a week from all over the country and I roar with laughter at them. I hope I am helping celebrate local papers; letting them know how much love there is for them.

So here are my top ten. You have to imagine them blaring out in big black letters on a waist-high board positioned right in front of you as you do your shopping:

1. PUDDLE SPLASH VICTIM VOWS REVENGE
   (*Weston & Somerset Mercury*)
2. POLICE STOP BOY SKIPPING IN STREET
   (*Chorley & Leyland Guardian*)
3. POODLE HOLDS CLUE TO DEATHS
   (*Brighton Argus*)
4. MAN'S LEGS STOLEN – WEDDING DREAM SHATTERED
   (*Manchester Evening News*)
5. DELIGHT AS MAN GROWS BANANA IN GARDEN
   (*Surrey Herald*)

6. FIRE CREW FREE WOMAN'S BUM FROM WALL
   (*East Grinstead Courier & Observer*)
7. BLACKBURN CLOWN PANIC
   (*Lancashire Telegraph*)
8. SHOCK AS POPE STEPS DOWN TWO YEARS AFTER
   BRUM VISIT
   (*Birmingham Mail*)
9. WINDOW CLEANER KILLED BY GIANT PENCIL
   (*Brighton Argus*)
10. BUDGIE'S DEATH NOW BEING TREATED AS
    SUSPICIOUS
    (*Cumbrian News & Star*)

Some of these headlines may smack of desperation – 'BLACKBURN CLOWN PANIC' is probably my favourite – but all of them are more interesting than most of what you read in a national paper. On Radio 2 we might draw the line at following up the *Express & Star's*

. . . but a programme that covered budgie deaths, window cleaner fatalities and people having both legs stolen on their wedding day sounds like it would be serious competition for mine. In fact it sounds very much like mine. If the police stopped a boy skipping in the street, we would be all over it.

When someone tweets me their local bill and it makes me laugh, I repost it for my followers with the phrase 'It's all kicking off'. So the *East Grinstead Courier & Observer* breaking the news 'POLICE CALLED IN OVER KILLER GOLDFISH' was my cue to post a picture of the bill along with the line, 'Looks like it's all kicking off in East Grinstead'. The people who follow me can see it, laugh and share.

But of course, sharing on social media is what caused the problem for newspapers in the first place. The first instinct of the modern age is to share. Sometimes the effects are terrible. When a young Gloucester hairdresser, Hollie Gazzard, was murdered by her violent ex in the salon where she worked, police were appalled that the first reaction of passers-by was not to help, or even to call them, but to stand there filming it all.

The other night I watched a man eating alone in quite a posh restaurant. The room was dimly lit and every time a course was brought – even a small bowl of olives and a piece of bread at the very start – he carefully arranged his cutlery and napkin around the plate, pulled his phone from his jacket and took a flash photo from directly above. Once he even stood up to get the angle right. Flash photos of food are always a bad move, because a sudden burst of bright white light makes even a five-star dish look like it has come sliding down the counter at Wimpy. But he seemed to have no worries that other diners, and restaurant staff, could see he was the kind of person who photographs his food – because these days everyone seems to be the kind of person who photographs their food. In fact I think I might be the kind of person who photographs my food. We use the hard drive on our phones as an extension of the brain cells nature gave us, like a brand-new garage attached to a tumbledown cottage. The problem is that the more we use the garage, the more we neglect the cottage.

The diner tapped away at his screen after he took each picture, so was doubtlessly uploading his food to a website. Maybe Facebook or Instagram. Or Photobucket or Imgur or Gifboom or Lafango or Phanfare. Or TripAdvisor, where you can now see thousands of plates of food looking like criminals – photographed with a flash from the front and the side – to help you choose which restaurant to book. Of course uploading a picture also means waiting for a response, so the man then spent quite a bit of time staring at his screen waiting for it to give him something in return. Eventually he replaced the phone in his jacket pocket and tucked into his cold meal. Enabled by his mobile, the man had become a publisher. In a way it's wonderful – being able to share your food like that.

What I love about local newspapers is that they still exist to tell us stuff, not just to help us share the things we know already. The headline 'FUGITIVE SAUSAGE DOG CAUSES MAYHEM' from the *Jersey Evening Post* is inspirational on so many levels (the dog, according to the copy, was 'making an ill-fated bid to escape the town on the No. 1 bus'). But there is something else that ought to help local papers survive this terrible time. The clue is in the name. The best news is local.

I was at a charity dinner once and found myself in the seat next to the Foreign Secretary, Jack Straw. The places had been set by Ed Owen, a near neighbour of mine who also worked for Straw. I thought, 'This conversation is going to test me', and started to run down the list of countries where stuff was happening and the Cabinet Minister was trying to sort it out. Iraq and Afghanistan, obviously. But there'd been trouble in Tibet, too. In South America – wait – Venezuela? Chavez? And hang on, hadn't he recently been to Sudan to try to broker some kind of deal where the south split from the north? I had been to Sudan. *What was the capital of Sudan?* Maybe that was the place to start. Okay. Solid ground. No – just a second. Burma. Wasn't something big breaking there, with the army and the monks and Aung San Suu Kyi? Bloody hell, I thought, *he is going to want to talk about Burma.* I nervously grappled with the bread roll.

'How do you know Ed?' the Foreign Secretary asked.

'We are neighbours.'

'Where is that?'

'Hammersmith. A little network of roads which they rather glamorously call Brackenbury Village.'

'Do you have a residents' association?'

'Er . . . yes,' I replied uncertainly. 'Ed and I are both members, I think. It is called the Brackenbury Residents' Association and it's very proactive. I had a friend once who came in late one night, a bit drunk, and she saw she had three emails from them in her inbox, and sent a rude one back asking them not to send her "any more of this rubbish", and it was disastrous.'

'Disastrous because she had to apologise?'

'No, I think she actually had to leave the area.'

Straw laughed.

'The residents' association goes by the name BRA,' I told him, 'and it is more powerful than NATO.'

'What sort of campaigns do they do, then?'

And we were off. Every single country in the world we could have spoken about, but our conversation ended up revolving around the two streets where Ed and I lived, and whether residents should have the right to paint over graffiti on council property. We never went near Tibet or Burma or Venezuela, and I did not have to remember Khartoum. Even when you are Foreign Secretary, all the stuff that really matters is just down the road.

*　*　*

The Nomadic Academy of Fools is a theatre group based in Somerset. In 2013, members decided to promote their latest production by standing in Glastonbury High Street wearing stage costumes and handing out flyers.

Nothing unusual about that. The production, showing nearby at the Assembly Rooms, was called *Fooling Around: Four Days of Plays*, and there were still tickets to sell. The costumes, however, were a little . . . different. The man was dressed as a large penis, and the woman standing beside him was dressed as a vagina. The production had been overseen by veteran actor Jonathan Kay, who is well known for workshops which push at the boundaries of theatre.

212

Unfortunately, one passer-by objected to the fact that people dressed as genitalia were drawing attention to themselves.

'He started shouting at me, saying it was disgusting and children could see us,' Chris Murray of the Nomadic Academy told a local reporter. 'I could tell by his body language that he was really angry. I tried to calm him down, I wasn't looking for a fight, but he grabbed my hat, tore it off and chucked it on the pavement.'

When a punch was thrown, the other actor tried to get between the two men to force them apart. The resulting headline in the *Central Somerset Gazette*

Woman dressed as vagina steps in as man in penis costume is attacked in Glastonbury

will probably not be bettered for at least a century.

If you looked carefully at my list of the best billboards, you might have noticed two mentions for the *Brighton Argus*. Somewhere on that paper works a bill-writer touched by genius. The paper is fighting the internet with some of the best headlines we have ever seen, and I love them for it. We could actually do a top ten just with *Brighton Argus* sandwich boards. Ready?

1. MOTH DIES IN SHED INFERNO
2. 12 REMAIN DEAD IN MORGUE FIRE
3. BRIGHTON 'MOST GODLESS CITY IN BRITAIN' (this rivals 'BYKER IS CENTRE OF WORLD DRUGS TRADE' from a newspaper in the north-east)
4. WORTHING RUNAWAY ELECTRIC BUGGY CHAOS
5. STUDENT ATTACKED BY SEAGULL
6. SEAGULL ATTACKED BY STUDENT
7. MYSTERIOUS GIRLS IN PUNCH-UP AT PETER ANDRE SHOW

(I showed this to Peter when I was on *Strictly* with him and he laughed so loudly)

8. LIFEBOAT CALLED OUT TO HELP WITCH
9. OAP CRUISES A27 AT 8MPH
10. MENTAL HOSPITAL GAVE LIGHTER TO ARSONIST

More than any other local paper, the *Argus* seems to have understood that they need to fight the internet with every weapon available, or die.

I became fascinated by the *Argus* and asked the team at Radio 2 if I could meet the person who turbo-charged their bills. In September 2016, he came into our Brighton studio. He was not what I expected. Martin Cooper was roughly my age (I had anticipated a keen-as-mustard recent graduate who was barely shaving) and by the time we met he had moved on from the paper.

But the encounter was inspirational. He had joined the *Argus* as the most junior member of its production staff, despite being in his forties. 'I started doing the bills as the junior,' he said. 'No one wanted the role as it always needed doing at the end of a hectic shift. But I wanted it to be a glorious thing.'

That single line is wonderful. Cooper realised the sandwich boards were seen by almost everyone in Brighton and yet the normal attitude to them was casual to the point of throwaway – someone would simply copy out the main headline from the paper and stick it on the billboard. 'Until then the unwritten rule was that you just put the front-page headline on the bill. My idea was to break the rules.'

Sometimes, he said, 'You had to try and intrigue them. On Sussex Day I wrote "DO YOU KNOW WHAT DAY IT IS?" because I liked the idea that people would stop and wonder.'

The billboard 'often had to be written in thirty seconds using four to six words. If I could come up with something that would pique people's interest, it was very satisfying.' His personal favourites? There was 'POLICE CALLED IN OVER CLIFF RICHARD POSTER' and 'COUNCIL CALLS IN COUNSELLORS TO COUNSEL COUNCILLORS', he tells me.

The first dance on *Strictly*, a cha-cha-cha, and the moment I shouted 'YOWZERS!'. The audience went completely crazy – and I will never forget the terrifying way the entire dance deserted me. Afterwards Karen Clifton asked, 'What happened?'

Karen's training regime for *Strictly* was continuous. Not only kicks in the gym – I never got my leg quite as high as hers – but stretches in the *Eggheads* studio too.

With the Eggheads: Chris, Daphne, CJ, Kevin and Judith (the first winner of *Who Wants to Be a Millionaire?*). I felt very sorry for CJ after an interview he gave led to him being accused of murder.

A beautiful collision of two of my worlds, as *Strictly*'s royal couple, the Cliftons, appear on *Eggheads*. Quizzer Barry Simmons is a huge fan, and a keen dancer himself, and was quite overwhelmed.

Right Recording the 50th anniversary of *Points of View* in 2011 with long-time producer Caroline Jones. Later I found this phone (*below right*) when we filmed an edition of *Points of View* in a disused gallery in Television Centre. It is a reminder that in the BBC nothing stays hot forever.

Below Probably the greatest complaint ever made to *Points of View*: 'Why did a bare bottom suddenly appear on the *Six O'Clock News*?' When we examined the footage we found an engineer who clearly thought he was out of sight.

With Hugh Bonneville, Gurinder Chadha and Angela Scanlon, presenting *The One Show* after an accident at the barber's. As Steve Wright said: 'You look like one of the wanted faces on *Crimewatch* with that haircut.'

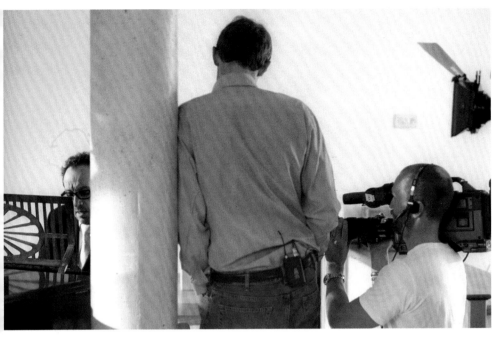

I am not sure Elvis Costello wanted this photo taken, which is why the taker hid behind a pillar. I had just interviewed my hero for a TV series, and he said, 'Tell me what you think of this,' and played a song he had just written. The moment was so intoxicating I felt drunk afterwards.

Tea and sandwiches with Kay Gilderdale, accused of murder. Sitting like this should have felt natural, but the wire on the carpet is the giveaway that cameras were filming us for *Panorama*. I reflected afterwards that the intimacy of radio is impossible on TV.

Left The black-and-white world. Three Vine children on the beach in 1974. Me aged nine, Sonya at four and Tim at seven. The reporter, the actress, the comedian.

Middle My little brother's name in the huge lightbox above theatre entrances. This was the Shepherds Bush Empire. There is unique joy in having a family member whose sole duty is to make people laugh.

Below Taking over *Crimewatch* in 2016. We dropped the 'Don't have nightmares' catchphrase because it seems to me a funny thing to say when you've just shown viewers an hour of end-to-end robbery and violence.

Two of my greatest friends in the world: Alex Armitage, my agent, whose grandfather wrote 'The Sun Has Got His Hat On', next to my wife Rachel, who can find a sun behind any cloud.

Photos of my father at different stages of his life. My parents gave their three children so much love that we felt we could do whatever we wanted . . . and we all did.

Sniper's Alley. But I clung to these two giants and they got me through. On the left is Anna. Martha has the cool shades. The blue tree I can't explain.

Two days before a general election, I thought my daughters would find it fascinating to sit at Dimbleby's historic desk. You can see from their expressions that they haven't yet quite grasped the full drama of an election night.

What I love about Martin's story is that he took the most hum-drum junior job in the office and, as he says, made it a 'glorious thing'. Usually such stories are told by hyperactive 23-year-olds but Martin was two decades beyond that when he joined the *Argus*. Maybe any job can be made a 'glorious thing'. Cooper's bills were so good they were often stolen off the streets – that had never happened before. 'Students and pubs used to take them. Students put them on their bedroom walls.'

Thanks to Brighton residents with smartphones and a sense of humour, many Cooper-bills went round the world. People in Vietnam and Alaska have now heard of the *Brighton Argus* when previously they wouldn't even have known of the town.

Listening to Martin speak, I think there are uncanny parallels with my show. The *Brighton Argus* and Radio 2 are both defiantly analogue – radio and newspapers pre-date television, let alone the web. Yes, we do our best to visualise and viralise to make the tidal wave of new technology work for us, of course we do, and I tweet like a crazy person, but the plain fact is that most people still listen to radio on radios. Many listeners still do not know what I look like: I met one the other day who said: 'I expected you to be short and rather rotund.'

Strange as it may sound, we are also *local*. At least we try to be. The stories that work best for us involve the name of a street and a reporter standing in it, then a listener saying: 'Yes! I've been there.' (If I ever announce, 'Next, Russia . . .' I can almost hear people switching off.) Your local newspaper is your friend, written by people who shop where you shop and get parking tickets from the same wardens. On a good day, we need to have that intimacy.

On Radio 2 we also have headlines. Each day the most junior member of the team selects two stories and – just like Martin Cooper did – combines them in half a dozen words or less for BBC text services. These headlines appear on the website and flow across the display of your car radio. (Let's pass over the misprint I saw while on holiday: 'VANESSA FELTZ SITS ON JEREMY VINE'.) The problem is that stories never make a tidy match when they are compressed so tightly. For example, our website announces:

and everyone starts messaging me that the Queen 'is not a drug user'. It happens all the time. In the past you may have clicked on our page or looked at the text running across your car radio display and been baffled by the following combinations:

Tamiflu and Oscar Pistorius
Owls and standing up in the office
Junk food in schools and Iran
Mr Whippy and Lyme Disease
Steroids and Maria Miller
Donald Trump and burst water pipes
Islamic State and brick shortage
Jeremy Corbyn and robots
Devolving power to the north and the menace of
amateur beekeepers.

Or, brilliantly, sent from a listener with a car radio:

The oddness of the combinations became such a feature that Radio 1 introduced a competition called '*Come Vine with Me*', where DJs had to choose which of the headline-pairings was made up: 'Was it "Railway trespass and gnomes" or "Monks and water meters"?' asked Matt Edmondson, who had invited fellow DJ Greg James to play along. 'Next, Greg, was it "The monarchy and wardrobes" or "Scottish independence and dog poo"?'[3] As I was writing this chapter I saw a tweet from the comedian Lloyd Hollett, complaining that his phone memory is now full up with previous programmes. The list was impressive:

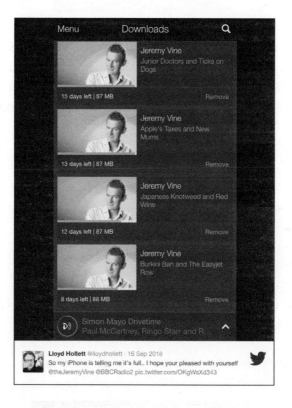

True, nothing quite beats the power of the *Lancashire Evening Post* billboard 'JOHN LENNON'S TOOTH TO VISIT PRESTON', but

---

[3] The real ones were 'Railway trespass and gnomes', and then 'Scottish independence and dog poo'.

we are on the same track. Maybe we can learn from each other to survive.

Martin Cooper left our Brighton studio after a great discussion about his billboards. Five minutes later, I remembered the one question I really wanted answered – what would have been his headline for our bat infestation story?

16. The Power of the Inanimate Object

We had a great question on *Eggheads*. In the theatre, what is the expression for any unusual item that, if it appears on the stage at the start of a play, will need to form part of the drama at some point?

For example, a pig's head. If a pig's head is sitting on a table as the curtains open for scene one, even if the play is about something unrelated like politics, and – let's say – a person playing the Prime Minister comes on, at some point the pig's head will have to form part of the action. It's a rule.

Presenting at Wembley with the actor Martin Freeman (*Sherlock*, *The Hobbit*, *Fargo*, *The Office*) for a big Radio 2 special on England's World Cup victory in 1966, I asked him if he knew the answer.

'No,' he said.

I realised that must be pretty annoying. Being asked a question about theatre by a non-actor, and having to say just 'No.'

The answer is Chekhov's Gun.

It was the Russian playwright Anton Chekhov who said: 'Remove everything that has no relevance to the story. If you say in the first chapter that there is a rifle hanging on the wall, in the second or third chapter it absolutely must go off. If it's not going to be fired, it shouldn't be hanging there.'

Looking around Radio 2, I wondered: do we have a Chekhov's Gun? Maybe not a rifle hanging on the wall, but somewhere in the building an inanimate object that keeps forcing itself into the proceedings? An item that almost has a personality, becomes part of the team?

In *Strictly Come Dancing*, we had a train. The celebrities arrived in a large locomotive and jumped out. That should have been the end of the matter. Unfortunately, it then emerged that the last time the 'Strictly Express' had been used was for a 26-minute Canadian porn film called *Nympho*, leading to the *Sun*'s front-page headline 'CHA CHA NUDEY CHOO CHOO' above a story which said: 'The BBC will be horrified to discover their flagship family show is now linked to porn.'

So if Chekhov had a gun, and *Strictly* had a train, what does Radio 2 have? My first thought is the downstairs lavatory. In a classic piece of BBC design, the receptionists at Radio 2 sit in front of an enormous toilet. The loo space – no cubicles, just one big room with an outer door – seems to have been plumbed by supporters of Eric Pickles because everything is just a little bit larger than the world can handle. The cistern is Olympic-sized, so the flush makes the kind of dramatic sound you would expect if the Kennedy assassination had happened with water.

Frequently an important guest will appear at the front desk – Dolly Parton, say, coming in to visit Bob Harris. Just as she tells the staff who she is here to see, there will be a loud explosion of water behind the receptionists as if the entire country music output of the radio station is hastily being disposed of. When Nick Clegg arrived to be interviewed on my show a while back, the flush coincided with his press officer saying the words 'Liberal Democrat party', which turned out to be an uncannily accurate prediction of the 2017 election.

You do not need me to tell you the obvious other annoyance when your reception is a modest room annexed to a supersized lavatory. Suffice to say, the occasional belch of bad air clears the ground floor more effectively than any fire drill.

At some point the workers at reception decided enough was enough. Unilaterally, and quite understandably, they took the lavatory out of action permanently by locking the door from the outside.

Which is how the loo stayed for more than two years. Door firmly shut. As out-of-use as those American shopping malls you sometimes see pictures of online, ghostly places where the escalator is covered in moss and the plastic chandeliers host a family of bats.

So far so good. But, rushing into the building one day, I happened to see the door was ajar. I needed a lavatory urgently and in my haste was not going to be too considerate. Quietly, I nipped into the toilet and firmly locked the door.

Peace! For a few minutes there was no sign of trouble.

Then I heard someone trying to get into the room from the other side. The person attempted to turn the handle, found it locked and said a tentative: 'Hello?'

My first thought was Lionel Ritchie, but it sounded more like one of the security guards. I did not reply because I thought there could be no danger.

That was, I now accept, a mistake.

What I had failed to realise was that the receptionists had been told a lavatory needed to be found urgently for Barry Gibb, the last surviving member of the BeeGees. Barry has one of the most distinctive singing voices in recording history and with his brothers made music that is the soundtrack to all our lives.

When the security guard tries my door and finds it locked – with no answer from the other side – he naturally assumes the normal arrangement is in place. The loo is locked and nobody is using it. Off he goes to get the master key while Barry Gibb quietly waits.

Inside, I am sitting perfectly happily – for now.

There is then what I can only describe as a terrifying sight. To my consternation I watch as the door handle *revolves on its own as if I am in a horror movie*. From the outside the security guard unlocks and opens the loo in a single movement that is so fast I don't even have time to move off the seat. Standing there in front of me is Barry Gibb. Yes, I am suddenly visible to the person who wrote 'How Deep Is Your Love' and 'Islands in the Stream'.

I react instinctively, with a high-pitched scream: 'AAAAA-aaaaaaaaaah!' And I realise I have made the situation worse, because Barry may recognise this as one of his own songs.

It's funny. When I plonk myself on the seat in my Radio 2 studio each day, I always think we throw open a window and in comes GB. It's better than throwing open a loo door and in comes a BeeGee.

The door quickly closes. The moment passes. By the time I emerge, Mr Gibb has left the building and possibly the music industry. I found myself wishing I had asked him for a selfie. Only later did the thought surface . . . *Is the lavatory Chekhov's Gun?*

* * *

The gun could also be the coffee machine. For several years BBC cutbacks meant that guests who arrived at the Radio 2 studios on the 6th floor – whether they were kings, Olympians or pop gods – were allowed only a PG Tips teabag or a spoonful of instant coffee. It did not matter who they were. Betty Boothroyd, Status Quo, Salman Rushdie . . . all were limited to a spoonful of instant or a single teabag. Milk was proffered from a small fridge.

The phrase you hear most these days in the BBC is: 'We have no money.' When I take visitors around Broadcasting House and show them the chutney of Latin engraved above the 1930s entrance, I tell them it translates as 'WE HAVE RUN OUT OF CASH'. Searching for headed writing paper one day in the Radio 2 office block, I found every cupboard bare. I don't normally need to print letters on corporation paper, but on this occasion it was an official thank-you which had to look smart. I went to other floors in our building – BBC 6 Music, BBC Comedy – but every other cupboard yawned back at me, empty.

'Have we run out of all stationery across the BBC?' I asked a harried assistant on my show.

He made some calls and came back to me. 'There are three sheets of Radio 2 writing paper in the building,' he said quietly, in case someone overheard. 'They are on the third floor. Julia has them. She says you can have one.'

The single sheet of headed paper was brought down from the third floor, handled as carefully as Russian porcelain. Unbearable tension followed as I tried to work out whether it needed to go into the printer face up or face down, painfully aware I would only get one chance. Eventually I took the plunge. Bingo. The letter printed and was sent. Now the radio station was down to two sheets.

Given that the same hard-line approach applies to every single item of expenditure, you can imagine the shock when the instant coffee stocks were suddenly displaced one day . . . by a stonking, shining, brand-new coffee machine. The thing flashed chrome hubs at us like a new Maserati. Staff walking past clutched each other for assurance. People came from all parts of the building to see.

The Radio 2 coffee machine now plays a role in all our lives. News of it has spread to other buildings. A funnel in the top contains coffee beans. It will foam your milk and treble your espresso. A notice on the front says

This machine is serviced three times a day

although, when it broke, it stopped being serviced for three weeks, so really the notice should say

**This machine is serviced three times a day
so long as it's working**

. . . but that sounds too much like a complaint. If a serious latte with heart-shaped milk froth costs £2.80 in a shop, and a hardy coffee-drinker uses the Radio 2 machine three times a day, that person is effectively being given £42 worth of free coffee per week. Across the year that is an extra £1,890. Since the benefit is not taxed, the sum equates to a pay rise of around £3,000 a year. The coffee machine may therefore have given some of the lowest-paid workers an effective 15 per cent pay rise. It is a brilliant thing.

Is the coffee machine Chekhov's Gun? The inanimate object that inserts itself into the action? It makes a hell of a lot of noise, that is for sure. When the raw coffee beans stacked in the funnel drop two inches into the grinder, the sound of them being dashed against the interior by a bladed propeller is reminiscent of the worst human rights abuses in Pinochet's Chile. That is not the only noise it makes. For some reason the machine's digital display will regularly announce 'CLEANING CYCLE STARTING' and a series of whooshes and bangs drowns out every conversation.

Beside the coffee-maker are some brown plastic sofas of the sort that are regularly wiped down after being used in adult movies. Opposite is a grand piano Elton John used to play.

One day I was due to interview Hillary Clinton about a memoir she had written. It was just before she announced her ill-fated run for the American presidency, so I valued the chance to meet her. Usually the famous and powerful run late, but for reasons that have never been explained she arrived a full *forty minutes* before the show was due to start – unaccompanied. The first I knew of it was when someone on the sixth floor called down to my office on the second and said: 'Hillary Clinton is waiting for you by the coffee machine. She is alone up here.'

Alone! The idea that a woman who had been First Lady, senator for New York and US Secretary of State was perched on her own on a sofa that gets wiped down daily with a J-cloth alarmed me. I raced up the stairs with Phil Jones, our preparation for the rest of the programme suddenly forgotten. There she was, sitting with her hands in her lap. We greeted her formally, urged her not to stand, shook hands. Conversation turned to the First World War, because she had noticed all the posters about the BBC's centenary commemorations.

'I am never sure I understand how World War One started,' I said to Mrs Clinton, thinking that as President Obama's Secretary of State she would have the lowdown.

'Well, we have to look at that gunshot in Sarajevo first,' she replied, and at that moment, right behind her, the coffee machine made an explosive bang.

She paused. I saw the coffee beans just above her head move in the funnel.

'There is no one identifiable cause, but essentially there were two empires clashing. Or maybe three.' The unit started to whirr and there was a loud crunch. Mrs Clinton frowned, glanced over her shoulder for an instant, and continued.

'The carnage was terrible – '

The unit burped. I heard the propeller start up as the innards rattled and the beans slid into the grinder.

'My understanding is that it was Germany, plus Austria-Hungary and Italy, and then you had Britain, Russia and France. And they all came together – '

BANG! CRACK! WHOOSH! A puff of steam came out of the front nozzle as the machine cleaned itself.

'The trench warfare was the most remarkable part of the story – '

Grrrrrrrrr. KSSSSSSSSSSSSSSSSSSt. The blades inside ground the beans. The body of the coffee-maker shook and bounced. It hunched its chrome shoulders and burped and gulped and hissed and belched.

The famous politician said nothing for a moment. She looked behind her at the machine, tipped her head, furrowed her brow.

I suddenly realised: *The coffee machine is recreating the First World War.*

*   *   *

But the coffee machine is not Chekhov's Gun. Too much of its time is spent just doing what coffee-makers do – make coffee. From the other side of the open space outside our studios the grand piano sits, that gift from Elton, turned slightly at an angle as if reluctant to share space with catering kit and bad sofas.

Could the piano be Chekhov's Gun? It is a candidate. For the first two years a notice sat on top of it, telling visitors

DO NOT PLAY THIS PIANO

and every day I saw the notice I got a little crosser. If there were a West End play called *Events at Radio 2*, and as you sat there the curtains opened on a scene with a piano in the middle of the stage and a notice on the polished lid saying 'DO *NOT* PLAY THIS PIANO', you would absolutely know, one hundred per cent, that at some point one of the actors is going to sit down and play it and there will be a row and someone will probably grab a rifle off the wall and all hell will break out, and that will be the turning point.

More than a decade ago, some consultants came into the BBC and were asked the simple question: where does the power lie in this organisation, and how should it be structured?

They toiled for more than a year and then left without any public announcement about their conclusions. Later I asked an executive: 'Why was it never published, that study?' She replied that the conclusions had so appalled the BBC they could never be made public. The consultants had discovered the most powerful people in the BBC were the presenters, so there was simply no answer to the question about how the place should be run.

How I wish it were true. Sadly, us presenters are not even able to get the heating turned down, and I struggled powerlessly with my upset about the sign on the piano. But – and this, I suppose, is the key to how the organisation works – at some point I mentioned it to a boss called Lewis Carnie.

At the time Lewis ran a large part of Radio 2 and we bumped into each other in one of two tiny lifts which force everyone to stand with their navels touching.

'I am so cross about that sign on the piano,' I said. 'What message does it send out? That we are the kind of place that doesn't like music? Every day I see it I get more upset.'

The next day the sign had been changed.

The sign was one of the greatest acts of management in the BBC's history and was swiftly followed by Lewis being promoted to run the whole station. We went from having a piano which could not be played, to a piano which should be. But it does mean the piano cannot be Chekhov's Gun, because these days it goes off all the time.

* * *

I mentioned the Radio 2 lift – or lifts, plural, as there are two. The twin elevators play a role in all our lives. They are barely larger than old-style telephone boxes. They seem to require servicing more often than the coffee machine. But they are a vital part of our building's personality.

You never know who you will meet in them. One lift plays Radio 2 twenty-four hours a day. The other has the cooler, more youthful BBC 6 Music pounding from the ceiling. It took me far longer than it should have done to work out which was which. Appearing on Ken Bruce's show one day to trail my own, I came out of the lift and ran into his studio, exclaiming: 'Brilliant to hear you giving X-Ray Spex a run-out!' He told his listeners, 'No, that was actually Lionel Ritchie', which must have been a most baffling exchange to hear on the radio. There was a similar mix-up involving 'New Rose' by The Damned and 'Rose of Cimarron'. Both were caused by my failing to realise I was not listening to Ken's show because I had stepped into the BBC 6 Music lift.

One day I headed up in the Radio 2 elevator and thought Ken sounded ill. Or – an incredible thought, this – slightly the worse for wear. I saw my reflection in the mirror as the lift beeped for different floors and watched as my face showed puzzlement, then turned serious. Ken's voice came through the speaker above my head. He said he was about to speak to me, although I was 'quite boring'. His normally crisp Scots lilt had turned into a rambling slur. I had memories of a famous debacle on Radio 2 when Sarah Kennedy called the visiting clergyman 'an old prune' and accused the newsreader Fenella Hadingham of soiling her underwear. Every few words, Ken would stumble or murmur something inaudible. It was undeniably the DJ, but his thoughts seemed disconnected. Plus, the remarks he was making about the records – 'That was the band Sweet. I do love a sweet' – were not of the normal calibre. He sounded like he had borrowed them from Smashie and Nicey.

It turned out many hundreds of listeners were thinking the same thing. They deluged our switchboards and inboxes to ask if the famous mid-morning presenter was drunk or suffering from the first signs of a stroke. One comment said: 'Ken Bruce has been really annoying this morning. Totally unlike him, but I for one am not impressed. There, I've said it now, rant over.'

The lift doors opened and I walked briskly to Ken's studio. We speak promptly at 11.30 each day.

'I take it you know what's going on?' said his producer.

'Nope.'

'It's not Ken.'

'It's not Ken?' I repeated.

I looked through the glass. What was all this? No sign of Mr Bruce at all. Instead his seat was taken by the comedian Rob Brydon, who was trying to pass himself off as the famous DJ for the entire two-and-a-half-hour show . . . and whose impression was bewitchingly good. The date should have been the clue. April the 1st.

It was a genuine surprise for me. Unusually, we had not had the radio on in the downstairs office. I had arrived late that morning at 10.20 for my briefings. In the hubbub no one had thought to tell me that Ken was not Ken, possibly because of the danger that a stray tweet might give the game away if too many people were in on the joke.

Only in the BBC.

'In you go,' said the producer. 'Play it straight.'

PLAY IT STRAIGHT??! Yes, I actually had to read out my list of prospective stories – politics, a violent crime, plus our medical special – while Brydon grinned at me, occasionally saying in Bruce-speak: 'That, Jeremy . . . sounds like . . . a very . . . serious issue.'

He used the same phrase in response to every story. How neither of us burst out laughing I have no idea.

When his show ended at the stroke of twelve, 'Ken' compounded the indignity by introducing me as Tim Vine.

So the Radio 2 lift has a piece of every action. It is like the radio station's spinal column, wiring every movement. One day a young researcher on my show was asked to collect a blind guest, David, from reception. The guest confirmed his name and the researcher very thoughtfully took his elbow and started to lead him carefully through the glass security gates, explaining each change of direction and each pause.

'We are standing just by some glass gates, David, which go up to about chest height, and in a moment Judy on reception will open – ah, they are opening now, thanks Judy, and here we go, we're walking through to the lift.'

They got into the lift. Just the two of them in that cramped space, the music playing from the ceiling. The researcher described to David how small it was – 'The interior is a kind of silver mesh. Luckily there's no one else in here today' – and which buttons were lit up. 'Next to you are the lift buttons, David, a couple of them are glowing. So it looks like we will stop on the third but then we go straight up to the sixth.'

At the sixth, the lift announced the floor number and the researcher took David's elbow again. 'We are turning left now, just a few yards, then there's a big door and I have to get my pass out to open it. Just stop here if you can. This is a light area, the sun is coming in through the windows.'

The door clanks open.

'The door is now opening outwards towards us, no need to move, we are a couple of feet back.'

Finally he steers the guest down the last stretch of corridor to the studio. 'Just a few more yards.' He is still gripping David's elbow, using it to steer him. 'Come through the main door here.'

When the entrance to the studio control room opens and my editor Phil Jones sees David he realises – *this is the wrong guest.* The researcher has in fact brought David Davis to the studio, the Conservative MP. He has perfect sight and does not even need glasses.

Amid the apologies, David Davis says: 'Yes, I did wonder what was going on.' The researcher goes back down to reception and collects the other David, who is indeed blind.

So the Radio 2 lift is a focal point. It was central to affairs when one of our producers, Tom Bigwood, made an approach to the building management team about having several Shetland ponies in our studio.

No, you didn't mishear me. *Several Shetland ponies.*

A few weeks earlier, we had done an item about large dogs. A breeder brought in an enormous Dane, which did not like me saying its name in an intimate way and knocked me over with the kind of nonchalant shoulder-barge darts players do when they are carrying a trayload of foaming tankards across a crowded pub. The reaction to me sprawling on the studio floor – thousands of people sharing the video clip because it was so funny – made us think we should broaden our minds a little. The studio is a space. The space is a bit like a stage. Things should happen on the stage. What about ponies next?

The problem with bringing Shetland ponies into the studio was our elevated position on the sixth floor. Could they fit into the phonebox-lift?

At this point we are about to meet the BBC's health and safety person, Wendy Pelaez. She will become a hero of the story, which begins with the following email from Tom.

Email Number 1

From: Tom Bigwood
Sent: 22 October 2015 17:44
To: Wendy Pelaez
Cc: Jon Skelton
Subject: Shetland Pony

Hello Wendy

I know Jon has been in touch with you about our item on Monday 14 December when we are previewing the Shetland Pony Grand National at Olympia.

We plan to have one of the competing Shetland ponies in studio 6C at Western House. One of the child jockeys and the Shetland pony's owner and Shetland Pony Grand National organiser Vera Akehurst will also be part of the item.

Vera says her ponies are comfortable in lifts they fit in. She is able to come to London next Tuesday or Wednesday to have a look at studio and route to it.

All the best

Tom Bigwood

@thetombigwood

BBC Radio 2's Jeremy Vine Show

Western House

99 Great Portland Street

London W1A 1AA

Tom, a seasoned producer later promoted to a job on *Panorama*, had possibly glossed over some of the complexities of his plan. The words, 'Vera says her ponies are comfortable in lifts they fit in', will have rung alarm bells in Wendy's office. A day later came her reply.

Email Number 2
From: Wendy Pelaez
Sent: 23 October 2015 09:09
To: 'Tom Bigwood'
Cc: Jon Skelton
Subject: RE: Shetland Pony

Hi Tom

Yes. Jon mentioned it yesterday. It's not a common scenario – so I do need to think about this one. There are some 'what if?' questions. Obviously my first suggestion would be to do this outside the building on the piazza, but I understand you don't want to do that. I am about on Tuesday, so would very much like to meet the Trainer if I can. That way I can ask some safety questions (as I don't know much about Shetland Ponies).

I can do Wednesday at a push, but it would mean me having to change a few things in my diary. I wasn't planning on being in the building that day. I am waiting to speak to one of the Senior Facilities Managers, as I have a few building-related matters I want to check with him. My main concern is obviously the welfare of the animal. Specific issues I will need to consider are –

a) Arrangements for feeding and watering the animal while on site
b) Arrangements for collecting and disposing of animal waste, and cleaning the studio afterwards if there is an incident
c) What sounds/environments/activities/things are known to 'spook' a Shetland Pony?
d) How will we get the animal in and out of the building? The Radio 2 lifts are really small and would be a confined space for the pony
e) If the lift gets stuck, how will we get the animal out in an emergency?
f) How would we manage evacuation of the animal (and the occupants of the building) at the same time, if the fire alarm goes off?
NB The fire alarm is a very loud siren. It might also spook the animal.
g) I am sure all lifts in the building go straight to ground if the fire alarm is activated, so in the event of a fire we would have to get the Shetland Pony down six floors of stairs. *Is it possible to lead the animal down*

six floors of stairs along with the occupants of the building at the same time?

h) Will the animal (and the usual production staff and a child) fit into the studio on the 6th floor?

i) Do we have to make sure the studio temperature is cool/warm for the animal?

j) Do any staff working in the area have any specific allergies, connected with animals or specifically Shetland Ponies?

So I have a few questions, which I am happy to discuss further with the trainer, when he/she comes in next week?

W

Wendy Pelaez
BBC Safety
BRITISH BROADCASTING CORPORATION
The BBC Safety App is here: http://www.bbc.co.uk/safety/resources/safetyapp/

Wendy obviously thought quite carefully about the issues raised by elevating an unspecified number of Shetland ponies, for she then followed up with an email to a senior colleague.

Email Number 3

From: Wendy Pelaez
Sent: 27 October 2015 12:29
To: Tony Wood
Subject: Shetland Pony in Western House, 14th Dec

Hiya Toan

See below. This came through to me, via Jon. The production team initially spoke to him about it.

After sending the below out, I had a chat with Scott Nobel (who shared the same questions as me). The trainers are now coming in on Monday at 1400. I am meeting them and the production and I have invited Charlie Muir (the FM).

Nothing for you to do – this is just FYI.

We didn't want to bother you about this when you were on leave, as we knew it could wait until you got back.

W

We are seeing into the heart of the BBC here. Good people, burdened by responsibility, all trying to make the programme happen while conscious of the obstacles.

Email Number 4

From: Tony Wood

Sent: 29 October 2015 20:01

To: Wendy Pelaez

Cc: Phil Jones-LBH; Jon Skelton

Subject: RE: Shetland Pony in Western House, 14th Dec

Hiya – I am sceptical this can happen in the studio to be honest.

What if the lift is broken on the day, what will the show do then? Also, what if it works on the way up and then breaks so we can't get it down again until it is repaired? What is the SLA on the lift repairs? What is the weight limit on the Western House lifts? Can the lift accommodate the animal and its handler? As you say, the evac situation is an interesting poser. We can hardly have a PEEP for it, security staff cannot be held responsible for its safe evacuation.

Phil – as you know, I'm totally all for pushing the boundaries but I think there is a strong chance there will be some risks we cannot realistically mitigate. Even if the visit on Monday shows that the route would work, there are plenty of other risks we may not be able to satisfactorily deal with. I have not shared these thoughts with Tom because I absolutely do not want to dampen any creative endeavour but as editor it is something that definitely needs to be on your radar sooner rather than later. What do you think?

Thanks

Tony

At this point the project looks doomed. The Shetland ponies will have to stay outside the building, and the team will only be able to make the item work by coming down to meet them on the stone piazza. But then Wendy turns superhero.

Email Number 5

From: Wendy Pelaez
Sent: 02 November 2015 15:31
To: Tony Wood; Phil Jones-LBH
Cc: Charlie Muir-EXTERNAL
Subject: RE: Shetland Pony in Western House, 14th Dec

Hi both
If I am honest, my initial thoughts on this idea were sceptical – I really didn't think this was going to be possible.
But I was wrong. I just met with Charlie & Nikki (Facilities Managers for the building), Tom (Jeremy Vine Show) and Trainers from the Shetland Pony Grand National. We ran through the plans and discussed the below:

a) <u>Arrangements for feeding/watering the animal while on site.</u>
The animal will have been fed/watered before and the Trainers will have snacks (Polo mints) to give the animal during their visit.
b) <u>Arrangements for collecting/disposing of animal waste (and cleaning the studio afterwards, if there is an incident).</u>
Trainer confirmed that the pony usually disposes of his waste in the horse trailer (as it is excited that it is going out, so usually gets rid of

*waste during the journey). But the Trainer will bring some material
which can be placed on the floor, to collect any waste from the animal.*
c) <u>What sounds/environments/activities/things are known to 'spook' the
animal?</u>
*The trainer will bring the calmest animal they have – the animal which
is taken into Great Ormond Street to see sick kids. The animals are
given a small dose of a specific drug, which is used when they travel on
an airplane. It can be used to calm the animal if required.*
d) <u>How will we get the animal in and out of the building (our lifts are
really small and would be a confined space for the animal)?</u>
Trainer confirmed that the animal and its owner will fit into the lift.
e) <u>If the lift gets stuck, how will we get the animal out in an emergency?</u>
*If the lift gets stuck, there is an onsite lift engineer to deal with lift
issues. The lift to be used on the day is also used to evacuate people in
wheelchairs from the building in an emergency. If for any reason the lift
is out of action, the animal can be carried down the stairs.*
f) <u>Evacuation of the animal (and occupants out of the building) at the
same time, if the fire alarm goes off (the fire alarm is a very loud siren
and might spook the animal).</u>
*If the alarm activates inside the studio, occupants of the building can't
use the lift. So the special Evacuation Lift can be called to the 6th floor
and the animal can be evacuated in that lift, while staff in the building
use the stairs. There is a disabled button on this lift which, when
pressed, will take you directly to the ground floor. The trainer confirms
that the siren will not spook the animal – they are used to loud noises.
Charlie Muir will be here on the day and will brief the security staff of
the arrangements for the day.*
g) <u>I am sure all lifts in the building go straight to ground if the fire alarm
is activated, so that would mean getting the animal down six floors (is
that possible?), along with the occupants of the building at the same
time.</u>
See answer to (e) and (f).
h) <u>Will the animal (and the usual production staff and a child) fit into our
Studio on the 6th floor?</u>
Yes, plenty of space.
i) <u>Do we have to make sure studio temp is cool/warm for the animal?</u>

The studio is cool and the trainer confirms this is a good temperature.
The temperature can be adjusted if needs be, on the day.

j) <u>Any staff working in the area have any specific allergies, connected with Shetland Ponies?</u>
Tom will check with staff working in the area.

k) <u>What if the lift is broken on the day, what will the show do then?</u>
See answer to (e) and (f).

l) <u>What if the lift works on the way up and then breaks so we can't get it down again until it is repaired?</u>
See answer to (e) and (f).

m) <u>What is the SLA on the lift repairs?</u>
Charles confirmed there is an onsite lift engineer.

n) <u>What is the weight limit on the Western House lifts?</u>
600kg or 8 People. The trainer confirmed the animal weighs approx.10-15 stone. There will only ever be one animal and one owner/trainer in the lift at any one time.

o) <u>Can the lift accommodate the animal and its handler?</u>
See answer to (n).

p) <u>Additional info:</u> It was decided that two ponies (1 x foal and 1 x pony) will be brought on the day. The owners will accompany their animals in the lift and into the green room area on the 6th Floor of Western. But the two ponies will be accompanied into the studio by their trainers and a Jockey. The ponies will be brought in one at a time. A carpet will be put on the floor of Western House Reception, for the pony to walk on. This is because the pony will have shoes on and the floor is tiled in reception. The piece is due to go on air at 1230 on Dec 14th, so it was agreed the two ponies will be brought up to the R2 Green Areas on the 6th Floor, 10 minutes before they are due on air. It is envisaged that the two ponies and their trainers will be in Western House for approx. 20/25 mins.

q) Myself and Tom will get together to write the RA for this planned activity.

Both Charlie and I don't see any reason why this can't happen, if the above arrangements are put into place.

W

Reading this exchange of emails gives me the feeling you get when the Proms play the loudest, most rousing tune at the very end, or Springsteen goes 'ONE, TWO, THREE, FOUR' at the climax of 'Born to Run'. My goodness – the BBC really is full of amazing people who want to put shows out, even if they don't work in programmes themselves, even if they work in Health & Safety.

The Shetland ponies duly came up to our studio on the sixth floor. To ensure they didn't hurt their shoed hooves on our tiled reception area, a red carpet was laid from the pavement to the lift, which was more than Angelina Jolie got. As I watched from behind my microphone six floors up, a blur of movement in the corridor outside gave way, finally, to a beautiful sight – the studio door opened and in came two ponies with children on their backs in a scene that could have been a Norman Thelwell cartoon. No accidents happened, the lift cables didn't snap, the carpet wasn't ruined and at no point was I knocked over. Result.

So Wendy, even though we've never met, I absolutely love you.

And Radio 2 lift – you are indeed Chekhov's Gun.

17. Have You Ever Been Pecked in the Eye by a Gannet?

The old model of journalism – the broken, clapped-out model that strangely most broadcasters still seem to use – is that your programme first finds an important person, then asks them an important-sounding question.

'Prime Minister, what is the future?' is the typical formulation.

The Prime Minister will then answer: 'You know better than to ask me a hypothetical question.' (James Callaghan actually used this answer in almost every interview.)

The interviewer will press: 'But we are talking about the future. The future matters. And you are the Prime Minister.'

The Prime Minister then chuckles: 'The future is taken care of, as you well know.'

'Thank you, Prime Minister,' sniggers the interviewer.

When did you last hear an interesting interview with an important person? Probably you never have. We have begun to realise, nearly a century after the broadcast interview was invented, that *people become important by not giving interesting interviews*. In 2013 the editor of *Newsnight*, Ian Katz, accidentally tweeted a rude comment about an interview with the Labour MP Rachel Reeves, saying it was 'boring snoring'. He quickly retracted, but in a *Financial Times* article a year later he substantially modified his apology, saying 'a large proportion of political interviews *are* boring snoring'. Even that was an underestimate.

In the article Katz lavished praise on the Conservative politician William Hague – 'candid, witty and emotionally intelligent' – but these qualities were ones he had only discovered outside the television studios in personal encounters. The article went on, hilariously: 'I honestly can't remember anything about any broadcast interview William Hague has given as Foreign Secretary, except perhaps that it involved Angelina Jolie.'

Now remember, this is a guy whose job depends on us believing the important person on his show later tonight might say something worth staying up for.

The problem is not that people who are uninteresting become important. It is that people who are important become uninteresting.

For example, the Foreign Secretary, Francis Pym, gave an interesting interview during the 1983 general election campaign where he said the public would be best advised not to give his boss, Margaret Thatcher, a big majority in the next election. He was quickly fired by her for saying it, so he was now an interesting chap who wasn't important any more. Gerald Ratner made an audience laugh by saying most of his jewellery was 'crap' and saw his entire business crater as a result (I met him recently – he said the disaster had caused him so much distress he had to spend seven years in bed. But he gradually came back to life, and is now an inspiring speaker and business leader, wiser and warmer than before). Rebekah Brooks told a parliamentary inquiry her newspapers had paid police for information and she had to endure the stress of a criminal trial with the threat of jail.

They all learnt the hard way. You can be important or you can be interesting, but you can't be both.

At home I sat down with Martha to watch *The World at War*, the all-time greatest documentary. It was made by Jeremy Isaacs in the mid-seventies. I thought it might be good for my daughter to see the Second World War explained country by country, year by year. At one point Hitler's secretary, Traudl Junge, begins speaking about her time in the Berlin bunker in the final days of the war. What she says is spellbinding. Then Hitler's valet Heinz Linge appears, describing how he removed the Führer's body ('dragging it, with my arm around his neck') after Hitler and Eva Braun had killed themselves.

'Isn't it funny,' remarked Martha, twelve, 'that the most

interesting people are the ones with the most boring jobs.'

As they say in darts: One hundred and eighty. She was bang on.

If you doubt the notion that *important people never give interesting interviews*, just try this test:

1. Think of an American president before 2016
2. Think of an interview he gave while in office
3. Think of a particular thing he said in the interview
4. Bet you can't do (3) or even (2)
5 Don't worry, I can't either.

So if high-profile people always give dull interviews, might it follow that low-profile people are the ones to listen to? Every time I see audience figures that put my show ahead of Radio 4's *Today* programme – ahead even though theirs is an hour longer, has four times as many staff, five times as many presenters, six times as many big-name guests and should be unbeatable with a breakfast slot – I wonder if it is because my 25,000 callers are just naturally more . . .

Er, how do I put this . . .

Um.

Compelling?

#awkward.

Of course, for an interesting answer you usually need a good question.

In July 2011, Michael Buckland discovered an injured gannet on a beach in Wales. The 38-year-old Cardiff man, walking with his girlfriend Alison Stanley, 48, found the bird apparently unable to walk or fly as the tide approached. They decided they should take it to higher ground in case it drowned. Buckland lifted the gannet from the sand and began carrying it across the beach on Gower.

He told BBC Wales: 'We were just walking along the beach . . . I was going to take it to the sand dunes. A family walked up with their dog. The dog was jumping up trying to get the gannet's tail and, as I looked down at the dog, all I saw was a beak coming straight towards my eyes.'

His left eyelid was slit in two and his right eyeball was left dangling from his face. Buckland staggered across the sand and tripped beside a rock pool. 'I put my right hand to my face and I felt there was a big hole where my eye was meant to be.'

A surgeon said the gannet had pecked him three times at least. 'The beak went through the centre of one eyeball.'

The eyelid needed twelve stitches and the surgeon said the right eye was unlikely to function again. Luckily the poor man had saved the sight in his left eye by blinking just in time. But Michael would have to give up his job as a welder.

The horrible story prompted a discussion on my show and the single question which is the title of this chapter.

Steve Wright came into my studio during the programme, looking serious. 'Oh —"Have you ever been pecked in the eye by a gannet?"' he repeated incredulously. 'That is the best question you have ever asked.'

Remarkably another listener rang who had also been pecked in the eye by a gannet, and although he was less seriously injured he told us you should never attempt to rescue an injured bird with a large beak. That single sentence is more interesting than anything a British politician has said on television in the last forty years. Maybe Rachel Reeves should have used that line on *Newsnight*.

I asked Eleanor Kiff, one of our producers, whether there were any questions we had asked on the programme which she remembered especially clearly.

'Yes,' she said, 'because we had a period where there was a run of remarkable ones and I noted them down.' She emailed me the list:

- *Did your glass coffee table spontaneously explode?*
- *Does your town have antisocial seagulls?*
- After a bus driver desperate for the loo veered off his route, and police had to set up a roadblock to stop him

going the wrong way down a one-way street – *Did you have a moment of madness when you were desperate for the toilet?*

- *Is your kettle louder than a lawnmower?*
- *Have you been showered with foul-smelling innards when the stomach of a dead whale exploded?*
- *Do you have an unsightly crack?* (The guest was a structural engineer.)
- *Have you been seduced by a Buy-One-Get-One-Free deal and regretted it?*
- *Have you ever been attacked by a goose?*
- *Did a glass paperweight set your house on fire?* (The answer, from about half our callers: yes. An ornament left on a windowsill will focus the sun's rays like a magnifying glass, 'and if I hadn't smelt burning I would have lost the house'.)
- *Have you never sent a text or an email, have the reading age of a two-year-old and are financially illiterate – yet, like Harry Redknapp, you have been very successful in life?*
- When Marks & Spencer are accused of 'selling a handbag that smells of fish' – *Have you ever had to return something because it smells?*
- After a tiny Nissan Micra is photographed carrying two sofas on its roof – *Have you carried something far too big on the roof of your car, and did it fall off?*
- *Is being a house-husband just an excuse to watch* Countdown?
- *How did you try to remove your wart?*

Ah, that last one. It was triggered – wrong choice of word – by the actions of Shaun Murphy from Doncaster. He had visited his doctor for the umpteenth time about a wart on his finger, and was prescribed yet another ointment which he knew would not work.

Murphy, a security officer at Markham Grange Nurseries, decided his Beretta shotgun was a better weapon against warts than any pill or cream. He had found the firearm in a hedge – *Have you ever found a shotgun in a hedge?* – and hung on to it without a licence. The day after seeing his doctor, Murphy drank several pints of Yorkshire bitter which he hoped would work as an anaesthetic. He sat down outside his caravan, stretched out his left hand, and aimed the shotgun at the wart.

There are a number of problems with this method of wart removal. A shotgun is not as accurate as, say, a surgeon's scalpel. A shotgun needs to be gripped strongly and aimed carefully, which is not really possible if you are firing at one of your own hands. It also has powerful recoil. Strong beer may work as an anaesthetic, but it also makes a person less accurate with a firearm.

'I didn't expect to lose my finger as well as the wart when I fired the shot, but the gun recoiled and that was it,' he told local reporters afterwards. 'The wart was gone and so was most of my finger. There was nothing left of it, so no chance of reattaching it.'

The noise of gunfire also alerted police to the weapon he should not have had, and he was prosecuted. In court Richard Haigh, defending, said Murphy had been 'a victim of his own stupidity'. After being given a suspended sixteen-week prison sentence, the man himself insisted he had no regrets.

'I'm happy with that,' he said outside Doncaster Magistrates' Court. 'The best thing is that the wart has gone. It was giving me a lot of trouble.'

It is fair to say that Shaun Murphy may not have been the smartest person on God's earth. He is possibly not the man you want in charge of the Large Hadron Collider, or indeed a wart treatment unit. Personally, I don't like the word 'stupid', because it is so often used maliciously. Everyone has a right to exist and Mr Murphy's life has as much value as yours or mine or a cabinet minister's. His *actions* were undoubtedly stupid. And stupid actions do make formidable lessons.

After 25,000 calls there are at least two discoveries that surprise me. Important people do not say interesting things; and stupidity is the best teacher.

Somehow they seem linked. The best person to do an interview about safe swimming at high tide is not a lifeguard. It is someone who went in when there was a red flag, got pulled under by a current and nearly drowned.

Stupidity is not the preserve of the stupid. All of us make dreadful blunders. I went to a formal drinks reception at the Chinese Embassy, just down the road from Broadcasting House. One of the deputy ambassadors had only just arrived in London, and, in faltering English, she was politely asking me all about the BBC. 'We are – very close – to you,' I explained, doing the British thing of raising my voice and speaking in staccato.

Trying to help her recognise the building, literally fifty yards beyond the window, I explained that it was 'shaped like a ship', but as I could see this was only causing confusion I drew the outline on a napkin. 'This is the front, the doors are here, and you walk in this way.' With my pen I showed where a visitor should approach to reach the entrance doors and the reception area. To my intense puzzlement she looked horrified and moved quickly away.

I was also appalled when I looked back down at the napkin and saw what I had drawn.

From that incident I learnt to think carefully about using a sketch in the event of a communications problem. I was stupid. Everyone is stupid at some point. Sophie Ellis-Bextor famously sang, 'Heartbreak make me a dancer'. Well, stupidity makes a great teacher.

In Florida a woman called Katie Gaydos walked past a street worker using a leafblower. It bellowed debris into her eyes.

Unable to see for a moment, the mother-of-two begged the blower-man to reach quickly into her handbag for her eye drops. He accidentally pulled out a tube of superglue. Katie promptly glued both her eyes shut. She said later: 'As soon as I felt it burn, I screamed and called 911.'

Doctors saved her eyelids and her sight (after briefly refusing to treat Katie because her insurance had lapsed). Remarkably, when we covered the story – *Have you ever mistaken superglue for eye drops and glued your eyes shut?* – we had no fewer than *four* listeners call us to say they had done exactly the same. Two had simply picked up the wrong bottle from their bedside table in the night.

As a newspaper journalist, you could search for a fortnight for those four stories and not find them. But a live show with millions listening is such a powerful research tool, a turbo-dragnet.

* * *

If wise people don't have much to teach us, and important people are boring to listen to, then this is the perfect moment for me to introduce my hero.

Larry Walters was an American who, as a boy, had dreamed of being a Top Gun pilot. Sadly, poor eyesight meant he had to be content with a job as a trucker in North Hollywood. But he never totally let go of his dream. Despite not having a pilot's licence, he would often sit in the backyard of his house and watch planes fly overhead.

One day Walters, by now aged thirty-three, hit on an adventurous plan. He bought forty-five weather balloons from a local army surplus store and, stacking them in five tiers, lashed them to a tethered lawn chair bought from Sears. He sat in the chair with a large bottle of fizzy drink, a CB radio, a parachute, a camera and an airgun – thinking that, once the chair was released, he would float gently upwards. If he went too far into the sky he could shoot some of the balloons and return slowly to earth.

There are various accounts of what went wrong for Larry. The first suggests that he had lashed the chair to the bumper of his Jeep, and after a while he simply got bored of only being thirty feet above the ground and ditched the safety line completely. The second is that he boarded the deckchair on the roof of his girlfriend's house while friends pulled on the guy ropes to stop it flying away. But the guide ropes were sliding back and forth against the sharp edge of the roof, and before they knew it one frayed and snapped and the friends instinctively let go of the others.

All the accounts we have agree on this point – on 2 July 1982, more by accident than design, Larry flew into the sky above San Pedro as if shot from a cannon. He reached for his CB radio and sent a message that he was sailing across Los Angeles Harbour towards Long Beach, into the huge area of controlled airspace around Los Angeles Airport.

On the ground, a group of local CB enthusiasts calling themselves 'REACT' picked up Larry's signal and recorded the conversation.

REACT: 'What information do you wish me to tell the airport at this time as to your location and your difficulty?'

Larry: 'Ah, the difficulty is, ah, this was an unauthorised balloon launch, and, uh, I know I'm in a federal airspace, and, uh, I'm sure my ground crew has alerted the proper authority. But, uh, just call them and tell them I'm okay.'

Larry Walters had begun at thirty feet. His eventual altitude was not thirty, or three hundred, or even three thousand feet. At sixteen thousand feet – *three miles* above the ground – he levelled off. But he was now drifting into the flight path of Long Beach airport. Two pilots reported the presence of 'a man, in a lawn chair, with a gun'. This was a fully fledged emergency.

To force a landing – since at that height Larry was now freezing cold and feared losing consciousness – he fired pellets at several of the balloons but then accidentally lost his grip and dropped the gun.

Looking downwards, the balloonist saw the expanse of grass belonging to Long Beach Country Club and tried to force his craft to land there. As he approached the area he became entangled in power lines. There were sparks but miraculously, because of the plastic sheathing on the balloon tethers, Walters was not electrocuted. Fire crews arrived and cut power to the area. Parts of Long Beach were plunged into darkness while rescuers slashed the lines to the helium balloons.

Eventually the lawn chair dropped to a place where Larry could gingerly climb out onto the top of a wall. He disentangled the lawn chair and gave it to some local children as a souvenir.

He straightened up and looked around.

An onlooker apparently shouted: 'Why'd you do it, Larry?'

Larry Walters replied: 'A man can't just sit around.'

I love that line so much. There is a whole life of learning in those six simple words. *A man can't just sit around.* Can I have that on my tombstone?

After Larry's disastrous flight, the authorities announced they were throwing the book at him. The Federal Aviation Authority said they would take away his flying licence but soon realised he did not have one – either for planes or balloons. They settled on a fine of $4,000. Regulars at a local bar raised the money. Larry went on to make small sums on the chat show circuit, worked briefly as a motivational speaker and appeared in an early 1990s print advert for Timex watches.

© Martha Vine

The picture shows a good-looking, rugged man with an uncomplicated gaze, who 'apparently wears our moon dial watch'. Yeah, right.

After the advert, interest waned. There was no internet back then to allow the adventure to be globally enjoyed and analysed. You saved a story by scissoring it from the page and filing it in a metal cabinet. Those cuttings, like memories, literally faded; they grew yellow in newspaper libraries. Something similar seemed to happen to Larry. His confidence faltered. He began working as a security guard, telling colleagues he was saving to finance a second flight to the Bahamas. There was a broken relationship too.

On 6 October 1993, 'Lawn Chair Larry' hiked to one of his favourite spots in Angeles National Forest and shot himself through the heart. He was forty-four when he died.

He has since become more fabled than he could have imagined. There was a movie based on his flight called *Danny Deckchair*. The story is taught in American high schools, where teachers pose the question: Was Larry a fool or a pioneer? The founder of the Darwin Awards, Wendy Northcutt, who highlights fatal acts of human idiocy, named Larry as an early inspiration but said he could not be among those 'counting the human race down to extinction' because his folly had not cost him his life. She made a speech about him which I expected to hate for its mockery of a genuinely enterprising man – but actually, watching it, I sensed Northcutt's admiration for what he had done.

He also inspired others, with sometimes disastrous results. In November 1992, Yoshikazu Suzuki attempted the Larry Walters style of flight in Japan. He lifted off from Lake Biwa with helium balloons in a cluster. Suzuki was spotted floating above the Pacific Ocean by a Japanese coastguard and never seen again.

In April 2008, a Brazilian priest, Adelir Antônio de Carli, used a chair and – astonishingly – one thousand balloons for an ascent. His aim was to raise money to build a spiritual retreat for truck drivers. Sadly, the priest underestimated the power of helium.

He was last seen alive drifting out over the sea. Oil rig workers found his body.

The fact that people died trying to copy Larry Walters suggests there was a kind of madness in what he did. But genius and madness are brother and sister, as we all know. Many now see 'Lawn Chair Larry' as an aviation pioneer in the mould of Lindbergh or the Wright Brothers.

'It was something I had to do,' Walters said after his escapade. 'I had this dream for twenty years, and if I hadn't done it, I think I would have ended up in the funny farm. I didn't think that by fulfilling my goal in life – my dream – that I would create such a stir and make people laugh.'

There is a man exactly like Larry who is still alive.

When young people come to Radio 2 on work experience and are keen to help somehow, I always say: 'Can you get Philippe Petit on the show?'

I warn them it won't be easy. The Frenchman became known as the 'Man on Wire' – the title of a movie about his death-defying high-wire walk between New York's Twin Towers in 1974. He is another one whose lunacy electrifies me, possibly because I know my cautious, risk-averse, mapped-out life doesn't reach to those heights.

No one has yet managed to get hold of Petit for my programme, but one day a trainee will wave a phone at me and say: 'Jeremy – Mr Petit is on the line, just asking how long you want the interview to be.'

Then we could pose the question to our listeners: *Have you ever put a cable between two tall buildings and tried to walk between them?*

Or, had we been around in 1982 and covered Larry Walters: *What happened when you attached forty-five balloons to your garden chair?*

And I bet someone would ring us on both.

Strange, isn't it? All the power and focus of modern news programmes are dedicated to rounding up presidents and prime ministers, who sweep into the studio with their entourages and then tell us . . . nothing at all. Given the choice, wouldn't we far rather hear from a man or woman living an otherwise unremarkable life who has lit up our skies with a single flash of madness? We can learn more from a moment of foolishness than a lifetime of wisdom. To sum it all up in five words:

From the ordinary, the extraordinary.

18. 'It's Big, and the Cat's Gone Missin'

This is the best thing I ever saw on TV. It was on a satellite channel. I was tuning around, found it and hesitated at the image.

A professional animal-catcher – complete with net on a pole and ranger's hat – emerges from his Jeep, which has drawn up in the driveway of a middle-aged woman.

She emerges from the house in 1950s spectacles, with a hairdo that makes me think of the Jeff Foxworthy line: 'You know you're a redneck when your wife's hair gets caught in the ceiling fan.'

She tells the ranger: 'Thank GAWD you came.'

I can tell from the accents the pair are in the southern states of the USA. The man asks the homeowner what the problem is. She replies with the immortal words: 'I don't know what it is, but it's big, and the cat's gone missin'.'

Drawn in, I check to see what the programme is called. The digital listing says something like 'I'VE GOT A WILD ANIMAL LOOSE IN MY HOUSE'. The man is now pushing his fingers into what look like washing-up gloves. The woman says: 'It's hidin' in the garage.'

I can feel the tension, and I'm watching from a distance of thousands of miles. He goes into the garage.

The ranger – who, the commentary tells me, is someone whose job is to find and remove home-invading wild animals – searches the garage carefully. When he pulls off the top of the biscuit tin there is a snarl. Back down goes the lid.

'I think we need the other gloves.'

Honestly, I'm sure he said that. He fetches a much bigger pair made of green rubber. The animal hiding in the garage turns out to be a possum, which looks like a badger with a hangover; razor-sharp teeth and furious eyes. When the man opens the barrel again he is wearing the mega-gloves. He makes hypnotic movements with his hands as if waving away smoke, and grabs the animal.

Ten minutes later, with the possum safely locked in a cage in the boot of the Jeep, the cat skulks back into the house. The lady reacts with a scream of joy. Her pet had not been eaten, it had fled.

When people talk to me about all the new frontiers in media I think of the bespectacled lady with the deep south accent, and us all standing around in our fifties specs with bemused expressions. *'I don't know what it is,'* we are all saying, *'but it's big, and the cat's gone missing.'* There are so many reasons to look down our noses at new social platforms like Facebook and Twitter. My former colleague Jeremy Paxman, who now styles himself as a kind of Olympic grump, signed up to Twitter[4] towards the end of his time on *Newsnight* to see what the point was. The result was hilarious. Paxman joined on 24 January 2012, and launched his account with a tweet which said: 'Had a bath this morning.'

This was followed with: 'Just occurred to me. Where would we be without bath plugs?'

And finally, as he gave up the ghost: 'Grey skies. I think I might take an umbrella with me when I go out.'

He managed seven tweets in four years. Some people send forty a day.

It is pretty clear what happened here. A young producer on *Newsnight* told Jeremy that he really should be on Twitter. She enthused about it infectiously as only a young producer can, and the presenter – who would probably listen more to a junior than a boss, which is greatly to his credit – reluctantly got stuck in and found the whole experience meaningless.

---

[4] Just in case you haven't ever used it, Twitter allows a person to send messages to other people – but crucially, the exchanges are public. It's a bit like pinning a letter to a noticeboard. You can also upload brief thoughts which are seen by everyone who follows you.

Paxman elaborated in an interview a few months later. 'Twitter? This is an activity for people who have got nothing going on between their ears, or nothing going on in their lives. I don't want to lead anyone anywhere. I want to find things out. I have no thoughts that I want to share with people . . . I don't want people to follow me.'

Nothing going on between their ears, or nothing going on in their lives. Let's not make this easy by pointing out that Stephen Hawking is on Twitter. Or the Queen, or the Pope. As well as Usain Bolt, Stephen Fry and the Dalai Lama . . . or that a search of proper philosophers with more than a thousand followers identified 345 of them on Twitter . . . or that you can also find the so-called 'science Kardashians' – people like Brian Cox, Richard Dawkins, Michio Kaku (theoretical physicist), Tim Berners-Lee (invented the web), Neil deGrasse Tyson (New York astrophysicist with 5.92m followers) or Marcus du Sautoy (mathematician). No, we can find a better rebuttal.

If Jeremy were to interview himself, he might well take issue with the statement: 'I don't want followers.'

'Really?' he would say. 'I put it to you' – he is now leaning forwards across the studio desk towards himself – 'that as the longest-serving presenter of *Newsnight*, a nightly news programme that only survived because people watched it, you have spent your entire career wanting followers. In the *Newsnight* office they would have been called 'viewers'. But viewers and followers are the same. You would not have had a programme without them.'

'Um –' the Paxman-guest would start, cowering a little.

'OR WOULD YOU HAVE BEEN PREPARED,' continues the Paxman-host in his most menacing key of foghorn, 'to sit in a dark room and read the news to a wall? OH, COME OFF IT!'

There is nothing wrong with wanting followers. Jesus Christ started with twelve of them. Jane Austen wanted them – she wrote for people she had never met. Rembrandt painted portraits for drawing rooms he had never entered. It didn't make them trivial people.

The last of Jeremy's objections is perhaps the most serious. He has 'no thoughts I want to share'.

I remember presenting *Newsnight* with Jeremy Paxman in the early 2000s. He was the main man. I was the spotty kid who did the show when he was busy elsewhere. Basically I got three years' flak for not being Paxo and then left for Radio 2 by the same exit they used for the bins. My leaving do was held *in a pub garden in the middle of winter*. But there were some superb moments along the way and I ended up genuinely admiring my senior colleague, who, behind that blunderbuss exterior, always seemed quite tentative, even a little shy.

One day an envelope arrived on my desk with the word JEREMY on the front. Thinking it was for me, I opened it. Inside was a large photo of the three *Newsnight* presenters (Paxman, Kirsty Wark and me). On the white strip at the bottom was written a single, mysterious sentence:

I have absolutely nothing to say.

This was very puzzling. I couldn't fathom it at all. I sat there staring, wondering what it meant. Was the line aimed at me – could it be some kind of threat? Or a coded message of encouragement to the junior presenter?

But then I found a sheet of paper inside the envelope with the following typed on it:

> Dear Jeremy,
> As this is for auction, we wondered whether
> you might be able to elaborate a little on this
> one sentence? It would help us very much.
> Yours sincerely. . .

And I understood. I had opened someone else's post. Guiltily sliding the photo and note back into the envelope and resealing it, I had a pang of pity for Paxo. A charity asks him to inscribe a photo with a meaningful message, he does the decent thing and writes a line that is actually quite profound when you consider who he is, and the people then send the photo back to him to ask for more. To me, 'I have absolutely nothing to say' is a great one-liner from a man paid to speak.

When Jeremy Paxman says about Twitter, 'I have no thoughts that I want to share', I have a lot of sympathy. The bathplug tweet underlines the difficulty of being interesting. But having 'absolutely nothing to say' does not debar a person from social media. Having spent the last five years on Twitter quite a lot, and Facebook just a little, I think I have only recently grasped the fundamental principle behind them all. The Bible told us: 'It is better to give than to receive.' But social media is the opposite of the Bible.

On Twitter, it is better to receive than to give. I laughed on a bus when I saw this, posted by @alicewhitey – someone I don't even know – when Leicester City were close to clinching the Premiership: 'Well done to my boyfriend for jumping up and shouting "FUCKING YES!" when Leicester scored, while we're in the middle of a christening.'

After a UKIP councillor in Oxfordshire said storms and floods in England might be caused by the government's support for gay marriage, an account called @UKIPWeather started announcing a series of made-up news stories:

UkipWeather @UkipWeather · 19 Jan 2014
A lingering look between 2 men at a gym in York has sparked concerns from residents living near the River Ouse

UkipWeather @UkipWeather · 19 Jan 2014
High winds at a garden centre in Kent after 2 men were spotted heading towards the plants without stopping to look at the ride-on lawnmowers

UkipWeather @UkipWeather · 19 Jan 2014
Council gritters are on high alert after a man in Peterborough went into a pub and ordered a glass of white wine

Another example came in while I was writing this chapter. I switch on my phone and can't stop laughing. A reporter I follow has shared this screengrab from a person called James Doleman, who captioned it 'Still my favourite journalistic line ever':

CNN reports that, according to a senior park official, Cecil the lion's brother Jericho, who is also a lion, was killed on Saturday in Zimbabwe's Hwange National Park.

I show it to my wife. She laughs too. Then I do what you do these days, and share it with my 600,000 followers.

Later I looked at how @jamesdoleman describes himself. He is a 'freelance legal/tech reporter' based in Glasgow. But he could equally have been in Alaska. For a second James and I were connected. I follow him and see he is tweeting every minute from the courtroom where the trial of Mazher Mahmood is taking place. A complicated story, the case of the 'fake sheikh' journalist who framed a celebrity to get his scoop. I discover I am fascinated by Mahmood and follow every twist. From a lion to a snake.

So yes, I may have absolutely nothing to say myself. But if, like Paxman, 'I want to find things out', a place where 320 million active users keep bumping into each other is a great place to start.

Some of those users are as dull as emulsion. Others are geniuses without even knowing it. Within four weeks in 2013 there was news of Margaret Thatcher's death and the resignation of Sir Alex Ferguson from Manchester United. One person with only a few dozen followers tweeted, 'Thatcher dies, Ferguson resigns. Somewhere in Liverpool there's a Scouser with a magic lamp and only one wish left' and the tweet was shared by millions. To me that is a poem in 114 characters. It is written by an ordinary mortal – a milkman or a magistrate – not for money but for joy. Why would you depend on paid hacks to tell you what the news is and what they think of it? Why did we ever let so-called 'professional journalists' control the supply lines?

There is a sweet moment of dialogue in Hitchcock's *Rear Window*, made in 1958. James Stewart plays a slightly self-important photo-journalist out of action with his leg in plaster, sat by his back window. Trying to persuade him that their relationship is the key thing and his precious career in journalism may not be as important as he thinks, Grace Kelly tells Stewart: 'It's ridiculous to say it can only be done by a specially anointed group of people.'

No wonder everyone in my industry is frightened. In an old house, the pipes bang in the night. In journalism the noise you hear is knees knocking.

My father-in-law used to get the *Independent* delivered to his out-of-the-way home in Devon by a man in a van. The fellow pootled up the steep driveway, dropped off the paper, did a laborious three-point turn and drove away. Feeling I was watching something that future generations would not believe had ever happened, I even took a picture of him heading back down the drive one day:

Let's not even think about the environmental impact. The arrangement looked preposterous. Someone in a vehicle carries news written on sheets of paper to a house . . . where that news, written yesterday, is read and dropped in a bin . . . then picked up tomorrow by another man in a slightly bigger van who drives it away to incineration. Surely something had to give?

In the end it was not the man with the van who vanished, as I had expected, but the newspaper. The *Independent* stopped printing. And that is a scything message to professional journalists – *We, the audience, no longer need you to tell us what is going on and what we think of it. We are just going to tell each other.*

That message is just a version of the i-Power being celebrated in this book. Paxman is an insurgent, a rebel, a man who likes to tear down the houses of the holy – why would he hold out against social media? Twitter is just doing the job he retired from.

I mentioned the magic lamp. There was a similar moment of joy – and realisation – when an investigation revealed that Findus Beef Lasagne contained horsemeat. I don't know whose tweet this was originally, because so many people copied it, but I was so angry I hadn't thought of it myself I swore at the ceiling. 'Mafia are getting lazy. Woke up to find half a Findus beef lasagne in my bed.'

Not that I could have thought of it. Whoever wrote that is a genius.

* * *

In 2016 a 15-year-old boy was walking through a park in Romford. I will call him Ben. He was listening to music on his phone and, in the late autumn sun, life didn't feel too bad. Ben was the young lad we all know and perhaps the young lad we were ourselves – not especially tall, perhaps a little geeky, exuding the existential uncertainty which seems to be generated by the rapid transit from boy to bloke. He was casually dressed in dark tracksuit bottoms and a grey flannel top, with the mop of thick hair all teenagers get when they walk past the barber's a few too many times.

From what I can see in the video of the incident, Ben is waylaid by three older boys – aged seventeen, apparently – who start speaking to him. You see Ben's posture change very slightly, weight on his back leg, shoulder slightly turned away, as if his body knows something isn't right here. He has not noticed the fourth lad, standing off to the side, filming them all. We have already mentioned the case of the bystanders who filmed a murder; now we are about to encounter the criminals who film their victim.

Ben is listening to the older boys, two white and one black, still holding his phone while it plays music.

Suddenly a fist comes out of nowhere and connects with the side of his head. A single punch can kill. This one is delivered with colossal force. He had no warning – it's a classic 'sucker punch' of the kind cowards use. Ben falls to the ground and drops the phone. His legs give way as he struggles to stand. When he gets back on his feet, woozy, he is punched even harder in the head and his legs buckle. Now he is lying flat out on the ground, semi-conscious. The older boys draw closer, giggling and teasing him.

'You got dropped, bro,' one says. 'Get up big man, get up.' In the only moment of mercy, the lout with the camera calls out: 'Don't stamp on him.' Now he zooms in on Ben, still dazed and crying on the ground. One of the boys kicks him.

Again they taunt him. 'Why you crying on the floor, bro?'

Sadly, there are lots of videos like the one Ben is in. That is a powerful indictment of the online world. On the face of it, the internet seems to prompt cruelty, then spread it. We did once ask the question on Radio 2, 'Does the internet show how the Third Reich started?' because it seemed to us that one lesson of the web is that if you give people anonymity, a lot start behaving in a disgusting way. One listener said that having Twitter in the 1930s would have given Germans who liked to wear uniforms a safe space to be fascist in, and stopped them carrying out real-life invasions . . . I am not so sure. It could also have allowed Hitler to network more effectively.

We should also – while we go through the rap-sheet – mention trolling. Who are these people who sit in their bedrooms, presumably wearing anoraks their mothers bought them, firing off abuse at anything that moves? I saw one of my closest BBC friends, the weather forecaster Carol Kirkwood. She confessed she had been upset by constant messages from someone called Zak. I was cross on her behalf and said I would try to help. When I got back to the office I looked up the exchanges, of which the ones below are the least offensive.

I saved them by hitting screengrab. Then I messaged Zak with the screengrab attached. 'You're obviously a big guy. So instead of upsetting my friend with these horrible messages, can you tell us who you are?'

The message was public. The troll was silent.

'Don't send Carol any more of these disgusting messages,' I continued, fired by indignation (I hope I don't sound too sanctimonious). 'I am aware of your regular account changes to hide yourself.'

And finally – 'If it ever happens again I will take steps to find out who you are and expose you.'

At last Zak surfaced. Are you ready for his reply?

It beggars belief, doesn't it? *If she didn't like it*. In flights of fancy I think I should set up a troll-busting operation with the motto: 'CHANGING THE WORLD, ONE TROLL AT A TIME'. During our exchanges scores of other Twitter users piled in to condemn Zak and he withdrew injured. But maybe he will reopen his account tomorrow under a different name and spray juvenile fluid at another woman unlucky enough to be doing a job in the public eye. Even if he has been taken out, there are a million more Zaks. Troll-busting would be a full-time job for a nation-state, let alone a person.

When I said there were lots of videos like the one Ben was in, I used the wrong phrase. If you are Ben, there are no others. The film of his beating in Romford is the only one that matters – Ben seeing himself being beaten up and knowing that the images will probably be searchable on the internet for a thousand years. Hospital doctors examined him that day and discharged him, but I have a relative who got Parkinson's at the age of thirty-five and is convinced it came from a single blow to the head he suffered fifteen years earlier in London, when a man hit him from behind with an iron bar. So the news that Ben had the all-clear from the Romford doctors may not be as clear-cut as it sounds.

The distressing clip popped up on my timeline on Twitter, shared by a Radio 2 listener I follow. With mixed feelings I watched it and passed it on, urging people to get in touch if they recognised the thugs. Gabby Logan, the sports presenter, shared my post and thus the video travelled outwards across the online world with phenomenal speed, like the web shot from Spider-man's wrist. The police had names before sundown and made arrests.

There you have the good and bad of the new world. There used to be four dimensions, and now there are five. The world is now HWDTO – height, width, depth, time . . . and online. The internet is additional space. It may well be that Ben was beaten because the older boys wanted fame in the fifth dimension; it is certainly the case that they were identified because the web really did act like a web, trapping them within hours.

So – good or bad? Bad that Ben may have to see that video again because I am not sure it can be fully purged. Bad that the thugs may have been motivated by some perverse idea of 'fame' to hurt him in the first place. Good that decent people around the world expressed outrage at an event which, fifteen years ago, would not have got beyond the pages of the *Romford Advertiser*.

What happened to Ben meant something personally to me. I am not a big Facebook person, but I do have a page. Whereas Twitter compels its users to express everything super-succinctly, in 140 characters or less, on Facebook you can take more time and space.

So I started to type. As I typed, I got completely lost in my own thoughts about what had happened to Ben and what happened to me – at the time an ungainly 15-year-old just like Ben.

Because it was the same thing.

The same punch.

I wrote most of my post at Paddington Station as I waited for a train to take me to the Appledore Book Festival in Devon. When the train pulls out of the station just after 3 p.m., I click 'Publish' and send it to my Facebook page. Then I open a book and think no more about what I have written.

<If anyone knows the victim of the Romford bullies please could they pass this letter on to him.>

Dear Romford 15-year-old – who I'll call Ben –

I don't know your name, and it's good that I don't, because I am sure you do not want to be associated with that video of the bullies savagely punching you to the ground.

Bullies? They are worse than that. I was really shocked by what I saw. Loads of people were disgusted.

You are just fifteen. The lads who attacked you without warning are apparently seventeen. Grown men.

Ben, something similar happened to me. I was a sensitive young teen, always trying and failing to be cool . . . never athletic enough, never hip enough, a late developer, crazy hair, with uncool parents who thought church was the main event. I worshipped indie bands – Joy Division especially – in the way that sensitive souls do. I wanted to be a jock, but I was a nerd. Maybe you recognise that.

One day I was at a party and spoke to a girl. Apparently she was the girlfriend of someone important. He sent his friend to beat me up. The friend said, 'Excuse me, can I tell you something?' and because he was shorter than me I had to lean down to hear him. Having moved my head within range he punched me as hard as you got punched. I had never been hit before. The shock was unbelievable – violence does that. I went down immediately just like you. My mates, also sensitive souls, were too scared to help. They were gutted afterwards.

You feel humiliated. Your pride is hurt, your head is hurt – I had a gigantic black eye. A person can get very down over a beating. Some people think depression evolved in us as a way of keeping us safe if we lose a fight – the mind and body working together to prevent you re-entering the conflict for your own safety. It took me ages before I wasn't scared of being hit again. You look over your shoulder for a while, and you feel a primal fear. That is natural, Ben.

So I watched your video and saw myself. That guy who distracted me in 1980 could be the thug who hit you from behind in 2016 – such a coward.

Can I give you some advice? Don't think you have to be hard like them. I tried to be a tough teenager afterwards and closed myself off like a drum. I reacted to nothing and felt nothing. I especially struggled to tell anyone I loved them because I thought it was a sign of weakness. Then I got to university and found people like me who would never dream of punching someone, and my life opened up like a flower.

A kind lecturer was shocked when I proudly and foolishly told him I had never read a poem. He said, 'We'll change that,' and helped me understand the power of poetry. One day in my student room I read a poem and cried. I was alive again. Sure, I would never win a fight – I have never hit anyone in my life – but you don't need to hit people to succeed in your life. Quite the opposite.

The courts will decide who assaulted you and how to punish them. (To be clear, I have no idea whether any of the arrested individuals are connected to the crime.) In our society, what happened to you is thankfully now taken very seriously. But let me tell you something about the lads in the video.

In twenty years, when you're with the person you love and hopefully in a career you have a passion for, they will still be scumbags. They will be doing odd jobs for twenty quid – nothing wrong with that – but they will also be listening to shit music. Their cupboards will smell of gym sweat and cheeseburgers; they will always carry a knife. Each will own one suit which he wore to the funeral of a friend who died doing a wheelie on a motorway – by the way, they all wore the same baffled expression at the funeral service. They've gone from making the weather to being rained on, and they complain about it constantly. Two of them will have a bad drug habit, they swear profusely, and they are all, without exception, violent and contemptuous towards the women in their lives.

Those three are not something anyone wants to be with – their lives are already over. They hit you because they saw you have something different, a complexity and intelligence they can never understand.

Five per cent of people are good at fighting. I'm not one and nor are you. It is very important we let the five per cent fight each other. Live by the sword, die by the sword: the thug who beat me up was in hospital himself a year later after someone broke a bottle across his face.

Meanwhile, you and I can read poetry and listen to our favourite bands, and if we sometimes cry, there is no shame in that. To cry is to live. The people who attacked you are the walking dead.

Come into Radio 2 sometime and I'd be happy to show you around.

Yours, Jeremy

I took some flak from a couple of liberal friends for my choice of words. According to one of them the thugs 'might well be re-formed one day'. I was wrong 'to write off their chances in the future' and should 'remove the word cheeseburger' from the text. One friend seemed more worried about the thugs than the victim, but I took her point. Well, you live and learn. Maybe on another day I would phrase it differently, but the internet is always the first draft. That's what makes it feel so true. The point of the post is that it came from my heart. It wasn't planned and, with only 40,000 Facebook followers – on FB they are called 'page likes' – I never expected what followed.

The post was uploaded on that train to Devon on Friday. A million people had seen it by the following lunchtime. Looking at it now, four days on, Facebook tells me it has been seen by 1,390,107 users.

What is more remarkable are the comments appended to the post. There are more than 1,300. Many are from people intimately telling their own stories.

Ian, a little older than me, writes: 'Yes, I am 57, I remember at school being on a school trip and sensing I was going to be tar-geted. I could see by the looks on certain boys' faces they had me in their sights. I hung back on the trip and kept a safe distance. I saw the same boys chuck one lad in a river. I was told the same would have happened to me. I was not a big lad and had many friends but to this day it still hurts me.'

It is such an intimate story. So are scores of others. Daniel wrote: 'Never since I stopped it happening to me have I cried over the bullying. Like you said, I closed myself off and for the longest time couldn't express myself beyond basic interaction . . . In the years since it all got much better . . . Yet I have never cried about it. Much to my amazement, your post brought tears to my eyes.'

266

From Clare, a mother: 'I read this to my 15 year old last night as he was hit twice in the head and kicked in the face. 30 stitches later, one tooth lost and a black eye, I hope he took something from it.'

And now a different Clare, also a mum: 'I was bullied at secondary school for having ginger hair! Although mine was only teasing and humiliation – as a 13 yr old girl it did at the time feel like the end of the world! Now a mum of 3 (and so very proud of my fabulous red hair) I'm able to share that tough time with my kids and hopefully make them realise that all people can become a target of bullying and what doesn't kill you makes you stronger!'

Then a reply, not to me, but to Clare-with-red-hair, from Pixie: 'Clare, ditto! I tend not to say much on these public forums but I was bullied through most of my school life, again for being a bit "different" with auburn hair and freckles. I even wasn't moved up in senior school as my bully was in that class, meaning I could not do 'O' Levels. I worked bloody hard later as if to try to prove to someone. As a result I am now a young persons counsellor. I can't say I'm glad of what happened but I now love my auburn hair and freckles and my deeply satisfying career.'

Gradually I found myself checking my smartphone more and more to see each new post below my original. There were so many other touching stories like the ones above, so many moments where an adult felt they could finally share what had happened to them in childhood, or maybe speak about the difficult fix their own child was in. And, as with the Clare–Pixie exchange, conversations started *between* different readers. Which was remarkable to me.

The dad-dancing post I mentioned earlier – the one written about *Strictly* – was more like an old-style article, the journalist telling the reader something. That made my jaw drop because of the number of people who saw it, more than the entire circulation of a national newspaper.

But this was different. In the end it was not about Ben in Romford (who, by the way, happily came to the BBC for a tour of Radio 2 and beyond, and seemed to be recovered from his awful experience in the park). The post was not even about my reaction. It became about the experiences of the people who looked and responded. With the Romford post, I was not a leader but a reader . . . just as, on my show, I am the listener.

With old media, the key word was *tell*. You pay for a newspaper or switch on a TV and they tell you something. The key word of this new era is *share*. Social media is a conversation. And it's changing everything. It's so profound I struggle to describe what's happening . . . I just know it's big, and the cat's gone missing.

19. Mistakes Happen

They really do. When I arrived at the *Today* programme in 1989 to start my first BBC job, sitting underneath a dangerous shelving unit stacked with reel-to-reel tape recordings in fake leather jackets, the office was full of talk about what was described as 'a terrible moment'.

Naturally I asked for details. I was told a man had been booked to speak about playing tunes with his armpit. He would take off his shirt and place one hand under his arm. By moving the arm up and down like a chicken, at various speeds, he would entertain people with notes that sounded as bold as a French horn. It had taken him years of practice to be able to control the pitch. He was able to play 'Come On Eileen' in this way.

He duly appeared for a pre-recorded appearance. The man was speaking down the line from the BBC radio studio in Newcastle, so I was told. He was asked to say a few words to help the technician set the right recording level. They were about to start the interview when the producer in London pointed out that they should also listen to the volume of sound emitted from his armpit.

'Before we start,' the producer said, 'can we just hear you play a tune from underneath your arm?'

Silence at the other end.

'By putting your hand under your armpit,' she elaborated. 'I don't know if you need to take your shirt off to do it.'

More silence in Newcastle. For a second the producer wonders if the line has gone down.

Then, at the other end: 'I'll try.'

There was some rustling.

'Could you play "Come On Eileen"?' the producer said.

More silence.

Then a faint sound at the other end. An armpit exhaling. But only quietly, like a kitten breaking wind.

The producer is concerned.

'Are you able to play "Come On Eileen"?'

'I could try,' he said, 'but this is an odd way to take the recording level, I must say.'

The producer has a feeling in the pit of her stomach. 'You *have* come in to show us how well-known songs can be played from your armpit, haven't you?'

'No. I am here to talk about the pressure on manufacturing industry in the East Midlands.'

It turned out this was the Derby studio. The armpit man was sat in silence in Newcastle with no connection to London. The man in the Derby studio had been patched through by mistake while he waited for a slot on regional economics. It says something about the power of long-standing, trusted programmes that he actually *tried to play a tune from his armpit* when instructed.

The *Today* programme does have a lot of power. I remember, when I was working on it, feeling that you could usually ask for an interview and people would usually say yes. When I joined Radio 2, there was a definite sense that we were a couple of rungs lower on the BBC ladder.

This was confirmed when Sir Terry Wogan announced his retirement. He was presenting the breakfast show on Radio 2, and I recall the morning vividly. It was a Monday, and I was trying something new – walking the seven miles to work. I was wearing earphones so I could hear Terry chatting about this and that. The eight o'clock news came on, and then Wogan broke the biggest story when the newsreader handed back to him.

'I think this is the hardest thing I've ever done,' he said, and announced his retirement. It was 7 September 2009 and Terry would leave at the end of December.

I found it very touching. I can picture exactly where I was – on foot, in a long coat, emerging at the top right corner of Hyde Park, where the racetrack that is Park Lane meets Marble Arch. The sky was blue but the air had a wintry chill. That chill took me back to childhood. I was a seven-year-old in grey flannel shorts, sitting in our chilly family kitchen on a school morning. The dark was slowly lifting outside as Terry chatted on a tiny radio perched on the family breakfast table, the volume set so low his records could have been playing in a house two doors down.

From shorts to overcoat, Wogan had been my radio companion from the age of seven to forty-four, broadcasting his show across five of my decades with a break for television work between 1984 and 1993. There was no pressure on him to go even now. He was doing the most difficult thing in broadcasting, telling the world he was leaving before the first call for him to step down.

Wogan was a private man. He was extremely friendly to me when I arrived at Radio 2 – *I met him as he lived* – but later I found that even people who had known Terry for years were not sure how close to him they ever got. I once planned an evening out with an old university friend, whom I will call Ryan. He arrived at my office promptly, just before five o'clock. In those days Terry was on the breakfast show, but for some reason he was standing in reception too.

'Ah, Terry,' I said. 'I must introduce you to my old friend.'

'Not that old! Who have we here?'

'Ryan,' said the friend, shaking Terry's hand.

'Welcome to the madhouse.'

Since we were in the building, would Ryan like to look around? We said goodbye to Terry and headed upstairs to the studios. In the lift I told my friend how sorry I was that I never got to meet Kenny Everett properly. I have always thought of Kenny as the greatest DJ. Like his friend Freddie Mercury, he succumbed to HIV/Aids just before life-saving antiretrovirals came to the rescue. Had he lived, I told Ryan, I felt sure Kenny would be sharing this lift with me and I could tell him how much he inspired me as a teenager. I choked up a bit as I said it. He was the best.

'Not John Peel?' asked Ryan.

'Definitely in the top two,' I said as the lift doors opened on the sixth, feeling my own love of radio burst through. A lot of the music I still listen to was introduced to me by Peel on Radio One. New-wave bands from the period after 1977 like Theatre of Hate, Joy Division, Magazine, The Undertones.

'Did you meet Peel?'

'Nearly,' I replied. 'I blocked his car when I parked in Duchess Street in the eighties, which was a really chaotic BBC car park they closed down years ago. When I went to collect my car I was told he had been so furious he had to be restrained from kicking the door in. A shame, because it would have doubled in value with John Peel's footprint in the side.'

On reflection, I accepted my story did not exactly constitute a close connection with the great Peel.

We walked into the studio area. Steve Wright bounded towards us. Thirty-five years on the radio and still with the vocal energy he had in the eighties. Again, I introduced my friend. Wright was super-friendly as always.

'Now let's see if we can give Chris Evans a wave,' I suggested. At the time Chris was on the drivetime show. Sure enough, we poke our heads round the door of the control room for his studio – the same studio I use today – and Chris sees us and starts calling out on the air: 'Hey!! It's Jeremy Vine AND A FRIEND! Come in, friend and Jeremy!'

We walk into the studio itself and lark around a bit.

'You haven't been to the pub have you?' says Chris.

'Not yet. We're heading there now,' I reply, knowing my answer will be audible in that voice-on-the-other-side-of-the-room way.

'Who's your mate?'

'Ryan.'

'Ryan! From where?'

'We met at university.'

'Hi Chris,' says Ryan.

'RYAN FROM UNIVERSITY!' shouts Chris.

My friend and I head back down in the lift.

'Do you know,' I say, 'what happened there is quite remarkable. The five greatest DJs in the history of British radio are Kenny Everett, John Peel, Terry Wogan, Chris Evans, and Steve Wright. Two are dead – but you just met all three living ones in the space of twenty minutes.'

The lift doors opened back on the ground floor.

'Can we go to the pub now?' said Ryan. He is an investment banker, so he is not interested in other people.

All of those memories crowded my head as I emerged from Hyde Park on the morning Wogan announced his retirement. The weight of traffic increased as I approached Oxford Street and, wanting to hear a bit more from the man himself, I turned up my radio.

To my surprise, the great broadcaster said no more for at least ten minutes. Instead of him speaking about the momentous announcement and reflecting on how he felt – which is what I wanted as a listener – all I heard was a series of records. What had happened to him?

By chance, I saw his producer Alan Boyd later that day.

'It was very touching,' I said, 'but then Terry seemed to disappear, just as I wanted him to be speaking about it.'

'Ah,' said Alan, a charming Scot who had the most fantastic relationship with his presenter. 'What occurred was this. As soon as Terry announced it, the news started to spread. And the *Today* programme rang the studio straight away and wanted him on.'

'What?' I laughed. 'They wanted him to appear on Radio 4 *during his own show*?'

'Yes,' said Alan. 'They spoke to me. And I explained to them, "We are actually on the air at the moment."'

'So how did they respond?'

'The person at the other end just said, "This is the *Today* programme", as if I hadn't heard him right.'

I laughed.

'I tried again,' Terry's producer told me. 'I patiently explained that it was Wogan's job to present his own show before he appeared on anyone else's.'

273

'What happened?' I asked, fascinated.

'The voice at the other end just repeated more loudly – "YOU DON'T UNDERSTAND. THIS IS THE *TODAY* PROGRAMME."'

In the end Terry did indeed break from his own show while a series of records were played, to give an interview to the BBC's flagship news outlet. So while I was pushing my earphones deeper into my ears to hear even a word of explanation on Radio 2, Wogan was away on Radio 4 giving them the full story.

The corporation has those unwritten seniorities. For example, an obscure man at the heart of BBC News called Steve Mitchell actually ran the entire department for years without it ever being officially recognised. 'Steve' was the answer to every question. He sat in a small office in grey hair and a grey suit and pretended not to be important, when everyone knew there was nobody more central to the operation. Mitchell worked himself into the ground for his colleagues, but disaster struck when *Newsnight* became embroiled in the Jimmy Savile scandal. There was an inquiry. Conveniently for his bosses, 'Steve' was the answer to every question at the inquiry too. He bravely took the blame for the whole thing and, without a murmur of complaint, was eased out of a high window.

If the BBC has unspoken seniorities, it is also guided by its mistakes. 'We must never do that again' is a common call, as if a cyclist makes herself safer by constantly looking backwards. Every wall we hit comes as a total surprise.

Terry Wogan used to revel in all of this, of course. All his best jokes were about the BBC. I took the baton from him when he stopped presenting *Points of View*. If someone had had a meter that could measure levels of sarcasm and subversion and placed it next to Terry while he read the autocue on that programme, the device would have exploded.

The show is another example of the way the most old-fashioned formats are suddenly cutting-edge. The GITLUK shows – 'Get in touch, let us know' – are suddenly seen as the vanguard of the digital world. For years it was regarded as laughable that a programme could open the rear doors and invite viewers onto the back seat. In the twenty-first century the audience expects to pile into the front and take the wheel. Of course we all have to pretend the idea is brand new, when at least two of the shows I present (Radio 2, *Points of View*) have been doing it for decades.

Opinions are shifting and the change is fascinating to watch. In the nineties an adaptation of *Lady Chatterley's Lover* on BBC1 drew an avalanche of criticism. It was 'too steamy', 'too sex-obsessed', said Points-of-Viewers. The show was presented by Anne Robinson back then. She described how members of the public were seething about the close-ups, including 'a bare bottom'. The sex scenes between Lady Chatterley and the gardener were variously described as disgusting, primitive, unreal and unholy.

Spool forwards. In 2016 the BBC remade *Chatterley*. This time viewers reacted differently. There was, they said, *not enough sex.*

Terry would have loved that. But he was not around to enjoy it. The cancer he suffered took hold quickly. He hid the speed of its progress from anyone outside his immediate circle. His death was shattering for Radio 2 – if the station had a Mount Rushmore, all four of the faces carved in rock would have been his. He was the central figure of the old station and the new. Only rarely does a broadcaster bridge generations.

My producers were told that Wogan's memorial service would start at noon. The entire event would therefore be aired live on my programme and it was a hugely important moment for the network and the entire BBC. For the first time in anyone's memory, the news bulletin at noon was cancelled. Because my show normally starts at twelve, executives decided it would be safer for me to go on air half an hour early. That way I could be sure to hand to the outside broadcast team at Westminster Abbey well ahead of the formal start of the service.

It was made clear: *The beginning of the memorial service must not be crashed.*

The start time was fixed, to the second. For five minutes before twelve o'clock, an organist would play 'incidental music'. At bang on noon – not a second later – the Abbey choir would start singing. If I handed over late, and we interrupted the choir, it would be viewed as a major calamity.

Struck by the gravity of all this, I decided to hand over to the organ music at two minutes to twelve. That way there could be no danger of speaking over the choir.

As planned, Zoë Ball introduced my programme at eleven thirty. At 11.58, I announced: 'The news has been cancelled today. We are now going to join Sir Terry Wogan's memorial service at Westminster Abbey. You will hear some reflective organ music until exactly twelve o'clock, when a choir will start singing.'

This was what actually happened:

11.58	Organ music (serious, slow)
11.59	Organ music (slightly louder, graver)
12.00	Organ music (subsides, but continues)
12.01	Organ music (lots of twiddly bits now)
12.02	Organ music (shades of the Old Spice advert)
12.03	Organ music (quietening – something is about to happen)
12.04	Organ music (suddenly urgent again)
12.05	Organ music (into the theme from *Apocalypse Now*)
12.06	Organ music (*The Man with the Golden Gun*)

Eventually the man at the keyboard finally stopped, the choir piped up and the service began. What had happened? Apparently the Queen's personal representative arrived late – too posh to push, I guess – and we all had to listen to *eight minutes of organ*. Shall we take a moment to think of what Terry would have said about this, what facial expression he would have pulled, how he would have laughed with his happy band of colleagues – Ken Bruce, Alan Dedicoat, Pauly Walters, Fran Godfrey, John Marsh?

In a service which tried so hard to say the right thing that it felt too seriously suited and too wan for the colourful life it was celebrating, those eight minutes of accidental organ were the perfect tribute. Terry was celebrated most joyously by mistake.

*   *   *

For years I kept a collection of broadcast mistakes. When they happen I edit the clip and save the file. Then a Radio 4 newsreader, Diana Speed, read a story about Albert Speer's spell in Spandau Prison and I stopped collecting clips, because I could not imagine there would ever be a better one.

It happened as the newsreader introduced *Albert Speer's Walk Around the World*, a play by Michael Butt about the imaginary journeys of the Nazi architect during his time in prison.

The World at One had just gone off air and Diana Speed read the following: 'At two fifteen, Patrick Malahide stars as Albert Speer, or Prisoner Number Five as he was known throughout his twenty years in Spandau Ballet.'

She corrected it instantly.

' – in Spandau Prison, rather.'

The correction was not quick enough to stop Spandau Ballet trending on Twitter, with *Have I Got News for You* tweeting that twenty years in the New Romantic band 'would have been punishment enough'.

The joy of mistakes is that you can never really iron them out of a system, however good the system and the people in it are. 'It's Friday the fourteenth of October, let's tell you what's coming up on the programme,' said Naga Munchetty on BBC *Breakfast*. 'We are going to be joined by Scottish First Minister Nicola Sturgeon – we will talk to her about plans for a second referendum on Scottish independence.'

'I'm sorry,' interrupted her co-anchor Charlie State, 'we have very clearly run the wrong pictures. My apologies there.'

Throughout Naga's introduction, the show had run a full-frame image of a gorilla leaning against a tree eating a piece of bamboo.

The *Guardian* headline may not be bettered for several years.

BBC sorry for showing footage of gorilla instead of Nicola Sturgeon

Host tells viewers Scottish first minister is due to appear on breakfast show as video of escaped London zoo gorilla is broadcast

Errors spread ruin and a special kind of joy. When Jim Naughtie interviewed the Health Secretary Jeremy Hunt in 2010 and accidentally swapped his surname with the Rudest Word in the World, that should have been the end of the matter. Naughtie said later: 'I was there with lots of bits of paper and someone was shoving headlines in front of me and I said, "After the news we'll be talking to Jeremy C— " and all I could see behind the glass were arms going up in the air, as in "We surrender". And the guy who was passing the news bulletins to the late Rory Morrison went under the table laughing.'

As I say, that should have been the end of it. But mistakes have a tendency to spread themselves.

At our programme meeting that morning we decided we could not ignore the Naughtie bungle, so we would do a story where we asked listeners for occasions when they said the one thing they knew they should not have.

After the meeting I followed what was my routine back then – popped down the road to Daley Bread for a cup of their 90p tea. The modest café hidden in a side road off New Cavendish Street was run by a couple called Lyn and Rob, now retired. Without knowing it, the couple gave a profoundly effective counselling service to all their regulars.

'How are you?' 'Don't work too hard!' 'Get yourself in here for a cuppa, and we'll look after you. . .' 'Toast as always, Jel?' 'Would you ever move out of London? I don't mean out – I mean *out.*'

Their retirement was a terrible shame.

Unbeknownst to me, while I drank my second cup of Daley Bread tea, Andrew Marr was embarking on a discussion of the James Naughtie mishap on Radio 4's *Start the Week* with one of his guests.

David Aaronovitch: 'We heard this morning one of the primary examples of the Freudian slip that we are likely to hear on Radio 4.'

Andrew Marr: 'We are not going to repeat it quite in the terms that it happened, but – '

David Aaronovitch: 'But almost anybody now listening, who was listening this morning, will be aware of something that happened – '

Andrew Marr: 'Jeremy Cunt, the – (*Gasps, muffled laughter*) – the Culture Secretary had his name Freudianally transposed.'

David Aaronovitch: 'He did.'

So it had happened again. Any programme that uses the word 'Freudianally' should probably be considered for closure, but life must have seemed very unfair to Marr and his team that day. They had fallen down the hole in the street marked 'DO NOT FALL DOWN THIS HOLE IN THE STREET'.

When I got back to the office the editor was just putting the phone down after taking an important call.

'I don't think we can do the Naughtie story,' he said.

'Why on earth not?' I asked.

'It's too risky. I have just been speaking with the Head of Radio's office. There's been an edict from the Director General. He says the next presenter to say the word "cunt" on the air will be fired.'

We cancelled the item. And for a couple of weeks I had a Post-It stuck to my computer which bore these words in big thick marker pen:

THE NEXT PRESENTER TO SAY
C*** ON THE AIR WILL BE FIRED

because it seemed to me that really was the maddest, silliest thing the organisation had ever said to me.

While we are on bad language and mistakes – and hoping that I'm not straining your patience with all the swearing in this chapter – it was another c-storm that taught me a really important lesson about the internet. But once again, the lesson came via a mistake.

I had set up an alert on my phone. The phone would vibrate every time something with my name on it was uploaded to the internet. Google allows you to do this. The only small problem is that it is disastrous. You end up monitoring every corner of the internet for mentions of yourself, even parts no one else is visiting, and if you have any public profile it turns you insane quicker than inhaling mercury.

My phone buzzed one day. A link took me to the webpage, freshly uploaded.

The embarrassing photo had been taken during one of Radio 2's regular drives to appeal to younger listeners. Apparently people under thirty are more likely to listen to a programme if they sense the presenter is wearing bright green trousers. After this picture was taken it appeared in the *Observer* newspaper, which is how it came into the hands of the 'RESISTANCE IS USELESS' website. Underneath the snap – which clearly had not impressed the website authors – was a poll. I imagine you are heartily fed up of reading the c-word in this chapter, so I have scrubbed out the offending mentions.

> In the above photo,
> does Jeremy Vine look:
>
> ○ A c⬛⬛⬛
> ○ A prize ⬛⬛⬛
> ○ A total prize ⬛⬛
> ● A massive, biblically humungous mega-c⬛⬛t
> ○ All of the above
> ○ Very stylish (us c⬛⬛ must stick together)
>
> [Vote]   Results

Looking at this poll late one evening after my smartphone had buzzed with the Google alert, I felt some consternation. I was in the kitchen at home and it was time for bed. Of course it was possible to ignore the website. Shut the phone down and forget it. But that was a little tricky now I knew a poll was running. I wanted to see what sort of message the poll was sending me, how many thousands of people had taken part.

The problem was that I could not see the current tally of votes unless I cast a vote myself.

Sitting with the screen of my phone glowing in the dark kitchen, staring at the webpage, I realised I would have to vote and weighed up the options.

281

Going for the least critical (Option One: 'A c—') seemed to me to breach the BBC's guidance on impartiality. The same for the last (Option Six: Very stylish), which didn't feel right either. On the other hand, I did not wish to be overly condemning of myself. Voting for Option Four ('Massive, biblically humungous mega. . .') felt too harsh.

So I would go for the centre. Carefully, I drew my index finger across the screen and touched the circle next to 'A total prize c—'. Straight down the middle, Option Three.

The page refreshed, and now I saw how the voting was going. There had only been one vote, and it was mine.

20. What Makes Us ~~Human~~ Angry

Twenty-five thousand calls. 33,400 songs played. 3,000 hand-over conversations with Ken Bruce, totalling 200 hours. 12,000 jingles aired. 390 visits to the official allotment. One finger up my bottom.

Eh? Oh, sorry. The programme adopted an allotment in Wales right at the very start. I travelled there for a feature on prostate cancer after our allotmenteer, Terry Walton – TW the Second – fell ill with the disease. Rhondda's grow-your-own guru had been lucky to catch the symptoms early. He said all men over fifty should get themselves checked. So the BBC sent a doctor to his allotment in a van, which parked up by the cucumbers. Along with half a dozen of Terry's friends I joined the queue for digital inspection. The doctor wore latex gloves and there were curtains. I got the all clear; happily for Terry's wife Anthea and his adorable family, after a successful course of treatment he did too.

Increasingly, TW2's regular allotment slots strike a markedly different tone from the rest of the programme. Our gentle giant with the green fingers is all too often an oasis of calm in two hours of turbulence; a port in the storm. The programme seems to become more argumentative every year, and I am not sure why. Is bickering a national pastime? Why would we be crosser about things now than we were twenty years ago?

Our very-slightly-upmarket philosophy strand, which gives famous people the chance to talk about the life lessons they have learnt, has the title *What Makes Us Human?*. It has so far featured more than sixty voices. The rest of the show could be called 'What Makes Us Angry?' and has featured tens of thousands.

We are certainly inventive when finding things to grind our

teeth over. At the start of the book I mentioned lollipop ladies and Tony Blair. Maybe it is not surprising that people think Mr Blair can't see a country on a map without wanting to bomb it. But when we ran an item about lollipop ladies and a number of listeners railed at them because 'they block the roads, sometimes only taking one child across at a time', that did rock me back on my heels.

In 2016 we ran a story about public demands for the police to 'do something about clowns'. There was what journalists call *a spate* of clown sightings. Oh, we should point out that these terms you often hear on the news can be a little misleading . . .

SPATE	Something that happens all the time, but journalists have only just noticed it
TREND	Something that happens all the time, but an expert drew a graph
SURGE	The graph has a right-angle in it
CRAZE	Something that happens all the time, but a journalist's son or daughter has just started doing it
FAD	Something that never happens.

Your typical misleading headline – 'The number of people dressed as clowns has gone up by 100 per cent' – makes it sound like *every single person in the country* is now wearing a curly purple wig and Ronald McDonald shoes. In fact it just means there used to be fourteen clowns, and now there are twenty-eight.

Anyway. In this case there genuinely seemed to be more clowns than usual. Police asked fancy-dress shops to 'remove clown masks from sale' after sightings in Plymouth, Cardiff, Cumbria, Selby, Bracknell, Stanford-le-Hope and Peterborough. Brunel University was said to be 'in lockdown' because of a clown seen outside the student lodgings.

One listener, David Giles, suffered a disastrous combination of coulrophobia – the profound fear of clowns – and a weak heart. His angina had led to three heart attacks in the last twelve months. 'I have always hated clowns', he told me. 'It scares me to death and could literally scare me to death.'

'You have had three heart attacks in the last year?'

'Yes.'

'How many of them were caused by clowns?'

'None,' he told me. 'But this spate of clowns could bring on an angina attack. I am not trying to ruin anybody's fun.'

'David, what would you say to someone thinking of going out dressed as a clown?'

If this had been TV, he would have turned to the camera and addressed it direct.

'Don't do it because you could kill somebody.'

David is right to be cross. No one could be anything but sympathetic with a man who is one clown away from death. But the news headline at the start of my show, '. . . AND THE POLICE ARE URGED TO ACT AGAINST CLOWNS', made me wonder if we might all have gone a tiny bit mad.

Another subject that causes bug-eyed fury is cycling.

I discovered this entirely by accident, simply by buying a cheap bicycle so I could travel to work. I thought I was joining a mobile gym – 'a machine powered by teacakes', as a member of the House of Lords put it. Turns out I was taking up a weapon on a battlefield.

One day I was cycling down the centre of a street made narrow by vehicles parked on both sides. All cyclists dread the car door that suddenly opens. The official advice is to stay well clear of parked vehicles, but some drivers see that as deliberate obstruction. A car came rushing up behind me with the driver hooting their horn. I braked a little to see what the problem was and looked over my shoulder. Big mistake. The driver, a bespectacled middle-aged woman with bright red braided hair, started bouncing up and down with fury because I had slowed down.

Out of instinct – if there is danger, slow down or stop – I came to a gradual halt. I immediately wished I had not. She slammed on her brakes behind me, sprang out of the car, ran up to me and screamed obscenities in my face. I tried to explain I had to stay a door's width from the parked cars – my heart was racing and I went all wobbly voiced when I said it – but realised the explanation wasn't helping, and I was on the verge of being punched. More out of instinct than anything, I climbed off my bike.

This made the driver even angrier, and because I now had both hands on the handlebars I was totally unable to move or defend myself. Her fury was a physical thing. I expected a fist, maybe a knife.

The lady's weapon of choice was her right boot. She began kicking me and my bike and swearing loudly. She shouted, 'YOU LOT PISS ME OFF', which made me realise that in her own mind she was confronting a whole class of person.

Back on the cycle, I pulled in at the first available opportunity to let her pass, and she was gone. But then – as is the way in London, where a bike is faster than a car – I caught up with her at the next set of lights. A few weeks earlier I had been given a pair of cameras by a small-business owner who was selling them online and wanted me to try them out. They were switched on that day, but I had no idea whether they were recording or saving the images or had even been pointing at the commotion. So I thought I should take a photo of the lady's car with my smartphone.

Unfortunately she saw me raise the phone and point it at her car. Out she jumped again.

'Don't assault me,' I said as she bore down on me.

'If you take another picture of my car I'm going to knock you out, because that's my personal belongings!' she yelled.

In the nineties I had been a political correspondent at Westminster, and now I racked my brain to remember when they voted on the law that said you could knock a person out for photographing your personal belongings. With that, she climbed back into her car. I drew alongside and looked in through her passenger window. There was an older bloke in there, large and embarrassed. She leant across him, formed her hand into the shape of a gun, pointed it at me, moved her thumb as if cocking it and fired. I had been shot by two fingers. The lights turned green and she was gone with a screech of angry tyre. I felt breathless and upset and did not sleep very well that night. I guess I'm not cut out for urban warfare.

Later I was grateful to the chap who sent me the cameras. The images were crisp, the sound cringingly clear. They showed the lady almost colliding with a parked car as she drove off after confronting me. I uploaded the expletive-ridden footage, commenting that drivers did not always understand why a cyclist takes the centre of a lane. The film spread. News websites posted it alongside the story. Five days later a BBC person told me it had probably been viewed by between *ten and fifteen million people.* The BBC News take on the kerfuffle was the most-read story in the UK for seven hours the following day.

England | Regions | London

Motorist launches foul-mouthed verbal assault on Jeremy Vine

⏱ 30 August 2016 | London

The driver got out of her car twice to threaten Vine

A motorist launched a foul-mouthed verbal assault on BBC presenter Jeremy Vine as he cycled down a west London street.

But it was all more complicated than it at first appeared. I am guessing that even by taking the risk of telling you the details, I have forced you to take a side. You may be seething at me.

I had thought, as a victim of crime, people would automatically sympathise with me. That was naive. The footage was not seen in the simple way I expected. If you cycle in one of our major cities you are joining a battlefield that is both physical and ideological.

The physical part can be addressed with a good helmet, Marcel Marceau-style signalling and constant vigilance. The ideological part ... well, that's a little harder to deal with. Until my road rage incident I had simply not realised that if you climb on a pushbike, a lot of people will loathe you. For them, you are in the wrong 100 per cent of the time, even if you are sent flying by a truck with broken indicators driven by a drunken teenager wearing a blindfold.

So when the footage emerged I got hit by the anger. Of the 3,500 comments on my Facebook page, many criticised me.

'Wrap his bike around his skull,' wrote Paul Townsend.

Cindy Cunningham challenged him: 'What happened to patience?'

'It disappears when you get stuck behind a cockwomble dressed in Lycra,' was the reply.

Others were just as furious – at me, not the driver.

James Withers: 'If he wants to be in the middle of the road he should drive a motorbike.'

James Mah: 'This is why all bicycles should be banned from public roads.'

Jeremy Temple: 'Plenty of places to pull over to let traffic pass. You were causing an obstruction at worst, being ignorant at best.'

Nathan Dakin: 'You were being a massive bell-end.'

Gary Hollern: 'Vine you were being a prick.'

Zeb Black: 'Trouble is that cyclists are always trying to prove a point or establish some non-existent right, but maybe car driver could have been calmer.'

Was that a moment of sympathy? It didn't last.

Andy Brooks: 'Unusual for a cycle being in the road, they are normally on the pavement.'

Konstantin Sembos: 'Instead of being a fucking, self-centric c***, you could have pulled over either between 2 parked cars or on the huge space that was on your left where you stopped. But no, drivers must be considerate to cyclists, and cyclists can be perfect assholes to drivers!!! Clarkson was right on this one!!!'

Ah, Clarkson. The former *Top Gear* presenter also weighed in after the footage spread. 'He can be seen cycling down the middle of the road, deliberately blocking the cars in his wake, and when one gets too close he stops — still in the middle of the road — so he can record the woman driver's foul-mouthed tirade. The message is clear. He's been verbally assaulted while on a noble quest to save the polar bear.'

There was more from my former colleague. 'Hang on a minute, Vine. How did you know that the woman in the car behind wasn't rushing to see her injured child in hospital? How did you know there wasn't a pregnant girl on the back seat who was about to give birth? Can you imagine how frustrating it would be to be stuck behind a sanctimonious cyclist when you really are in a genuine, tearing hurry?'

The barrage took up almost the whole of a page in that Saturday's *Sun*, underneath a photo of Clarkson looking like he was about to hit someone. I was in a coffee shop with my young daughter Martha and could see her trying to judge her father's reaction as he read it. My brow furrowed. 'Are you okay, dad?' she asked me. I got to the last line – something about cycling in a city not being safe, so it shouldn't take a genius to work out that the solution was not to cycle – and roared with laughter. 'I'm fine, darling.' In fairness to Jeremy, the column was a brilliant read.

It did not exactly prevent my Facebook page turning into the equivalent of a brawl in a bike shop. Cyclists were now getting stuck in as well. But many are sensitive souls, and were finding themselves outnumbered by petrolheads.

From Toni Contini: 'Anyone who wants to live in London is a fucking loser, anyone who wants to cycle in London's Scottish oil invested overcrowded streets, is a loser and anyone who moves there to further their career is usually sucking someones cock . . . there you go, sorted.'

Enter a cyclist, slightly in the manner of a man joining a sword-fight carrying a toothpick.

Philip Smith: 'What a vile creature you are.'

Tom Neale: 'Look at the gap in front of you when you decide to be a knob and stop blocking the road.'

Mark Ammell: 'That is totally uncalled for.' (Again, surely a cyclist.)

George C. Bridges: 'At least four times you drive past a place where you could have pulled over and let a faster moving vehicle pass . . . you sir are totally to blame for this incident you are just trying to provoke people because you are a sad sad person.'

Another more moderate response from June Armstrong: 'But imagine this was her driving test. Would she have passed?'

Louis Thompson rolls over her: 'WHAT I DON'T UNDER-STAND IS WHY YOU DIDN'T JUST LET HER PASS!!! IT'S A DIRECT PROVOCATION!!! LEARN TO BE A RESPONSIBLE ROAD USER VINE!!!'

George C. Bridges, back for more: 'Jeremy Vine should be arrested as well for starting the whole issue.'

You get the gist. In the end, a person can go mad looking at screeds of messages like those. The best thing was just to withdraw.

If I open my Facebook page today, I can still see that video with the subtext: 3.5K COMMENTS. But after the first couple of hundred, my spirit was broken and I could not face the other 3,300. What is so interesting is that the anger was most conspicuous among motorists taking the side of the perpetrator.

As the journalist, trying to see both sides, I have to take off my cycle helmet and consider this objectively. The balance shifted dramatically towards motorists in the decades after the war as the UK went from a country of 1.5 million cars in 1945 to 34 million in 2010. Pulling road space back from motorists – wider pavements, cycle lanes, etc. – has created serious conflict. But it has not happened quickly enough in cities to cope with the massive upsurge in cycling. When I leave the house to cycle the seven miles to work, I say goodbye to my wife with the finality of a Japanese pilot in 1944. Cyclists with a battlefield mentality cut across pavements and parks in a way that drives pedestrians potty. They think they are doing it for their safety, but it puts others in danger. I am a driver, pedestrian and cyclist and I know the fury of walking across a road when the green man is lit, only for a cyclist zinging through red to brush the bristles on my chin.

Bizarrely, motorists feel threatened too. 'They are like flies, biting me!' a West African taxi driver told me the other day in London, patting his shoulders and elbows for effect.

'Look at them. And I can't see it getting any better,' growled a licensed black cabbie, indicating the six-strong peloton in the stop box ahead of him. 'What they don't realise is cars were here first.'

But the incident in which I was involved was pretty simple. I was the victim of an aggressive driver who also turned out to be a violent person with sixteen previous convictions, including one for biting a shop assistant and a community support officer when she was caught stealing belts at a fashion outlet on the Kings Road (she had run off, leaving her lipstick, which the police successfully scoured for DNA). After the bike madness, Scotland Yard had so many calls asking what action the police were taking that they decided to take some. The lady, Shanique Pearson, was arrested and charged. An officer came to see me at Radio 2 and took a statement. Such is the power of the internet that people had been able to scan Pearson's number plate and find she had no tax or insurance.

She pleaded not guilty, was convicted, and appealed. I was asked to go to court a second time and sit through a repeat of the entire case. She was convicted again. The judge looked exasperated when a barrister began slowly reading the list of previous offences, including theft, robbery and assault. He told Shanique Pearson, 'You have a very bad record for dishonesty and violence' and activated her suspended sentence for the Kings Road meltdown. She went to prison for eight months, only one of which was for the attack on me.

I took no pleasure whatsoever from the conclusion to the case and wished Shanique had simply said: 'Sorry, I'm having a bad day', which would have washed the slate clean. But I had been particularly upset when, during the original trial, her barrister asked me: 'Aren't you guilty, Mr Vine, with your remarks about Ms Pearson mock-firing a gun at you, of the worst kind of racial stereotyping?' No, I was not. I had simply told the truth about the one thing my cameras did not capture – the gun gesture – and it never occurred to me that this was 'associated with the black community', as her lawyer put it. He had a series of head-and-neck twitches that grew in intensity as he put the point, which I took as a sign that he knew it was nonsense. It was an own goal for Pearson, too. The 'racial stereotyping' accusation was a cheap shot from an expensive lawyer and persuaded me to cancel a day at work to ensure I could give my evidence in person at the appeal.

After the case concluded I was tempted to return to the Facebook page and respond to the many insisting that no cyclist should block a car because 'cyclists don't pay road tax'. It turned out that in the now-famous conflagration with Shanique Pearson, only one of us was paying tax and insurance on a car – and it wasn't her. 'Hey everyone!' I could write. 'I'm in the clear. It's official – I did nothing wrong! Turns out the other person was the criminal after all!'

But what would that do?

Yep. Start the tumbrils rolling again. I guarantee it. I just can't face it. The anger out there – in response to certain triggers – is astonishing. It takes your breath away.

Cycling is one trigger, for sure.

Banking is another. Bankers make people FURIOUS. For a while after the 2008 crash, which caused massive financial distress in every sector of the audience (although I don't think we have many city types listening), we used to bet on how quickly bankers would be denounced in the programme. Even if the first item was about nicotine or Nicaragua, somehow a caller would introduce the B-word: 'This situation is so bad I am starting to think bankers must be involved.' The classic formula is one where a group of people are not helped by our government, and then listeners point out that it's one rule for them and another rule for the bankers. The collapse of Woolworths?

'If Woolworths was a bank, it would have been bailed out.'

The demise of the Farepak hamper firm, which ran a voucher system to help poorer families save for Christmas – meaning many had lost their entire annual savings?

'Of course if the customers had been swanning around in pin-striped suits and ties in the City, drinking Peroni and doing swaps and derivatives and whatnot, the government would have been falling over itself to shower them with money. Because they're poor families, they don't seem to matter.'

Soon after the banking crisis the Labour government announced debt figures that were eye-watering. The sequence leading up to this sorry state of affairs was pretty clear – the boom in the 2000s created huge tax revenues; the government budgeted on the basis that they would continue ('no return to boom and bust'); the Conservative opposition endorsed the high spending, so everyone went all-in; the crash not only created a monster bank bailout bill but also wiped out the tax revenues. Thus Labour had to borrow enormous amounts to keep spending – otherwise, they said, the economy might capsize altogether. Gordon Brown lent himself £450m every single day in the year 2009/10, but it was hard for the Conservatives to complain because they had supported the spending in the first place.

The upshot: carnage.

Listeners drew the straightforward conclusion – the economy was going really well until bankers took all the money.

We had one discussion involving the socialist campaigner Hannah Sell and über-posh ex-banker Venetia Thompson. You can probably guess who got the rotten tomatoes as this conversation came out of radios across the country.

Venetia: 'I don't think it was the bankers that got us into this mess. It was originally a problem with fat, lazy people sitting around and not working hard enough – '

Hannah: 'Fat lazy bankers?'

Venetia: 'No, fat lazy people who don't want to go out and

get jobs and who are living off benefits and the state – '

Hannah: 'Come on. Look. This was a crisis of capitalism and the banking sector and yet they're laughing all the way to the bank.'

JV: 'Venetia, is somebody rich if they're on £151,000 a year?'

Venetia: 'No, I don't think they are that rich if they're on £151,000 actually.'

Hannah: 'And yet you expect people on benefits to live on sixty-five pounds a week in London and have their benefit cut.'

Venetia: 'Get another job!' (*Laughs*)

Hannah (*furious*): 'There is mass unemployment. People can't get jobs. You try it. You go and live in the north-east of Britain and see if you can get a job.'

During the exchanges, I could almost feel the idea take a physical hold: *The country had lots of money, then the bankers took it.* Since then we have rarely had a programme where bankers have not been held up as objects of disgust.

There are other live rails. When fishermen and swimmers clashed in a row at Henleaze Swimming Club in Bristol, it was over the club's decision to cull carp from their private lake. At least fifty of the fish apparently needed to be removed to improve water quality for the swimmers. The carp would be electrocuted in the water, then pulled out dead.

For the swimmers the solution was regrettable but effective. But the lake was shared by anglers, and they were beside themselves. The fishers wanted to hook each carp individually. The *Bristol Post* headline

FISH CULL LATEST:
DEADLOCK AT BRISTOL SWIMMING LAKE
AS GATES ARE SUPERGLUED SHUT

showed how unpleasant things were getting, and hinted at a revelation that came to us over the course of several stories – any conflict, no matter what the cause, can only be worsened by the arrival of an angler.

A year later, totally unrelated, we reported on the Devon angler upset by naked pensioners swimming near his fishing spot. We were not ready for the voltage released. Fisherman Nigel Bond had been on the banks of the River Dart with his rod when he was disturbed. He wrote an angry letter to the magazine *Fly Fishing and Fly Tying*:

> I found the peace of the river shattered by several very aged, lily white and scrawny humans cavorting stark naked in what is one of the best pools on the lower river. To an angler, having paid good money to enjoy a little tranquillity by the river, the sight was altogether too much.

This kicked off an almighty row. It turns out that a lot of other river users – in fact a lot of other people, whatever their pastime, including the wives and relatives of anglers – see them as one of the most arrogant groups in society. The key word used as an insult these days is 'entitled'. Anglers feel they are *entitled*. But they are more than capable of defending themselves. Indeed, they seem to be in a constant state of warfare with the world. For a group of people whose hobby is to sit quietly on a riverbank waiting for a gentle tug on the line, anglers seem to have an urgent need for anger therapy.

Another day, another row – this time the comic Griff Rhys Jones put his head in the lion's mouth when he went on a tour of Britain's waterways and ended up concluding that the rivers 'no longer belong to the people'. He named anglers as one group who had hijacked them, along with 'stockbrokers and farmers'.

Dangerous talk.

Griff had spent a year canoeing, swimming and surfing along rivers and canals. 'Private fishing clubs have bought up the banks, controlling the water to the middle where they meet rival fishing clubs,' he complained. 'You cannot pass without permission.' Canoeists, he added, should 'disturb as many fishermen as possible'.

Flame. Blue touchpaper. Already-angry anglers became even

angrier. Sir Ian Botham stepped in. 'This man needs to stay in his little town and not come anywhere near rivers because he obviously doesn't have a clue about what's going on in the countryside,' he fumed. 'His stupid remarks are pretty irresponsible and when there's an incident, and there will be an incident, because of him telling canoeists to disturb fishermen, then let it be on his hands and let the salmon fishermen sue him.'

On the defensive, Rhys Jones clarified, saying his call for canoes to disrupt anglers was a joke. But he had unleashed the Furies.

'We take great exception to Griff Rhys Jones' calls for canoeists to cause disturbance to anglers,' said Mark Lloyd, chief executive of the terrifying-sounding Angling Trust. 'He has gone out canoeing and dreaming up this lovely, Constable-like, idealistic view. But he probably doesn't understand the delicate nature of some of our rivers . . . canoe in shallow waters at certain times of the year and there is a danger you will damage fish spawn . . . if you have someone coming down the river in a canoe the fish disappear and hide and it spoils the fishing.'

During the item, an angler called our studio. He too was furious about Griff Rhys Jones, but he had a different story of the hazards of being on a riverbank. His expensive rods had all been carefully laid out, reaching across the river. He was sitting calmly by the towpath when . . .

A cyclist tore down the path and went straight over all my rods.

The arrival of the cyclist in the story was so unexpected, so dramatic, that I remember looking up at the ceiling of the studio as if I had just been hit by a falling tile. A cyclist came speeding down the towpath?

And went over all my rods, and broke them, and they were very expensive.

Entitled anglers versus arrogant cyclists. The snapping of rods, the scuff of tyre on grass. All we needed now was a banker to arrive on the scene and we would hit Peak Anger. The whole studio could explode and take me with it.

Yet bankers, cyclists and anglers are not the only ones who create a surge of audience indignation.

In fact banking, cycling and angling are not even the subjects which make people most angry.

The Thing That Makes People Most Angry is in the next chapter.

21. Intergenerational Warfare

As a child of 1965, if I want to know which generation I officially belong to, I can look up a table and find all the different names. But the answer I get is slightly confusing. Baby Boomers were conceived after the map of the globe was redrawn in 1945 – when every adult grabbed another adult and had the best kind of sex, which is post-World-War sex. You are a Baby Boomer if you were born up until the release of 'It Ain't Me Babe' by Bob Dylan.

Why is that confusing? Because the Dylan song was fading as I entered the world. It came out in 1964. I came out in 1965. Had I been born only six months earlier I would be in the same generation as my dear father-in-law Chris. He is the definition of a Baby Boomer – born in 1946.

Any measure that puts us in the same bracket seems a little inaccurate, since everything about Chris suggests his seniority to me. He owns a gravy boat. He has a beard and pauses before answering a question. He can slice a Sunday roast without doing himself a mortal injury. A volunteer sidesman at his local church, Chris is trusted with counting the weekly collection in a secure room. He keeps a bottle of meths to deal with oil stains, is a grandfather of four and drives a ride-on mower. There is simply no comparison.

As Nirvana said, *Nevermind*. (Chris would never quote Nirvana.) The spreadsheets say I squeak into the post-boomer generation, or 'Gen-X' as it is officially called. Think Billy Idol not Billy Fury. 'Smells Like Teen Spirit', not Smells Like Methylated Spirit. I guess I should count myself lucky.

Here is the full breakdown for you:

Traditionalists or Silent Generation:	Born 1945 and before
Baby Boomers:	Born 1946 to 1964
Generation X:	Born 1965 to 1976
Millennials or Gen-Y:	Born 1977 to 1995
iGen, Gen-Z or Centennials:	Born 1996 and later

In my studio the other day I interviewed John McTernan, one of Tony Blair's political strategists, along with the rumbustious Corbynite Owen Jones. As they left I mentioned the 25,000 calls and how I was writing a book about them. John said: 'So what's the theme?' Owen moves at speed from one studio to the next, but even he stopped to hear my answer.

What's the theme? I froze. Great question. It made me think. For a second the 25,000 calls became a giant Jackson Pollock painting, brutal spatters of paint whipped across the room in every colour, me aproned up beside the canvas drenched in scarlets and blues and livid greens trying to make sense of the chaos.

And then I had it.

In that half-second, the spatter resolved itself.

'Intergenerational warfare,' I said. 'That makes people even angrier than cycling.'

It's true. If I go back over all those programmes and all those calls, the issue that comes up again and again and fires so much conflict is the idea that the older generation had it better than the younger.

It generates more anger than cyclists or bankers. More even than anglers. More even than a cyclist going over an angler's rods.

I discovered this huge crevasse in the audience when, soon after the financial meltdown, a thoughtful graduate in his twenties called George arrived in the studio to say there was a moral duty on retired people to provide monetary assistance to twenty-somethings, even ones outside their own family. His case was both understated and explosive. In a quiet voice he described how the Baby Boomers – and those born before them – had plundered the country. They had hoovered up:

- ☐ Free education
- ☐ Cheap-as-chips housing
- ☐ Jobs for life
- ☐ Pensions
- ☐ Holidays
- ☐ Unsustainable amounts of NHS attention

and should now pay a windfall tax to his generation, possibly being forced to move out of their large homes into flats. The phrase I remember was 'rattling around'. Older people were 'rattling around' in five-bedroomed houses, while young people starting their careers with a mountain of student debt were lucky if they could find a spare sofa to sleep on.

Another young caller added that in addition to grabbing all the houses and the steady jobs, and forcing the NHS to treat them for years beyond their natural life expectancy without paying the tax to cover the cost, pensioners were the generation responsible for climate change. They had 'destroyed the planet on the way out'.

What was being described was the opposite of the Facebook party all parents dread. In the conventional story, mum and dad go on holiday, their teenager invites a few friends round on Facebook, the post spreads online, half the country turns up un-invited and trashes the house. In George's view the opposite had happened – teenagers had arrived on the doorstep to find their parents had trashed the country.

George claimed his generation would be overtaxed for the whole of their lives because of the selfishness of the Baby Boomers. Quite soon, young people would have no houses left to live in and no planet left to live on.

It seemed to me to be an extreme and one-sided argument, but then extreme and one-sided arguments often make you think . . . and the other side was not long in coming.

Within minutes of my thanking George for his 'controversial contribution' (code: presenter puts on crash helmet) the phone lines were deluged with incandescent pensioners. They were outraged that George had been given a free platform, and desperate to take his case apart point by point. They replied that young people:

- ❑ Want a flat-screen TV before they have a job
- ❑ Did not fight in the war
- ❑ Never had to scrimp and save
- ❑ Worship people like Kim Kardashian, instead of Keats and Yeats
- ❑ Would never use an outside toilet
- ❑ Drink alcohol on a nightly basis

and much else besides. When a 75-year-old exclaimed, 'We fought in THE WAR!' younger listeners pointed out that he would have been parachuting into Arnhem as a ten-year-old. Even if a person was a cook's mate on one of the D-Day ships, they would still need to be at least eighty in 2010 to be a veteran. People who bore arms in the Second World War are now in their nineties – so if a seventy-something claims to have 'fought in THE WAR!' it is almost certainly untrue, unless they have a more recent war in mind, but that would be very misleading.

Intergenerational warfare turns out to be as bloody as the real thing. Because the first person to lay out the case against the Baby Boomers on my show was George, none of us was ready for the speed and power of the response. He must have felt like a swimmer in Union Jack Speedos surfacing on Omaha Beach.

Since George, we have seen the power of those pensioner gun emplacements again and again. We will discuss something, even a subject as mundane as the merits of disposable nappies, and suddenly the rip tide takes us across to those dangerous beaches and BANG, the slits in the concrete pillboxes flash and the hot metal starts flying and it's the first twenty minutes of *Saving Private Ryan* all over again.

It happened the other day with fonts. Yes, the simple question of typeface design, and whether there could be a different way of writing a capital 'O' so it did not get confused with a zero.

WiFi passwords and number plates were a particular source of confusion. Where, you might ask, is the dividing line between the generations in this innocuous story?

Peter Rickett, phoning from Gloucester, showed us.

'If people can't tell the difference between a 0 and the letter O they should not be allowed to use technology. It's not the pensioners having these problems – it is the entitled younger generation in flip-flops and skinny jeans who just want everything in life to be made easy for them.'

But it cuts both ways. After Brexit a young man called Nicholas Barrett, posting on Twitter as @nbarrett100, uploaded his own howl of pain. Outraged by the feeling that his generation had been yanked out of the EU by older voters having a trash-the-house party, he wrote: 'The younger generation has lost the right to live and work in 27 other countries. We will never know the full extent of the lost opportunities, friendships, marriages and experiences we will be denied. Freedom of movement was taken away by our parents, uncles, and grandparents in a parting blow to a generation that was already drowning in the debts of our predecessors.'

In a single paragraph he had summed up the resentment. As did Maxwell who emailed me: 'Absolutely the young have been shafted by their grandparents' generation whose final act of selfishness was to remove the right of the young to work anywhere in Europe.'

But the older generation are unshiftable on the subject and respond with fury. They point out that retired voters were more dutiful about casting their votes in the Referendum – one analysis of the turnout for Brexit found that on average an 80-year-old was 2.3 times more likely to vote than an 18-year-old, even though the 18-year-old presumably finds it easier to use his legs.

It is not just Brexit. When we covered research showing workers now in their mid-thirties were poorer than the people of the same age had been in the 1990s, I did not feel the dangerous pull of the tide until we were suddenly in the sights of the older generation, who felt they were being blamed once again and unleashed a volley of bullets and shells.

From Robin in Birmingham: 'My savings and hard work are subsidising the young muppets' mortgages currently at 2% or 3%. I paid up to 15.5%. Didn't have a car or foreign holidays, big TVs etc etc etc and I had three jobs.'

Teresa in East Molesey: 'When I was in my twenties we didn't have the bank of mum and dad . . . if you needed something, you worked an extra job to pay for it. Young people today just expect everything instantaneously and don't understand the concept of living within their means.'

Simon in Chester: 'The under 30s have grown up with more extravagant spending, such as phones, online shopping, midweek and weekend drinking and meals. Their personal debt is too high.'

A constant theme is *things*. Older people name all kinds of *things* they didn't have, and suggest the reason young people cannot buy a house is because all their money has gone on *things* – so this argument about people is actually conducted with inanimate objects as the proxy.

Caroline in Hitchin emailed: 'Years ago we had a bottom drawer and saved for things & didn't have to buy the latest smart phones or have a huge TV and computer & heaps of DVDs in our bedroom, or have heaps of clothes and shoes; or have foreign holidays or have a car. Today's 30-somethings have had far more "stuff" but have not saved for the future.'

Deana in Lancashire: 'Isn't the issue down to those born in the early 80s wanting things "now"? We were happy with a week in a leaky caravan' – there are lots of mentions of caravans, by the way, and constant use of the word 'scrimped' – 'not a fortnight on some exotic beach drinking expensive cocktails. We didn't possess mobile phones . . . eating out or having a takeaway was a rare event.'

By definition, older people have had longer careers. They have lived more years so they have worked more hours. But the extended logic of this is that they have 'worked harder' than the young. One listener claimed he had been 'in work for seventy years', which I suppose is possible. Ray in Milton Keynes spent 'fifty years working for what I have. I left school to go into paid employment at fourteen.' Elderly listeners – the core of my audience, by the way – do the 1950s facepalm if ever the programme explains how youngsters are spending longer in education, especially if they hear there are university degrees in Golf Course Management and Surf Science.

A common theme emerges when the older listeners answer back. There is a difference in attitude. 'We did not expect to have everything NOW and waited till we could afford it,' Brian emailed. An anonymous lady followed up with: 'My husband and I are in our seventies and did not expect to have it all when we wanted it. WE WORKED AND WE SAVED.' Her capitals.

Reg in Essex, age sixty-nine, wanted young people to understand how hard it had been in the past. 'Wives having to have their housekeeping increased due to inflation on a monthly basis. No carpets or holidays when you bought your first house. And saving for a deposit which involved staying in. Our taxes have contributed to new hospitals, roads and schools. I doubt they would believe it.'

Wayne wrote: 'The old had to get a job – The old didn't have kids so could live on benefits – The old had to pay board to their parents – The old paid their own tuition fees – The old didn't run up a 40k bar bill whilst supposedly at university – The old didn't have a gap year that was funded by their parents – The old paid tax and insurance all their lives. But the poor young have to sit on the dole waiting for their parents to die so they can have a house and some money to live on. Could the young for once get a life and get a job and become what they despise so much . . . a person who earns a living and amasses assets?'

Patricia sent an email which was a little more gracious in tone, but seemed to sum up the disconnect between the generations.

'Jeremy, I can't get through on the phone. This subject is always coming up and we never seem to get the chance to reply.

'I am almost 70, I brought up my two children in a house with a loo at the bottom of the garden, no fridge, freezer or washing machine. Bath in the kitchen under the worktop.

'When my husband left there wasn't any financial help, I had to work and at times had to leave the children (then 10 and 7) on their own.

'No free childcare, child benefit for the first child only.

'After I remarried (at the Registry Office), I had to prepare the food for our party in the evening – bring a bottle. It was a fabulous evening. I did two jobs as well as caring for the children to help save the deposit towards a home. We put money away in an envelope each week to pay the bills.

'At one time the mortgage rate was 16/17 per cent. We had a week in a caravan about 30 miles away for our holidays. Nothing was bought unless we had saved the money.

'We saved as much as possible once the children had left home to put away for our old age. Now the lowest interest rate in history!

'Yes, house prices are ridiculous – and I feel sorry for the young people, especially those who forgo the latest phones, evenings out and foreign holidays but a majority of young people will one day inherit from their parents which our generation did not.'

The tone was conciliatory, even touching. But Annette, a pensioner in Lincoln, came roaring up behind her.

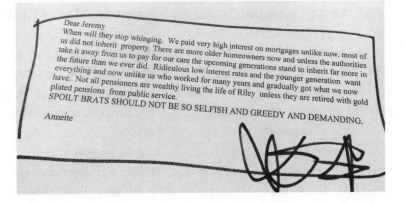

Dear Jeremy

When will they stop whinging. We paid very high interest on mortgages unlike now. most of us did not inherit property. There are more older homeowners now and unless the authorities take it away from us to pay for our care the upcoming generations stand to inherit far more in the future than we ever did. Ridiculous low interest rates and the younger generation want everything and now unlike us who worked for many years and gradually got what we now have. Not all pensioners are wealthy living the life of Riley unless they are retired with gold plated pensions from public service. SPOILT BRATS SHOULD NOT BE SO SELFISH AND GREEDY AND DEMANDING.

Annette

And there it is. The subject which causes the most aggravation on my show is Intergenerational Warfare. I look around and see it reflected everywhere now. David Willetts, a Conservative MP who went to the House of Lords and was nicknamed a 'one-man think-tank', wrote *The Pinch*, about the way Baby Boomers had locked in the country's wealth, a great book described in the *Guardian* as 'a hard-hitting account of the generation that took all the houses, jobs and welfare – and is having all the fun'.

But if you are reading this in your sixties or beyond and crossly feeling got at, and angry at the way you are being blamed, there are two great rebuttals you should have to hand.

The first is that the reason politicians bend over backwards to protect your pensions and bus passes and winter fuel allowances is simply *because you vote*. In the 2015 general election campaign, Ed Miliband spent an evening gurning away in front of Russell Brand in the mistaken belief that Twitter was a part of the voting process. He tragically discovered that the more people who support you on Twitter, the less electable you are. Twitter is just a left-wing version of the *Daily Mail*. He ignored the Baby Boomers and he lost.

The second reason is simultaneously beautiful and tragic. A big boss at the BBC stopped me in the street at the back of Broadcasting House and asked me how I was. 'Fine,' I said. 'Just struggling away.'

'Ha!' the Big Boss laughed. 'At least we are not in our twenties. My son has just graduated and he can't find a job or anywhere to live.'

'And I guess he is loaded with student debt?'

'Forty thousand pounds, or thereabouts. It's shocking.'

I looked at the guy, a very well known executive right at the top of the Beeb who I won't name, but who had – I am certain of this – a pension worth more than five million pounds which he was just about to collect on.

'And do you know what?' I said. 'Your son wouldn't swap with us for all the tea in China.'

(People who use the phrase 'all the tea in China' and 'or thereabouts' immediately mark themselves out as past it.)

'Well,' laughed Big Boss, 'it's true, he is young.'

'I'm fifty. And I'd do anything to be twenty-two,' I added.

'Yeeeee-es,' he said uncertainly, as his eyes clouded with all those freshly minted fifty-pound notes he would lose if he wound his life back forty years.

Then: 'Yes, Jeremy, you're right. So would I.'

The old are being accused of having everything. But the young have youth. Oscar Wilde said: 'Youth is the Lord of life.' It is worth more than any pension. Youth is currency; youth is another kind of money. Old age is poverty, no matter how rich you are.

Which is why the old should never have to explain themselves to the young.

22. Bonapartes

That phrase — 'We fought IN THE WAR!' — made me think. When someone says it to you, on the radio or in conversation, it is totally unchallengeable. It ends every argument. It allows the speaker to say their piece without any more interruption.

The line has been spoken so often on my show that I have come close to confronting it head-on: 'You are in your seventies. Which war did you fight in?' But that would be very rude, and they might say Korea.

So I let it pass. Every time. Baby Boomers fought in the war — it's official. They genuinely feel they were part of a generation that did, even if they are mistakenly thinking of teachers and parents as friends and siblings — getting two generations confused. They would have lived with post-war rationing and traumatised fathers, so in that sense the war lived with them. Isn't this fascinating? Some things pass into the bloodstream as truth, flowing in and around us as truth, becoming part of the shared truth we all experience and understand together, even though they are completely wrong.

I call them Bonapartes — these beliefs so deep-rooted we count them as close friends. One of the best is the widespread certainty that Napoleon Bonaparte was a very short man. He certainly made the mistake of standing next to a tall chest of drawers in one of the most famous portraits he posed for. And he seems like the kind of person who would have been short, for why else would he decide to go conquering his neighbours to establish a European empire? Haven't all of our short friends tried exactly the same sort of thing? Didn't you have a short friend who went off the radar for a while, and when they finally reappeared down the pub they let slip they'd been out conquering Italy and Switzerland?

We retrofit the argument: Napoleon tried to invade the rest of Europe *because he was short*. We even describe people as having a 'Napoleon Complex' if they are (a) vertically challenged, and (b) extremely ambitious.

The one problem? It seems Napoleon was not short. Most historians now agree that, far from being a shade over five feet, Napoleon was probably five foot seven. The average height for a European male in the 1700s was five foot five. The mix-up over Napoleon's height seems to have been caused by a difference in French and English measurements – with France using feet and inches that were very slightly longer than ours – and also by his regular use of giant bodyguards who towered over him.

So a Bonaparte, as I see it, is something that is regularly presented as an agreed fact, and which no one has yet thought to challenge. Yet it is wrong. I like 'Bonaparte' because it sounds like a sister phrase to 'Fall Apart', which is what these notions often do the second you inspect them.

A typical Bonaparte is the statement: 'Teetotallers tend to die earlier than people who drink alcohol, therefore drinking in moderation helps you live longer.'

Wrong. It is true that teetotallers die earlier, but that is because a lot of them are ex-alcoholics.

Another is: 'Prostitution is the oldest profession.' When I said this on air once – just repeating wisdom handed down, the most dangerous thing – I had a brilliant response from Harold in Torrington, Devon: 'Jeremy said prostitution is the oldest profession, but that's untrue. It's widely agreed by archaeologists that the oldest profession is flint-knapping, the process of sharpening flint for arrowheads. That has been going on since the Stone Age, pre-dating civilisation as well as prostitution.'

In the end, who wins the battle of ancient flint-knappers and prostitutes may not matter too much today. But other Bonapartes are more fundamental to the lives we lead now.

One that comes up constantly on my show is this: *You are safer in the NHS than a private hospital.*

This one is interesting. It is created by love. In a rare example of an accident without a bruise, the nation has fallen head-over-heels for the National Health Service. I love it too, because I was born inside it. We look across the Atlantic at the walking shambles that is healthcare in the US, where most personal bankruptcies are caused by unpaid medical bills, and what we see reinforces a deep suspicion of private medicine. Think Wild West, but with stethoscopes.

Besides, the NHS feels very British. 'The closest we come to having an organised religion,' said former Chancellor Nigel Lawson.

A few years back I presented a *Panorama* on BBC1 about the shocking tale of a man in his prime who died at a private clinic in Bradford because a routine gallbladder operation went wrong and there was no blood for an emergency transfusion. I went around the country interviewing people and the narrative was all one-way. Why are we allowing NHS patients to overflow into risky private hospitals? They are profit-driven, these places, so isn't every procedure an exercise in cost-cutting? The Bradford clinic had already been torn apart by a coroner for 'Mickey Mouse' practices, so the goalmouth was open. Its apologetic defence – it was the first fatality in 22,000 operations – went unnoticed.

This particular Bonaparte comes up a lot. The NHS employs one worker in every twenty in the UK. Add in the partners and children of staff members, at least those old enough to ring radio shows . . . then include a few million satisfied offspring like me . . . well, you can see how powerful the fan base is. Our health service is crawling with regulators, say its supporters. Private clinics lack them. They're in it for the money. They don't even have A&E departments if something goes wrong. Why send patients somewhere which is not, and can never be, as safe?

To which the painful answer is – I hate to say this, but I must – that the worst mass murderer this country has ever seen was an NHS doctor. Harold Shipman, a GP in Manchester, managed to kill 215 of his patients before anyone noticed. (Incidentally, his NHS pension was not cancelled despite the carnage – his widow, Primrose Shipman, still draws it.)

Beverley Allitt, the worst lone female serial killer in my lifetime, was a nurse in Lincolnshire when she murdered four children and made attempts on the lives of another nine. To put it as gently as I can, she was not working in a private hospital when she did all this.

These are sad facts. They don't mean the NHS is any less safe or that we love it any less.

It is simply that *youaresaferintheNHSthanaprivatehospital* is a Bonaparte.

A similar one is the London-based: 'You are safer taking a licensed black taxi than an Uber minicab.' For obvious reasons, official Hackney carriage drivers hate the minicab trade. They have spent years learning all of London's streets – 'the Knowledge' – and now find a £50 satnav has better recall. Their response is to pay for huge mobile billboards warning people about the danger of being attacked by a minicab driver. Black cabs are thoroughly licensed and constantly inspected, their argument goes, so they must be safer.

This totally ignores the fact that London's most prolific rapist was an accredited black taxi driver who attacked lone female passengers after tricking them into drinking spiked champagne – he told them he had won the National Lottery. John Worboys was the prime suspect in eighty-five attacks on women of which only a dozen came to trial. We must assume that part of the reason he had access to these trusting women is because they had been told they were safer in a black cab.

In fact a whole host of Bonapartes seem to come from the idea that *things which are licensed are safer*.

In 2011 a hair salon in Nottingham paid compensation to Charlotte Jones, a young administrator at Trent University who booked in to change her hair colour from brown to blonde after breaking up with her boyfriend.

Unfortunately her hair turned ginger during the initial colouring, performed by a trainee. The inexperienced hairdresser tried to rectify the mistake by bleaching it a further four times. The £60 treatment took an incredible eleven hours, during which the trainee kept reassuring Charlotte that each step was improving her hair.

By the end the customer felt her scalp was on fire. She turned to look in the mirror and was horrified to see that she looked like, as she later put it, 'a scarecrow who had been in a car crash'. The 27-year-old took to wearing a hat and became a recluse for months, according to her lawyers at the Nottingham-based firm Mullis & Peake.

When Charlotte won a £5,250 payout, Mullis & Peake launched a tirade against the hairdressing industry. Describing themselves as 'the UK's first specialist hair injury compensation lawyers', they denounced the entire profession as woefully under-regulated. Solicitor Martyn Trenerry said: 'This is not an isolated incident. There are scores of people who are trying to take out claims against hairdressers. But the industry has very little regulation.'

Many of my listeners agreed wholeheartedly. They rang and texted with stories of shocking haircuts and cartoon miscolourings that would make your hair curl . . . or straighten. Bleach was a particular issue. Listeners appeared to think it was diabolical that someone could set up as a hairdresser without a licence. There were calls for regulation, inspectors, associations, licences, badges, Kitemarks, certificates – everything we can think of that makes us feel safer.

But hairdressers are already heavily regulated. They are regulated by their own customers. If you or I have a hair treatment that leaves us looking like a scarecrow in a car crash, we walk up and down our local high street with the hair showing and pretty soon the salon responsible has either changed its practices or shut down. That is the most powerful regulation you can have – *regulation by customer*. A customer is the toughest inspector.

The same issue arose after a bumpy Halloween in 2016. A number of incidents around the country suggested householders had been unsettled by 'teenage yobs' appearing at front doors demanding sweets. There had been a stabbing in Croydon, police attacked by fireworks in Tottenham and a road in Leeds forced to close after more than fifty motorbikers chose the night to congregate in what a resident said was 'a scene out of *Mad Max*'. So what was the solution if Halloween was getting out of control? Michael in Leicestershire told me he found the answer in the USA.

'I am a councillor in Leicestershire and live in a small rural village. Every year local people complain to me about teenagers dressed in bin bags knocking at their doors demanding money not sweets. When people don't give them any, they throw eggs at their windows and damage their cars. I was in Michigan in America one Halloween, and the town siren went off at six and again at eight. Trick-or-treating was only allowed during those two hours. There is also an age limit on children participating under the age of twelve.'

Once again, I thought, as I read that comment into the Radio 2 microphone, we succumb to the classic Bonaparte: *what we license we make safer*. Do we really think a siren sounded from the roof of the local council offices would cause those fifty motorbikers in Leeds to suddenly dismount and start singing 'Tiptoe Through the Tulips'? Or that an age limit on children allowed to go door-to-door would have convinced a villain in Croydon to leave his knife at home?

The NHS and the BBC both played host to Jimmy Savile, who was the Harold Shipman of paedophiles. This despicable man would have sailed through any licensing scheme. Savile even wrote books on child safety, one about *Stranger Danger* and the other (incredibly) called *Other People's Children: a Handbook for Child Minders*.

It defies belief that a child rapist could have operated so openly and avoided detection, but it seems to come down to the way we reach collective opinions on things – 'a weirdo, but basically a generous eccentric who has spent his life raising money for charity' – and then defend them until the moment they finally fall apart with a deafening crash.

In a shattering book called *In Plain Sight: The Life and Lies of Jimmy Savile*, journalist Dan Davies – who, like the documentary-maker Louis Theroux, got close to the DJ late in his life, but not

quite close enough to see through him – writes hundreds of pages about how the monster blagged his way past every gatekeeper, even getting the keys to Broadmoor Maximum Security Hospital so he could abuse the patients. In the book there is only one moment where a person in authority sees him for what he is. While travelling on a cruise ship, Jimmy Savile makes a series of lewd advances to a girl of fourteen. Her disgusted parents go to the ship's captain to report his behaviour. The captain makes no excuses. He orders Savile to stay in his cabin and then kicks him off the ship at the next port.

Reading the book, marvelling at the moral courage of the captain, I had that desperate, doubting thought: I wish I could say I would have done the same.

Among the repercussions of the Savile case was a sense that we should have listened to people – often our mums – who groaned when *Jim'll Fix It* came on and later explained: 'I never liked that man' or 'I always knew there was something fishy about him.' These observations are grouped under the powerful expression, 'There is no smoke without fire.'

'No smoke without fire' is now so close to being a global brand it could be printed on trainers. In Britain it took on even more power post-Savile, because the DJ was smoking like a blaze in a paper mill. But the saying is not exclusive to us. It exists in many other languages – not just the sentiment but the phrase itself. Georgy Zhukov, Stalin's general who took the Russian army to Berlin in the Second World War, reputedly said it many times in Russian: 'Нет дыма без огня', which sounds like '*Net dyma bez ognya*' and is an exact translation. In Hebrew it is '*Eyn Ashan Bli Esh*', in Dutch: '*Geen rook zonder vuur*'. The Finns say '*Ei savua ilman tulta*', and the Vietnamese '*Không có lửa sao có khói.*' And so on.

Yet it is one of the most dangerous untruths. Ask Cliff Richard and Paul Gambaccini, innocent men swept up in the post-Savile dragnet.

Still the smoke-Bonaparte persists. Imagine a proverb which said 'Every rumour has a solid basis to it.' No one would ever quote that because it sounds mad. But people all over the world say 'No smoke without fire' all the time. The Bosnians say '*Nema vatre bez dima*', the Czechs use the words '*Na každém šprochu pravdy trochu*' and my listeners type 'THERE IS NO SMOKE WITHOUT FIRE' in upper case.

We are all in error when we say it. There can be smoke without fire. Anyone who has been to a Genesis concert knows this.

* * *

Lighter matters. Well, perhaps not. A pensioner called Richard Phillips was asleep in his home in Goldhanger, Essex, when there was an ominous creak in the bedroom ceiling. Before he could work out what the creak meant, the entire attic of his house had fallen in on him.

Richard was trapped below 7,000 yachting magazines which he had stored in the loft over more than a decade. The magazines, all copies of *Traditional Sail – A Panorama of Heritage*, were piled in 150 boxes. Over the years the thick paper pages had settled and become heavier. Finally the ceiling joists gave up.

Unable to move, the 77-year-old stayed buried under the

yachting magazines for several hours. Then a neighbour, Tony Piercy, looked in. He said later: 'When I got to his room I called out and Richard just said, "I'm stuck." He kept shouting, "I can't move, I can't move." So I went into autopilot and just bashed his door in.

'He was very lucky. If one of the ceiling beams had landed on his head he could have died.'

The heroic Tony, seventy-two, alerted the rescue services. By the time my programme broadcast the story – *What are the signs that your ceiling may be about to collapse because of the weight of something upstairs?* – it was clear that Richard would be okay. Rescuers, including neighbours, had formed a human chain to pass copies of *Traditional Sail* out of the house through the upstairs bedroom window.

After the sea-loving pensioner was safely removed from his bedroom, the fire brigade said: 'Incidents like this show people should not overload their loft.'

During our discussion about what causes a ceiling to give way, we had plenty of listeners call with stories of bowed plasterboard and creaking beams. Then a retired builder rang with a Bonaparte so majestic I have repeated it many times myself. 'What you've got to remember,' he said, 'is that nothing in this world is heavier than paper.'

Well.

For many years scientists have told us that the main contender for weightiest substance on the planet is osmium, which at 22 grams per cubic centimetre is twice as dense as lead. Put another way, a litre of osmium weighs the same as twenty-two litres of water. Mercury is also incredibly heavy. So are plutonium and iridium. No scientist has yet mentioned paper.

I know what the builder meant – a pile of yachting magazines may be three feet high, but if you keep them in place for ten years they settle. Then you pile more on top and the next thing is there's a loud bang and a chain of firefighters and neighbours are forming a line from your bedroom window, passing one copy at a time along the line, occasionally noticing the title, *Traditional*

Sail – A Panorama of Heritage and marvelling at the way we all assume there will be time in the future when we sit back and reread yachting magazines at leisure.

That sentence – 'Nothing in this world is heavier than paper' – oh, I just tried saying it to myself, and the obvious untruth felt so good; it felt like a dare. Some Bonapartes have the power to make you want to believe them.

We had one on the show I presented an hour ago. This week's medical special was on Parkinson's Disease. We believe it is an illness suffered by pensioners, and certainly it gets more prevalent among older communities. But one sufferer in twenty is diagnosed before the age of fifty (in an earlier chapter I mentioned the close relative of mine who is a younger sufferer). If you add the figures for those diagnosed before they hit *sixty* – surely nobody feels old in their fifties – you get a sizeable cohort of sufferers dealing with Parkinson's when they might consider themselves to be in their best years. So it is untruthful to tell ourselves, 'That's a condition old people get' . . . . but understandable. We all know why we do it. Some Bonapartes survive because we need to believe them.

* * *

The worst lie is the biggest. The worst lie is the one we tell each other all the time. The Bonaparte a lot of us seem to live by. It comes up constantly, a hundred times more often than flint-knapping or hairdresser-licensing or even 'We fought IN THE WAR!' It is . . .

Tell you what. Let me introduce it through a listener who will do his best to persuade you of its truth. Andrew called from Elham, Kent, during a discussion about China. He was a middle-aged man with a Chinese wife who had been infuriated by the drift of our item, where we asked whether it was right for the Prime Minister to give the Chinese an earful about human rights during a state visit to Britain.

Many wanted the PM to let rip. In that one year, China had de-tained around 280 human rights lawyers and activists. Some were released within the day. But forty remained in custody, most in secret locations without access to lawyers or family, accused of being part of a 'criminal gang'.

Andrew objected to the tone of this. He knew China and he knew the Chinese. He felt our concentration on human rights missed a truth staring us in the face – China is a better country than Britain. This was how our conversation played out when he appeared on the line.

JV: 'We are joined by Andrew from Elham. Are you practical or are you thinking we need to take a stand?'

Andrew: 'Having just come back from China and lived amongst the people – my partner is Chinese – I can tell you that China is a country that actually works. Not like this rathole of a country where nobody works, nothing works and everything is as hard as possible. China is a wonderful place to live. It's light years ahead of this country.'

JV: 'Okay. But if we had – '

Andrew: 'Boris Johnson from London is actually making regular trips to China and copying lots of ideas from China, for example the Oyster Card – '

JV: 'Well, if – '

Andrew: 'The Oyster Card is a Chinese invention.'

JV: 'If they want to build a road – '

Andrew: 'Yes – '

JV: 'They're going to knock your house down. They're not going to ask you.'

Andrew: 'No, but they give you a new apartment when they do.'

JV: 'And how would you fancy that?'

Andrew: 'If the new apartment is better than the old one, what's wrong?'

JV: 'You think it would be?'

Andrew: 'I don't think it's a problem, no. It's a country where everything works . . . At the end of the day, it's the advantage for the population of the city, not the individual.'

JV: 'Does it worry you – '

Andrew: 'And sometimes some people have to stand back and say, "Well okay, if it improves life for everybody it is better."'

Andrew has played the ultimate Bonaparte. Did you catch it? 'A rathole of a country.' The phrase drops like four aces on a bridge table. It is show-stopping because it speaks to a deep conviction within us all: 'Things are getting worse.'

It happened on *Newsnight* in 2008 when Jeremy Paxman interviewed the hate preacher Abu Hamza. At the time Hamza was a free man; later he was jailed for life by an American judge. On *Newsnight* he railed against the UK, attacking its people, laws and customs – even though Britain had taken him in.

Paxman asked: 'If it is so detestable in this country, Mr Hamza, why don't you go and live somewhere else?'

Hamza replied: 'I am stuck. Like someone who is stuck in a toilet and there is a minefield outside.'

There was a slightly shocked pause and Paxman ended the interview.

This rathole . . .

This toilet surrounded by a minefield . . .

Bonaparte No. 1 comes in many forms. Probably the most famous one is: 'This country has gone to the dogs.' I tuned in to a local radio station in Kent once and heard the late-night presenter being asked by a caller: 'This country has gone to the dogs – why *are* things so bad?' and the host replied, voice as heavy as an undertaker's casket: 'I'll tell you why things are so bad. It's because the lunatics have taken over the asylum.'

When the band D:Ream sing 'Things Can Only Get Better', and Tony Blair uses it as the soundtrack for his 1997 landslide, and the result is the Chilcot Inquiry and a 1920s-style financial meltdown . . . for some, that is all the proof you need. *Things are always getting worse. Things only ever get worse. Things Can Only Get Worse.*

D:Nightmare.

Back on the radio, Andrew was not finished attacking his rathole. I did my best to make him pause with a question.

319

JV: 'Do you think this country, the UK, would be better if we executed three thousand people a year?'

Andrew: 'If you don't break the law you don't get into problems in China. China is a country that has virtually no crime. Can you say that about this country?'

JV: 'No.'

Andrew: 'No, you can't. Can you honestly say that if you put a six-foot mirror outside your house that no moron would come along and kick it in?'

JV: 'No.'

Andrew: 'You can in China.'

JV: 'You could put a six-foot mirror outside your house – '

Andrew: 'Yes.'

JV: 'And no one would kick it in?'

Andrew: 'No, they wouldn't. There is no vandalism. There is virtually no crime. There is no graffiti. People respect where they live. They look after where they live. They respect each other.'

JV: 'Right.'

Andrew: 'All of those values don't exist in this country any more.'

JV: 'But if there's no crime, why are they executing so many people?'

Andrew: 'If you don't commit the crime, you don't have a problem.'

I have to admit that this conversation took on the status of immediate legend in the Radio 2 office. First he plays the nuclear-tipped Bonaparte . . . then he says a six-foot mirror would not get broken if you left it outside your front door in China. It was a Bonaparte and a Witch's Post combined. Where exactly did the six-foot mirror come from? Was it being delivered or taken away? Or is there a tradition in China of keeping large mirrors outside buildings, presumably so people can check on their appearance before entering?

Let's try not to be distracted by the mirror.

The 'rathole' argument just shows how embedded our natural pessimism is. It is certainly in our nature to believe we are more threatened than we really are; more in danger than we have ever been. In the USA it was gently pointed out that, despite the focus on the danger to every citizen from homegrown jihadis, only nine Americans die on average each year because of Islamic terrorists operating within the country. More than twice as many are shot by toddlers.

Number of Americans killed annually by:	
Islamic jihadist immigrants[1]:	2
Far right-wing terrorists[1]:	5
All Islamic jihadist terrorists (including US citizens)[1]:	9
Armed toddlers[2]:	21
Lightning[3]:	31
Lawnmowers[4]:	69
Being hit by a bus[4]:	264
Falling out of bed[4]:	737
Being shot by another American[5]:	11,737

[1] 10-year average of terrorist attacks "Deadly Attacks Since 9/11," New America, http://securitydata.newamerica.net/extremists/deadly-attacks.html
[2] www.snopes.com/toddlers-killed-americans-terrorists/
[3] 10-year average of deaths by lightning, NOAA, www.nws.noaa.gov/om/hazstats/resources/weather_fatalities.pdf
[4] 10-year average, Underlying Cause of Death 2014, CDC, http://wonder.cdc.gov/

Yet Bonaparte No. 1 seems to play on a loop in our heads regardless. It is pretty clear that when a person says 'things are getting worse and worse', what they really mean is 'I am getting older and older.' For example, the statement that 'music was better in the sixties' just translates as: 'That's when I was seventeen.'

When a person rings my show and says the country was a far better place in the seventies, all she means is that she was a far happier person. She was happier because she was younger. We navigate through rear-view mirrors, always trying to find our way back to our youth, blaming everyone around us when we find the horizon only ever recedes.

Soon after the six-foot mirror incident we began the endless argument over Brexit. Listener David Hall rang from the Wirral to say: 'The referendum was a farce. Brexit is an extremely bad idea . . . People voted for Brexit because they pined for the good old days, and you can never get the good old days back.'

Hot on his tail was Ian Bell, a pensioner in Suffolk. 'And that is where it [the argument] all goes totally wrong. Our generation voted Brexit, but if you think about it our generation knew what Great Britain was like before we got dragged into Europe by Heath.' As David groaned and sighed in the background, I asked Ian if it really was 'that good in this country in the sixties and the early seventies'.

Ian: 'If you think about how it was in Great Britain after the Second World War, yes we suffered, but we were a good country and we were quite a prosperous country.'

David: 'He's proving the point.'

Ian: 'I can name you umpteen manufacturers that were in Britain straight after the war. If you look at our truck industry we had something in the region of ten truck manufacturers. We don't have a single one now. They all come from Germany. We were a more prosperous country in the fifties.'

We were a more prosperous country in the fifties? Maybe we were happier with less. Certainly, if we go back a century, 100 million people had just died from a worldwide flu pandemic and Britain was heading into two world wars on the trot. Rationing was in force. Teeth fell out. Life expectancy in 1910 was fifty-one for men, fifty-five for women; it is now seventy-nine and eighty-three.

Aged thirty-five I had an overactive thyroid that crept up on me so slowly I knew nothing about it until a clever doctor said: 'I am a physician. You strike me as unwell.' That condition might have killed me in 1920, unless someone had gone into my neck with a scalpel and slashed away at the racing gland; imagine the terror of that operation. In 2000 it was all sorted out with a daily pill, carbimazole, which was developed in the fifties, had no side effects and had me right as rain after ten months.

Crime is falling, violent crime especially. In the early seventies, while my dad was hand-cranking the car on a cold winter's morn-ing under the shadow of nuclear war, pregnant teenagers were being sent to 'mother and baby' homes run by nuns where their newborn was removed at birth and given up for adoption with-out them even being consulted. I know this, because last week I spoke to a woman not much older than me called Diana who lost her child just like that and had missed her every day since. Birth, adoption, back to school and try not to think about it.

But this country has gone to the dogs. It's official. Just like it was official that Enron was America's most successful company (before it collapsed and its executives were jailed). Just like it's official that people who live in rural areas of Britain walk everywhere and are outdoorsy (most of the ones I know have never even been to the end of their driveways on foot; it is city people who do all the walking). Just like it's official that the man who brought Aids to the USA was a Canadian flight attendant called Gaetan Dugas.

And that is a particularly sad Bonaparte, caused by the misreading of an official study of Aids patients in New York and California in the eighties. Gaetan worked for Air Canada and died of Aids in 1984, aged thirty-one. He was labelled as 'Patient O' in the study – the 'O' stood for 'Out of California' – but a researcher subsequently misread it as 'Patient Zero' and thus began the myth that he single-handedly brought the disease to the States. Featuring heavily in the eighties book *And the Band Played On*, Gaetan Dugas was only officially cleared in 2016 by a genetic study of blood samples published in the magazine *Nature*. He would have been sixty-three years old.

*　　*　　*

One of the most exciting live shows I have ever done was an attempt to recreate the sinking of the *Titanic* exactly a century after it went down in 1912. The studio was not quite floated out into the Thames and scuttled, but it would have sounded like it at times – the programme, produced by Phil Critchlow and Jonathan Mayo from the indie company TBI, was called *Titanic, Minute by Minute* and the billing said:

> Our programme starts at 11.35pm just before the iceberg hits and ends at 2.20am when the ship disappears. Jeremy Vine,

Dermot O'Leary and Penny Smith together with experts take us through minute by minute what's happening to the passengers and crew, the structure of the ship and the musicians who made up the ship's band. We have actors reading the accounts of over 30 eyewitnesses – from First Class aristocracy to steerage passengers. By sticking to the facts the programme gives you a better idea of what really happened than any drama.

It was the reference to 'the facts' that seems to have caused the problem. When we looked on social media we found that the sinking of the luxury liner was news to some listeners. They had heard the story, of course – but always understood it to be fiction. A public conversation started on Twitter between people who were genuinely shocked that a real ship with real people on board had hit a real iceberg.

The moral? We humans have a simply extraordinary capacity for error. Looking on a website called Ask, where you can pose any question and get responses from your fellow users, I saw this exchange under the heading RESOLVED QUESTION:

Manda Panda: '*Do you think humans will ever walk on the sun? I was just thinking and thought how crazy it was that a person walked on the moon and Mars. I was just wondering if you think a person will ever be able to walk on the sun too? I know it's really hot but I'm thinking if you go in the winter when the sun is like 30 degrees I bet they could do it.*'

Gummy Roach: 'Well, if they do, it would have to be at night.'

That inspirational reply from Gummy Roach was headed BEST ANSWER, CHOSEN BY ASKER. The tragedy of all journalism is that we think we are here to set records straight and put the world to rights, but it may now be overrun with Bonapartes. Correcting them is simply too big a task.

Charlotte Hall @charliobbsss
Is it bad that I didn't know the titanic was real? Always thought it was just a film
tↄ Retweeted by stefan

jas @jasaxx
only just found out titanic was real #wtf
tↄ Retweeted by stefan

brittany £izama @izamagang
Nobody told me titanic was real...? How am I just finding this out?!
tↄ Retweeted by stefan

Megz ♋ @_HopeDies
Wtf I never knew the titanic was real :/ thought it was just another movie I haven't yet seen....
tↄ Retweeted by stefan

NaiNai @BabyDoe22
Guys, the Titanic was real! #mindblown
tↄ Retweeted by stefan

oh, hey fee (: @0_0woahshere_
"@TheBestMFyet: I never knew titanic actually happened" it did ???
tↄ Retweeted by stefan

A n t w a n @TheBestMFyet
I never knew titanic actually happened
tↄ Retweeted by stefan

Sophie☺ @iSophloveBieber
Didnt know the Titanic actually happened :O i thought it was just a film!
tↄ Retweeted by stefan

Bibi Bagnall @BibiBagnall
I didn't know Titanic actually happened, thought it was just a film #fuckme
tↄ Retweeted by stefan

Dirty Dan. 🚬 @tiffany_br
I thought the Titanic was just a movie. I didn't know it was real tho
tↄ Retweeted by stefan

Mr. Dragon Slayer @themilfmadness_
The titanic was real holly shit im never gooing on a cruise
tↄ Retweeted by stefan

your name @Jess_McBride
Fucking hell ive just realised titanic was a real event!!
tↄ Retweeted by stefan

23. The Narrowing

A while back I made a resolution. From now on, I will only listen to music I don't like.

I stripped all that glorious Van Morrison and Bruce Springsteen out of my smartphone. Deleted 'Heaven' by Talking Heads and even 'Shadowplay' by Joy Division. Removing all traces of The Jam was particularly difficult. Then I joined a music streaming service – which was like tuning into a radio station that has been taken over in a coup led by armed teenagers. I told it nothing about my own preferences. Each week it gave me songs to listen to by artists I had never heard of or cared little for: Drake. Foxygen. Family of the Year. Ed Prosek. Jasmine Thompson. The Lumineers. I tried never to tell it what I liked. Sometimes I even up-arrowed a song I couldn't get on with at all.

Its suggestions got more and more unlike anything I had heard before, as if we were two people speaking on a crossed line. One day, under the label 'MUSIC YOU WILL LIKE', it recommended 'Btstu' by a band called Dot. It could not have been less like anything I was used to listening to. Hearing 'Btstu' I felt I had arrived on a foreign shore. In days gone by I would have called it garbage, but now Music Formerly Known As Garbage was my choice.

Why? Because I could see, as I entered my sixth decade, how our brains shrink. I see it in my audience, I see it in my family and I see it in myself. I see it in every person who is a decade older than they were ten years ago. Those deadly Bonapartes are created by the shrinking brain, which embraces prejudice as efficient thinking.

Taking Elvis Costello out of my life was especially difficult. Between 1977 (*My Aim Is True*) and 1986 (*Blood & Chocolate*) the god of British post-punk released ten classic albums in a row. Has any British solo artist bar Bowie done the same? Turning fifty, I was still listening to them all – and to one in particular. The cover of his second features a furious-looking Elvis standing behind a Brownie box camera, consumed with jealousy and resentment as he takes (we presume) a photo of a beauty queen. *This Year's Model* combines the anger of punk with a novelist's feel for the power of the well-chosen word. One song, 'Little Triggers', I must have played a thousand times: 'Little Triggers, that you pull with your tongue'.

It only made the song more fascinating when, finally tackling the Victorian novel *Middlemarch* in 2016 – written by Mary Anne Evans under a male pen name – I read the line: 'Our tongues are little triggers which have usually been pulled before general intentions can been brought to bear', and realised that, back in 1978, this archetypal new-wave anger management case had actually been referencing George Eliot from 1871.

But I had noticed The Narrowing in action even with Costello. Initially listening to all of his albums, I then reduced my field to those ten. Soon it was five. What would the future hold? By sixty would I only be playing *This Year's Model*? By seventy would I just have 'Little Triggers' left?

Age is a narrowing agent. It sounds like the title of a horror film – *We Must Resist the Narrowing*. Around me, my seniors were repeating the same collection of stories about themselves, even looking bored at their own punchlines. They refused to try anything new and sank into long-held views like broken sofas. Too slowly I realised that I was doing it too. Which is partly why I went dancing.

The narrowing is logical as much as biological. If all goes well, as a person gets older they take more control over their life. A young person exists in multiple situations not of their choosing. In middle age we believe we have taken charge. The 25-year-old has to deal with the awful boss and a thousand interactions that are out of their hands. The 52-year-old becomes the boss.

So it is with the whole of life. If all goes well, a person gradually gains the ability to stay away from people who annoy them and views they disagree with. We own our own front door, and we can slam it. But the ability to shut out annoyances is actually a curse.

When Kanye West declared himself 'the greatest artist in the history of the world', I tweeted a picture I had drawn comparing him to David Bowie but swiftly realised I was falling back into the old habits. What if Kanye West really were better than Bowie – as great as Walt Whitman or Renoir – and I had missed it because my Bowie-leaning neurons would not give him the time of day? Super-diligently, I listened to everything I could by the rapper. Okay, by the end, none of it compared to Bowie's *Station to Station*, and the way Kim Kardashian kept arriving in the story was distracting.

But I got a little fascinated and switched on by Kanye. I won't spell out the lyrics of the wild 'I'm In It', but suffice to say it contains a description of Mr West removing his girlfriend's bra while quoting Martin Luther King: 'Free at last, thank God they're free at last.' Then the song 'New Slaves' stops you in its tracks with a description of the racism that stopped Kanye's mother getting clean water.

I realised: this was not about me finding music I liked. It was just about me being open to the music others like, and seeing into the life of someone different from me.

Spending time with people you disagree with is part of the

joy of journalism. Every day someone comes into my studio and launches a boxful of bad tomatoes in the direction of the government, or the audience, or me, or just tilts at a distant wind turbine . . . and I find myself thinking: 'Say nothing. It's not your job to ask if they're wrong – it's your job to ask if *you* might be.'

* * *

Quick question. Kinda relevant to this. Do you believe in God?

My parents are rapturous about God, and I think I now believe the story of Christ. But I took the long way round.

I was brought up to the sound of tambourines. The church I was taken to every week by my mum and dad was a so-called evangelical church, meaning there were constant warnings about hell and all the fixtures and fittings were functional. The carpets were new and there was no stained glass. Everyone seemed to show a desperate kind of joy.

Take nothing away from them, there was true kindness among those folk in Cheam. At the heart of the message was the theme of forgiveness and salvation. You confessed your sins and you were saved. But that only raised a thousand questions for the anxious ten-year-old me. Hell was mentioned enough for me to become genuinely scared. How did you know you were forgiven – I mean, *really* forgiven? What if you weren't, what if God's Dyson had failed to suction up one or two of those lethal sins you had forgotten to confess . . . what if there was some sort of clerical error and you missed out on forgiveness? What was Hell like?

The Bible seemed written for people who thought they were okay, and needed telling that, actually, they were unforgiven sinners. But what about people who are constantly down on themselves, the disheartened and depressed? Do they really need the message that they are not good enough?

So many questions. The young me constantly wondered about hell, or HELL as it was always written on the overhead projector. Sermon after sermon described it. Apparently I could literally burn to death for infinity in a lake of burning sulphur. I knew

I was a bad person – that seemed to be the message of the Bible, and certainly I had a maths teacher who told me I was worthless three times a week for five years – but this ten-year-old seemed like a waste of so much sulphur. Anyway, how much real sin can a person build up over ten years? Is it possible that I had committed what is wildly referred to in the Bible as 'the unforgivable sin' . . .

Wait. There is an unforgivable sin?
(That's the voice of the ten-year-old me.)
'Yes. It's very clear. Jesus refers to it.'
(That's the voice of the helpful youth group leader at church.)
But what is it?
'Um, we don't really know.'
What do you mean you don't know?
'I wouldn't worry about it. It's very unlikely.'
Unlikely? So it's possible I have committed a sin which would mean I burnt in hell for infinity, and I wouldn't even know?
'It's not infinity, Jeremy. It's a thousand years.'

. . . That was my first interview, I guess. It was good practice for journalism, questioning hell. Later I realised that the problem with the hardboiled model of Christianity is that everything hinges on the blinding moment of salvation. 'Anyone who is in Christ is a new creation,' writes Saint Paul (yes, I know all the verses). 'The old has gone, behold, the new has come.' But if you have been taken into a tambourine-waving, in-tongues-speaking house of worship since you were literally a day old, where is the change moment? What happens if you have a couple of years off? Are you toast? Can you convert, unconvert, convert again? How many refresher lightning bolts can a person have?

So I drifted away. Basically I couldn't handle the level of certainty I saw in the eyes of evangelicals, who had a straight and clear answer for everything. I found myself getting very down when I couldn't *feel* God's love, which is apparently important. So I went to university and forgot all about it.

Only years later did I put the pieces back together, and then carefully. I gradually understood that I would never feel certain, only doubtful. And instead of seeing doubt as a problem, I realised it was the key component of faith.

I had always thought faith and certainty were twins. On the other side were ignorance and doubt – paired, mutually welded, going steady, a couple never seen apart. Sometime in my life, perhaps during my rocky mid-forties when I needed someone or something to pray to, I took a second look at the whole God thing.

Slowly I decided I had got it the wrong way round. It's not faith/certainty . . . ignorance/doubt. It is exactly the reverse. Those with the most certainty are the most ignorant. Those with the strongest faith have the most doubt.

So it is with life. The enemy is certainty. The person most certain that dinosaurs did not exist is the one who has never visited the Natural History Museum. Certainty is so much easier when you are ignorant.

The love of the easy answer makes fools of us. When Donald Trump won the White House in 2016 he partly did it with the votes of women and Hispanics – an amazing 29 per cent of Hispanics, despite having called Mexicans 'rapists and murderers' during the campaign. That confounded experts, who were convinced that Hillary Clinton's gentler pitch would simply switch all members of certain voting groups to her party. As if people behave like that – might not some Hispanics have been prepared to ignore Trump's motormouthing because they wanted the halving of business tax he was promising? *Certainty–ignorance.* In the face of a thousand polls all faithfully predicting a Democrat win, doubt was a beautiful thing.

Doubt is the motor of faith. Knowledge is just a fact surrounded by questions. People who feel certain about uncertain things scare me like the hell of my childhood. Faith is doubt. Certainty is ignorance.

Here endeth my own personal lesson. Twenty paragraphs that took me forty years.

*   *   *

The BBC is an unpredictable beast. When it agreed to release the salaries of so-called 'top talent' in bands, I did not think I would be anywhere near the summit. I confided in one female colleague on the understanding that she was much more famous and better paid than me. Alarm bells rang when an executive warned me I would be the BBC's number seven presenter.

When the list emerged, it was worse than I thought. 'Bloody hell,' I said when I saw the names laid out. My salary (I will spare you the gore) put me in fourth place after Chris Evans, Gary Lineker and Graham Norton. I had to exit the Radio 2 building and do what Americans call a 'perp walk' – usually reserved for bankers in handcuffs – where a forest of cameras followed me down the street. Idiotically, I then had to unchain my bike from a lamppost, which took a full two minutes.

The teenager wanted to be a successful journalist. The adult gets there and has to do a walk of shame like a criminal. Fair enough, I guess. The reason my salary was high was only because of something a manager said to me in 1999.

I was the third presenter of *Newsnight* and discovered I was paid far less than Jeremy Paxman and Kirsty Wark. 'Every time you walk into the building we save five thousand pounds,' the manager laughed. In thirteen years at the Beeb I had never previously spoken to a soul about money, but then and there I resolved to ask for better pay when I got the chance. When Radio 2 knocked in 2002 the chance came. Hiring an agent, I told him to charge at the facing players like a fly-half after ten espressos. He got a very decent fee for Radio 2. Then *Panorama, Eggheads, Crimewatch, Points of View* and the election graphics were all added. I am not trying to justify it; just telling you how it happened. I did five shows in parallel and was paid in numbers I would never dream of defending in the presence of my mother (who was a doctor's receptionist) or my father, the college lecturer.

There was some talk at Radio 2 of my taking the day off when the salary news came out. After everything I have written in this book, I thought that would be an act of utter cowardice. The whole point of my show is that it is my job to listen. I told the producer, Tim Collins, that he should decide which callers to put through and 'the only disaster will be if they all support me'. Whatever happened, I said, I wouldn't be cross. Put through the angriest.

The programme started on a bizarre note. The head of radio, James Purnell, arrived in the studio wearing a large beard as if in disguise. I asked him: 'I'm on this list as having a salary of between £700,000 and £750,000. How do you justify that?' Never in my life did I imagine having to challenge a boss over my own pay live on air. He said something about it costing each listener 1p a week.

When it came to the listeners, I need not have worried about them pulling punches. The first call was from Harry Jones, an ex-miner listening in Neath, Glamorgan. He paid me a fleeting compliment and then launched. 'Jeremy, I'd like to ask you a direct question. Are you embarrassed to pick up your pay cheque?'

I sighed. 'Do you know, I just feel very lucky every day, is the answer to that.'

Mr Jones came back. 'Do you think you're overpaid?'

In my mind I went through half a dozen possible answers in the space of a second. *It's the market . . . I work very hard . . . I was underpaid for fifteen years . . . Chris Evans gets three times as much as me . . . It's a question for the BBC . . .*

Each answer seemed lame to the point of offensive. So I laughed nervously and said, pathetically: 'Er – I don't even really want to answer that because I don't think it's the moment for me –'

He broke in. 'You spend your lifetime asking people questions. Now I am asking you a direct question. Do you think you and the rest of the BBC are overpaid?'

The directness of this was like a torpedo. The brevity stole my thinking time. I now knew I was in terrible trouble.

But as I began by conceding, 'Some are,' and wondered in a panic whether this could be the last on-air conversation of my career, Mr Jones launched into a tirade against all presenters and the red dot dancing on my forehead drifted away. 'Because I work with men in the coal industry, I work on construction, I see men buckle through working all their life, doing hard graft and nothing to show for it. How can you people justify the amount of money they're earning? All of you are grossly, grossly overpaid.'

It smarted. Because from his perspective every word he said was true – and on that day his perspective was the only one that mattered.

Afterwards I realised something important. Mr Jones was probably the greatest caller in the history of my show, and his demolition of me was not something I should regret. A pat answer would have infuriated him and the rest of the audience. He took me down, and he showed the great truth at the centre of this book. The listeners have the power now.

A bigger story quickly emerged from the BBC talent list. On programme after programme, women were being underpaid compared to male counterparts. That turned out to be the major scandal, and with two young daughters I felt as indignant as the first people to spot the differential. The female presenter I had quietly spoken to about the pay ladder before it emerged was an inexplicable number of rungs below me. How the BBC did not spot the peril in the numbers it knew it would have to publish, and right the wrongs in the story that would explode as a result, is beyond me. There is simply no explanation. The organisation seems to navigate by crashing into things.

Twenty-five thousand calls after I joined Radio 2, the person who founded my programme died. The passing of Sir Jimmy Young triggered an onrush of listener sympathy and sadness that was the opposite of the reaction to the pay imbroglio. Many heard Jimmy broadcast in the same slot for twenty-nine years. Towards the end of his tenure, there was a tide of change around him. Executives were quoted wanting 'a bit less pipe and slippers, and a bit less cardigan'. Jimmy bravely posed for a publicity shot *wearing a cardigan*. When you consider his livelihood depended on it, that was as dangerous a gesture as anything by the Sex Pistols. The famous broadcaster was undoubtedly very conservative in his views – his *Sunday Express* column after he left the BBC proved that – but behind the microphone he remained an enigma, his ears open for the next call, his mind available. Even during fourteen studio encounters with Mrs Thatcher, Jimmy somehow managed to hide his devotion. He did that impossible thing. He did not speak his mind.

After taking so many calls and hearing so many opinions, the only thing I am really sure of is that I must restrain my own. Every time I express a view it makes trouble because it closes discussion down. 'Photography is not art', was among things I have said that caused no end of bother because they were too categorical about an unknown. I also once said: 'Anyone who owns a chest freezer is probably a murderer', and also that 'Lawrence Olivier was not a very good actor.' They caused bother too.

Gradually it has dawned on me that a presenter can have values, but not views. A value would be: 'It is terrible that your daughter was killed by a drunk driver.' A view is: 'He should spend the rest of his life in prison.' Hating litter is a value; being angry about dirty hospitals is a view, because once a discarded burger wrapper drifts into a hospital it becomes political.

Anyway, it is actually easier to have no views when you are bombarded by them. Listener interventions are as pungent as ammonia. One messaged: 'There is so much shouting on your show I've had to turn the radio volume down from 4 to 2.' Nonetheless I do try to read all comments with the utmost conviction. An actor would boast they *inhabit* them – maybe a presenter can do a version of that. Some lend themselves to a full-throttle delivery, like this exhilarating line from the 'Enjoy Norwich' Twitter account: 'If you are a society that values nuclear weapons above libraries. Simply, you have failed.'

As I look around I notice, emanating from the team of producers I work with, an incredible openness to new and different ideas. The editor is a particularly good example of this. Phil Jones once briefed me about an item involving Lord Tanlaw, an obscure peer who had tabled a 'Lighter Evenings (Experimental) Bill', suggesting the UK stops changing the clocks twice a year.

'He was on the *Today* programme and they called him "Lord Tanlow" by accident,' said Jones. 'He got really cross and the interview was brilliant as a result. So I want you to get his name wrong as well. Introduce him as Lord Tanlow.'

Unconventional, can we agree?

One producer, Tim Johns, told me he had tried three times to join my show and the third job interview – the one where he was successful – was the most surreal. He was interviewed by Phil Jones, who told him to imagine it was April Fool's Day.

'Would it be acceptable,' he asked Tim, 'for us to run a spoof item about dogs which can kill if they hear a certain command – a code word – and for Jeremy to have someone on the line who owns an Alsatian that has been trained to do this, and for Jeremy to accidentally blurt the word out?'

He continued. 'This would be an April Fool. We would then play the sound of the dog attacking the owner.'

Tim thought about it. Finally he replied: 'I don't think you could do that, because it might upset some listeners.'

Jones changed tack. 'Okay. What if it wasn't an Alsatian? What if it wasn't a dog? What if it was a rabbit trained to attack? An attack rabbit?'

He actually said that. Tim replied that might be okay, and duly got the job for having an open mind. He also emerged with one of the finest ever my-BBC-job-interview stories.

I did a show once that entailed interviewing an ex-MI5 guy about his operations against jihadis in London. Then, one hour later, the Canadian spaceman Chris Hadfield came into the studio. One talked about a dangerous car chase in Stoke Newington, the other about exiting the International Space Station attached only by a hosepipe. That night I went to Worcester to interview the Archbishop of Canterbury at the sports arena. He spoke about his drunken father and losing a child.

In one day: an agent, an astronaut and an archbishop. If we keep our ears open, there is so much to hear.

Love, laughter, learning. Isn't that where we started? The three best things in life are all a function of openness. That must be the lesson of the 25,000 calls.

Even the one about the coats.

Even the one about the bats.

Thanks

The publishers at Orion are outstanding, especially Alan Samson, Kate Wright-Morris and Lucinda McNeile. I owe a particular mention to Sue Stapely, a friend of the Clark family who became so tragically entangled with Sir Roy Meadow and helped ensure that chapter is accurate. John Batt's powerful, wise book *Stolen Innocence* also assisted me with details of Steve and Sally Clark's life together and I am extremely grateful.

Great editors at the BBC are too many to mention: Sam Woodhouse who does all our elections; Rob Dean who produces *Eggheads*; and of course Phil Jones at Radio 2, who could be mentioned at least a hundred times in the preceding pages.

I am sad to say that the delightful Rowena Kincaid, who inspired me so much in the two conversations we had – mentioned in the first chapter – died in Cardiff on 2 September 2016.

My wife Rachel and my two daughters, Martha and Anna, were patient on the occasions when I chose the laptop over the local park – hopefully not too often. Thank you, girls, for your love and laughter. And more thanks than I could ever express are due to every single unmentioned presenter and producer at Radio 2 and BBC 6 Music, who make each minute, hour and year I have spent in what is now called Wogan House a revelation from start to finish.

Credits

The Publisher is grateful to Universal Music Publishing for permission to reproduce lyrics from the following:

'Love Is A Stranger' – Eurythmics
'Disconnected' – Keane
'Take Me I'm Yours' – Squeeze
'Alison Hand in Hand' – Elvis Costello
'Livin' Next Door to Alice' – Smokie

And to Warner/Chappell for 'Cat's In The Cradle' – Harry Chapin

For permission to reproduce the following photographs in the text, the Publisher is grateful to:

Guardian/Linda Nyland (page 113)
Barcroft Media (page 177)

And for the following plates:

Page 5, Newsnight campervan (*Hartlepool Mail*)
Page 7, The graphics set (Jeff Over, BBC)
Page 9, *Strictly Come Dancing* (BBC)